THE LAW OF
DIVORCE IN IRELAND

THE LAW OF
DIVORCE IN IRELAND

Muriel Walls BCL, Solicitor
David Bergin BCL, Solicitor

JORDANS

1997

Published by
Family Law
a publishing imprint of
Jordan Publishing Limited
21 St Thomas Street
Bristol BS1 6JS

British Library Cataloguing-in-Publication Data

A catalogue record for this book is available
from the British Library.

ISBN 0 85308 408 4

The Family Law (Divorce) Act 1996, set out in
Appendix 1, is reproduced with the kind
permission of the Controller, Stationery Office.

Photoset by Mendip Communications Ltd, Frome, Somerset
Printed in Great Britain by Butler and Tanner Ltd, Frome and London

BIOGRAPHIES

MURIEL WALLS

Obtained Bachelor of Civil Law Degree in University College, Dublin 1975

Qualified as a solicitor in 1977

Member of Family Law Committee of the Law Society

Consultant to the Law Society on Family Law

Member and former chairperson of the Family Lawyers Association

Fellow of the International Academy of Matrimonial Lawyers

Associate of the Solicitors Family Law Association of England and Wales

DAVID BERGIN

Obtained Bachelor of Civil Law Degree in University College, Dublin in 1975

Qualified as a solicitor in 1976

Fellow of the International Academy of Matrimonial Lawyers

Member of Family Law Committee of the Dublin Solicitors Bar Association

Consultant to the Law Society on Family Law

Member and former committee member of the Family Lawyers Association

FOREWORD

The enactment of legislation providing for divorce in this country, following on the constitutional referendum in November 1995, marks a crucial change in our legal treatment of marital breakdown. Since the mid-1970s, we have responded to the problems associated with the open acknowledgement of marital breakdown by the enactment of what has been described by Mr Justice Keane as an 'untidy complex of laws'. The enactment in 1989 of the Judicial Separation and Family Law Reform Act was the first attempt to deal with family law in a comprehensive and logical fashion. The Family Law Act 1995 continued and expanded this process.

The Law Reform Commission in its Report on Family Courts published in March 1996 (LRC 52–1996) stated:

> 'The last twenty years have seen a growing recognition by society of the wide variety of problems associated with the breakdown of family relationships. Substantive family law has undergone a transformation during this period, with the introduction of a wide range of remedies and rights designed to protect vulnerable or dependent family members in the wake of breakdown, and to secure the fair distribution of family assets.'

The Family Law (Divorce) Act 1996 now provides a legal remedy both for those who seek a clear ending of marriages which have irretrievably broken down and for those who wish to remarry. Many of this second group are already involved in continuing second relationships.

In their book, Ms Walls and Mr Bergin provide a comprehensive analysis of the provisions of the 1996 Act. They also provide a useful survey of the development of case-law, particularly since the 1989 Act. Since there has been no comprehensive textbook on the law affecting marital breakdown published in this jurisdiction since 1990, Ms Walls and Mr Bergin's book will be an invaluable resource for legal practitioners. The overflowing attendances at recent seminars on the new divorce legislation run by both the Law Society and the Bar Council clearly indicate the demand among solicitors and barristers alike for information in this area.

In addition to dealing with the more familiar areas of custody of children, the family home, maintenance and matrimonial property, this book deals particularly well with the complex areas of life assurance, pensions, and discovery, financial disclosure and anti-avoidance, in all of which authoritative and clear advice is badly needed by family law clients and, if I may say so, by family law practitioners.

The authors of this book have many years of extensive practice in family law. Not only are they thoroughly aware of the letter of the law, they have also developed an understanding of the particular and personal art of serving family law clients at a time of emotional and, all too frequently, financial crisis in their lives. Their book is not only a survey and analysis of the legislation but also reflects their own experience and understanding. Its publication will be welcomed by all who practice and, indeed, all who preside in the Family Law Courts.

Catherine McGuinness
Four Courts
Dublin 7
March 1997

PREFACE

In this book, we have attempted to give a comprehensive analysis of the provisions of the Family Law (Divorce) Act 1996, an analysis which is intended not only for family lawyers but also for non-lawyers who are involved directly or indirectly with marital breakdown. We hope that it will give the reader a clear understanding of how the Act will work in practice and how it will interact with existing family law legislation. Family law is now a specialist area of practice which requires a high level of expertise in many subjects including tax, company law, property and conveyancing, pensions, life insurance, trusts and foreign property.

The enactment of the Divorce Act is a significant step forward in providing another legal remedy for those whose marriages have irretrievably broken down. Marriage breakdown itself is traumatic for the persons involved and every assistance should be given to marriages and families experiencing difficulties. Those whose marriages do fail are entitled to have their cases dealt with in as civilised a manner as possible.

This book was suggested to us over lunch by our publishers, Jordans, in September of 1995 and we willingly accepted the challenge to write a commentary on the Divorce Act when passed. At that time, the referendum campaign was in full swing and no one anticipated the closeness of the final result. The following months were taken up with the High Court and Supreme Court hearing of the challenge by Mr Des Hanafin to the result of the referendum. The work commenced in earnest in June of 1996. Many interests and events were forsaken to ensure that the deadline dates were met but, thankfully, David managed to be present at the birth of his beautiful daughter Leonie on 7 January 1997. The decisions of the courts in family law cases remain largely unreported and this hinders research. We were greatly assisted in our work by the reports of significant cases contained in the Family Law Journal (Fam LJ) which is the quarterly publication of the Family Lawyers Association.

We both want to thank our legal partners and colleagues for their support and advice, our secretarial staff for their willingness to type and retype drafts and especially our spouses Eamonn and Ceara and families for their patience and understanding.

As neither of us had undertaken the task of writing a book before, we greatly appreciated the help and reassurance we received from Jordans in bringing this book to a conclusion.

The Code of Practice was reproduced by kind permission of The Law Society of Ireland.

Muriel Walls
David Bergin

Dublin
March 1997

CONTENTS

TABLE OF CASES
IRISH REPUBLIC

References in the right-hand column are to paragraph numbers.

TABLE OF OTHER CASES

References in the right-hand column are to paragraph numbers.

TABLE OF LEGISLATION
IRISH REPUBLIC

References in the right-hand column are to paragraph numbers.

TABLE OF STATUTORY INSTRUMENTS
IRISH REPUBLIC

References in the right-hand column are to paragraph numbers.

TABLE OF STATUTES
UNITED KINGDOM

References in the right-hand column are to paragraph numbers.

TABLE OF STATUTORY INSTRUMENTS
UNITED KINGDOM

References in the right-hand column are to paragraph numbers.

TABLE OF CONVENTIONS, ETC

References in the right-hand column are to paragraph numbers.

TABLE OF ABBREVIATIONS

the '1965 Act'	Succession Act 1965
the '1976 Act'	Family Law (Maintenance of Spouses and Children) Act 1976
the '1986' Act	Domicile and Recognition of Foreign Divorces Act 1986
the '1989 Act'	Judicial Separation and Family Law Reform Act 1989
the '1991 Act'	Child Care Act 1991
the 'Divorce Act'	Family Law (Divorce) Act 1996
FHPA 1976	Family Home Protection Act 1976
FLA 1995	Family Law Act 1995
GIA 1964	Guardianship of Infants Act 1964
ISPCC	Irish Society for the Prevention of Cruelty to Children
PAYE	Pay As You Earn
PRSI	Pay-Related Social Insurance

GLOSSARY

Abduction

The unlawful removal of a child from its country of habitual residence.

Access

The right of the non-custodial parent of a child to see and have the child spend time with him or her.

Adultery

Voluntary sexual intercourse between a man and a woman one or both of whom are married but not to each other.

Affidavit

A statement in writing sworn on oath containing the evidence of the person making the statement.

Affidavit of Means

A statement sworn on oath by each spouse setting out his or her income and expenditure, assets and liabilities.

Affidavit of Welfare

A statement sworn on oath by each spouse setting out details of, and arrangements for, the children of the marriage.

Ancillary Relief (Order)

An order which the court can make in relation to financial and property matters when granting a decree of divorce or judicial separation.

Annuity

An annual payment of a specified sum of money.

Appearance

Notice filed by a solicitor to say they represent the respondent.

Applicant

The person who commences divorce proceedings by filing a Family Law Civil Bill.

Camera, In

The hearing of a case otherwise than in public, ie only the parties and their legal representatives may be in the court during the hearing.

Civil Bill

The document which requests the court for a judicial separation or divorce and which sets out in broad terms the reasons for so doing.

Consent Order

An order made by the court in terms which have been agreed by the parties.

Counsel   Barrister, senior or junior.

Counterclaim   The document by which a respondent claims a
                           judicial separation or divorce on different
                           grounds to those set out in the application
                           and where different ancillary relief is sought.

Cross-decree   When an applicant is granted a decree on the
                           basis of the application and the respondent on
                           the basis of the counterclaim.

Custody   The right to the physical day-to-day care and
                           control of a child.

Defence   The document which sets out the defence to a
                           judicial separation or divorce.

Dependent member   A child under the age of 23 and in full-time
                           education or a child who suffers mental or
                           physical disability.

Desertion   Departure of one spouse from the family
                           home without just cause.

Disclosure   Full information on all financial matters which
                           must be given by each spouse to the other and
                           to their legal advisors.

Discovery   The process whereby the parties disclose to
                           each other on affidavit all documents relevant
                           to the case in their possession, power or
                           procurement.

Divorce Court   Circuit family court and High Court.

Domicile   The place in which a person resides with the
                           intention of remaining there permanently.

Equity (of property)   The net value of a property after the
                           deduction of the amount outstanding on foot
                           of any mortgage registered against the
                           property and the expenses of sale, ie
                           auctioneering and legal fees.

Exhibit   A document referred to in an affidavit which
                           is usually identified by a letter of the alphabet
                           and is signed by the person swearing the
                           affidavit.

Ex parte

An application made to the court without prior notification to the other party.

Family home

The dwelling in which a married couple ordinarily reside.

File or Filing

Leave or leaving documents with the court office. Each document is stamped with the date of filing and the original retained on the court file.

Guardianship

The parental rights and duties in respect of the upbringing of a child, for example, the duty to maintain and the right to make decisions on education, health and welfare.

Hearsay evidence

Evidence of a fact not seen by a witness but told to him or her by another, ie second-hand knowledge.

Injunction

An order of the court directing a party to do or refrain from doing a particular thing.

Intestate or Intestacy

A person who dies without leaving a valid will.

Interim relief

An order made by the court after an application has been filed but before the case has come on for a full hearing.

Legal Aid

A government funded scheme administered by the Legal Aid Board. See Appendix 4 for addresses.

Liable Relative Proceedings

Proceedings taken by the Department of Social Welfare against a person legally responsible for maintaining his or her spouse or children and who has failed to do so.

Maintenance Order

An order of the court which provides that one spouse must pay a periodical payment to the other spouse for his or her support and/or the support of any dependent child.

Mediation

A form of dispute resolution. See Appendix 4 for addresses.

Mortgagee

The bank or building society or other financial institution which lends money on the security of a property.

Mortgagor
The person who borrows money and who mortgages a property as security for the loan.

Notice of Motion
The document by which notice is given to the other side of whatever application is being made to the court, for example, notice of motion seeking interim maintenance.

Notice of Trial
The document which is served on the respondent, once a defence is filed, in order to fix a hearing date.

Pleadings
The Civil Bill, defence, counterclaim, affidavits, and motions in the court office.

Pray or Prayer
Formal request in the Civil Bill or counterclaim for the court orders which the applicant or the respondent seeks.

Respondent
The spouse who is not the applicant in the application for judicial separation or divorce.

Service
Each court document must be served on the other party. Service is usually made personally, or by registered post, on the other party unless a solicitor has agreed to accept service on behalf of that party.

Summons
A notice issued by the court office against a respondent to appear at court either in person or by his or her solicitor at a specified time.

Special Summons
Documents by which a judicial separation or divorce application is commenced in the High Court.

Testate
The person who dies leaving a valid will.

Third Party
A person unconnected with the case who may have documents which are relevant.

Undertaking
A solemn promise to the court to do or not to do something.

Without Prejudice
When this term is used it stops any communications which have been made during the course of negotiation either orally or in writing being made known to the court if the negotiations are unsuccessful.

Chapter 1

MARRIAGE IN IRELAND

1.1 GENERAL

Marriage is not only a close personal relationship between a man and a woman but it is a legal contract which gives rise to a special status recognised as important by the State. Article 41.3 of the Constitution states:

> 'the State pledges itself to guard with special care the institution of marriage, on which the family is founded, and to protect it against attack.'

The Constitution further provides at Article 41.1.1 that:

> 'the State recognises the family as the natural primary and fundamental unit group of society and as a moral institution possessing inalienable and imprescriptible rights, antecedent and superior to all positive law. The State, therefore, guarantees to protect the family in its constitution and authority as the necessary basis of social order and as indispensable to the welfare of the Nation and the State.'

Because of the importance of marriage and the family, the law requires certain formalities to be satisfied before a marriage is recognised as valid:

(a) each party must have the required age and mental capacity;
(b) they must not be within the prohibited degrees of relationship either of blood or affinity;
(c) neither party must be a party to a prior subsisting marriage;
(d) the parties must understand the nature, purpose and consequences of marriage and must fully and freely consent to the marriage;
(e) certain procedural formalities must be observed.

1.2 FORMALITIES

In this regard, recent changes have been brought into operation by the Family Law Act 1995 (FLA 1995).

1.2.1 Age

After 1 August 1996, any marriage solemnised between persons who are under the age of 18 years shall not be valid. As this is a substantive requirement, failure to comply with it will render the marriage void.

This applies to all marriages solemnised in the State and marriages solemnised outside the State between persons either or both of whom is ordinarily resident in the State (FLA 1995, s 31(1)(a)).

Any person (eg priest, vicar, rabbi, registrar) to whom an application to marry to made is entitled to request proof of age and if this request is not complied with or if the evidence of age shows either or both persons to be under the age of 18 then the application to marry must be refused (FLA 1995, s 31(2), (3)).

Any person (eg priest, vicar, rabbi, registrar) who knowingly solemnises a marriage between persons under age are guilty of an offence and are liable on summary conviction to a fine not exceeding £500 (FLA 1995, s 31(4)).

1.2.2   Notice requirements

After 1 August 1996, any marriage solemnised in the State will not be valid unless the persons involved notify the Registrar in writing of their intention to marry not less than three months prior to the date on which the marriage is to take place (FLA 1995, s 31(1)(b)). As this is a substantive requirement, failure to comply will render the marriage void. It is the duty of the Registrar to notify in writing each of the persons intending to marry of the receipt by him of the notification referred to above. This acknowledgement in writing cannot be considered as approval by the Registrar concerned to the proposed marriage. It is merely evidence of compliance with the notice requirement. The Minister for Health may make regulations in relation to this notification procedure but none as yet have been made.

As the requirement with regard to age and notice of three months could in some circumstances cause hardship, the court (either the circuit court or the High Court) may on application to it by both of the persons to an intended marriage exempt the marriage from the application of ss 31(1)(a) or 32(1)(a) of the FLA 1995 or both of those provisions (FLA 1995, s 33).

These applications may be made informally. They are heard and determined otherwise than in public and no court fees are chargeable. An order will not be granted unless the applicants show that the order is justified by serious reasons and is in the interests of the parties to the intended marriage.

1.3   EDUCATION

Although there is now a three-month notice period before marriage, there is no requirement to attend a pre-marriage course. Excellent marriage preparation courses are given by Accord, Marriage and Relationship Counselling Service (MRCS) and other agencies. As the decision to marry is probably the most far-reaching decision that a person can make, many couples find these courses very beneficial. However, education on relationships should take place in schools as part of a personal development programme so that young people can learn the skills to cope with future relationships.

1.4 DEVELOPMENT OF FAMILY LAW

Marriage breakdown is unfortunately alive and thriving in Ireland. However, because of the status of the family and marriage in the Constitution and its special place in society, Ireland has been slow to recognise the fact of marriage breakdown and slow to provide appropriate legal remedies.

Prior to the Family Law (Maintenance of Spouses and Children) Act 1976, the matter of maintenance for spouses was dealt with by the Maintenance (In the case of Desertion) Act 1874. The 1976 Act, for the first time, placed a statutory obligation on both spouses to support and maintain the other. It was also the first time that statute recognised the serious problem of family violence and gave protection to spouses from violence within the home. The Family Home Protection Act 1976 (FHPA 1976) gave the non-owning spouse protection from a sale or mortgage of the family home by the owning spouse. Since then there has been a plethora of legislation to provide a civilised system for separation.

Prior to the Judicial Separation and Family Law Reform Act 1989, there was a very limited form of separation. Under s 7 of the Matrimonial Causes (Ireland) Act 1870, a divorce *a mensa et thoro* could be obtained on the fault-based grounds of adultery, cruelty and unnatural practices. The 1989 Act provides a procedure for couples to separate from each other. The grounds for judicial separation include adultery, unreasonable behaviour, desertion, separation with consent for one year, separation without consent for three years, and on the basis that a marriage has broken down to such an extent that no normal marital relationship has existed between the spouses for at least one year prior to the making of the application. The reality is that marital breakdown is the failure of a relationship. Although the Act requires evidence of fault, the majority of applications are made on a neutral basis containing an acknowledgement by the parties that the marriage has broken down for more the one year.

The 1989 Act also gives the court wide powers to be exercised at its discretion, having regard to the circumstances of each case, to make whatever ancillary relief orders are necessary to provide financially for the dependent spouse and children. The financial relief that the court can make includes periodical payment orders, secured and unsecured lump sum payment orders, property adjustment orders and extinguishment of Succession Act rights. These remedies have been further extended by the FLA 1995 which allows the court to make financial compensation orders and pension adjustment orders. The FLA 1995 also provides that relief can be granted in the Irish courts to spouses who have obtained foreign divorces or separations. This is an important development as up to that time there were very limited procedures in Ireland for former spouses of foreign nationals to pursue their entitlements in Ireland.

1.5   FOREIGN DIVORCES

The law in relation to recognition of foreign divorces must be reviewed. Because of the constitutional prohibition on divorce, the rules on the recognition of foreign divorces were also very strict. Article 41.3.3 of the Constitution provides:

> 'no person whose marriage has been dissolved under the civil law of any other State but is a subsisting valid marriage under the law for the time being in force within the jurisdiction of the government in parliament established by this constitution shall be capable of contracting a valid marriage within that jurisdiction during the lifetime of the other party to the marriage so dissolved.'

There must be a serious question as to whether recognition should now be based on residence for a fixed period or ordinary residence rather than domicile.

1.6   NULLITY

The effect of a decree of nullity is to declare that no marriage ever existed between the spouses. Because of the non-availability of divorce, applications for nullity were often made in order to facilitate remarriage. Judicial developments over the years have modernised the law. The Law Reform Commission Report recommended as far back as 1976 that changes were needed in the law of nullity to give greater certainty in this area. The law still needs to be codified because at present it is difficult for persons to be sure of the status of their marriage as valid or invalid and it is difficult for legal practitioners to give definitive advice to their clients. Even with the introduction of divorce, nullity will still remain an important legal remedy for many people.

1.7   CHILDREN

A father and mother who are married to each other are joint guardians of the children of that marriage. Guardianship means the parental right to make decisions in relation to the children, their health and welfare. Custody means the physical care and control of the children. All disputes between parents are dealt with by the court on the basis of what is in the best interests of the child. Expert witnesses are often called to give professional and independent evidence of what they believe is in the child's best interests. Unfortunately, the cost of calling such expert witnesses must presently be borne by the parties themselves. Section 40 of the 1989 Act, s 47 of the FLA 1995 and s 42 of the Divorce Act allow the court to direct that a suitably qualified medical person carry out an assessment of the child's needs but the parties must pay the cost.

At present, the whole issue of parenting and custody/access needs to be examined and some new thinking brought to the issue. It is accepted that it is very important for children to continue to have a meaningful relationship with both parents and equally important that both parents (especially the non-custodial parent) play a full and meaningful role with their children and work with each other as parents for the benefit of their children even though their spousal relationship may have ended.

1.8 THE COURTS

The Law Reform Commission Report on Family Courts published in March 1996 paints a picture of a system in crisis:

> 'The courts are buckling under the pressure of business. Long family law lists, delays, brief hearings, inadequate facilities and over-hasty settlements are too often the order of the day. At the same time too many cases are coming before the courts which are unripe for hearing, or in which earlier non-legal intervention might have led to agreement and the avoidance of courtroom conflict. Judges dealing with family disputes do not always have the necessary experience or aptitude. There is no proper system of case management. Cases are heard behind closed doors, protecting the privacy of family members but offering little opportunity for external appreciation, criticism, or even realisation, of what is happening within the system. The courts lack adequate support services, in particular the independent diagnostic services so important in resolving child-related issues. The burden placed on those who operate the system . . . has become intolerable.'

The Commission made 67 recommendations, the most important of which are as follows:

(a) A system of regional family courts should be established located in approximately 15 regional centres. The regional family courts should operate as a division of the circuit court and in the context of a full range of family support, information and advice services. In deciding on the precise number and locations of regional family court centres, it will be necessary to take account of population, density, geographical accessibility.

(b) Each regional family court should have attached to it a family court information centre with responsibility for providing information to those who have begun proceedings.

(c) A proper system of case management will be an essential ingredient in any new system of family courts and it should be introduced and implemented by means of Rules of Court.

(d) A system of pre-trial review should be considered.

(e) Greater emphasis should be placed on the gathering of statistics in respect of the courts system. Such detailed information should be gathered on an on-going basis, recording the volume of cases being processed through the system and any delays experienced and identifying problematic procedures. Responsibility for gathering statistical information should be assigned to a member of the Family Court Office.

(f)   The court should, of its own motion or upon application to it, have power to appoint an independent representative for a child whose welfare is in issue in family proceedings, where this appears to the court to be necessary in the interests of the child. Where an expert is requested by the court to make a family assessment, it should be clearly understood by all parties that formulating a report and recommendations to the court is the primary role of that expert.

(g)   Bona fide researchers and students of family law should be permitted to attend family proceedings. Access by a bona fide researcher to family proceedings should not be refused by a judge except on the basis of compelling and stated reasons. The attendance of students of family law should be at the discretion of the judge.

(h)   A comprehensive national statistical database in relation to family law cases should be established.

1.9   CIVIL LEGAL AID

Although the Civil Legal Aid scheme has been in operation since 1979, it was only placed on a statutory basis in November 1996. The Civil Legal Aid scheme makes available to people of moderate means the services of solicitors and, if necessary, barristers at little cost. Those who cannot afford to consult with a solicitor in private practice can apply to any of the law centres. If an applicant is in receipt of social welfare payments he or she will qualify for legal aid. However, if an applicant is working, qualification will depend on the 'disposable' income – that is what is left over after certain allowances are made for dependants, rent/mortgage repayments, expenses in travelling to work, hire purchase repayments or some other outgoings. The majority of cases dealt with by solicitors in the law centres are related to family law matters. The number of centres now operating on a full-time and part-time basis has been extended so that no one should go without legal representation due to lack of means. Undoubtedly, the availability of legal aid for those persons who could not otherwise afford to consult a solicitor in private practice has increased the volume of cases going to the courts, and it is likely that with the introduction of divorce the work of the Legal Aid Board law centres will be substantially increased.

1.10   THE FUTURE AND DIVORCE

The causes of marital breakdown are many and varied. The problems presented to counselling services show lack of communication, abuse and substance addiction, infidelity, sexual difficulties and family problems among the causes of difficulties in marriage. The stresses and strains of modern life do not help couples who find their relationships already strained. Many thousands of citizens have suffered the breakdown of their marriages. The absolute prohibition on divorce was a source of further hardship for many of those couples. There are many who fear the consequences of the new divorce legislation and its effects on society. There are many others who see its introduction as a mark of our maturity and as an effort to create a pluralist inclusive society.

To minimise the effects of marital breakdown, it is essential that every support possible is given to marriage and the family. The establishment of the Commission for the family is, it is argued, a step in the right direction. Its interim report, *Strengthening Families for Life*, makes excellent recommendations. However, governments will have to be prepared to implement its recommendations. Despite the present Government's increased expenditure on counselling services, an annual grant of £900,000 to the 140 voluntary organisations to carry the burden of providing essential counselling services to support families in crisis is totally unrealistic. Those couples whose marriages do fail, and who need to make application to the courts to determine the issues relating to children and financial maters, are entitled to have their cases dealt with in as humane and civilised manner as is possible, and the process and court facilities should reflect this.

Chapter 2

GROUNDS FOR DIVORCE

2.1 INTRODUCTION

Until the passing of the Family Law (Divorce) Act 1996, (27 November 1996), it was not possible for a spouse to obtain a decree of divorce in the jurisdiction of the courts of the Republic of Ireland.

Now, for the first time, under Irish law, a spouse may bring an application to court to have his or her contract of marriage dissolved subject to certain conditions and subject to proving certain matters to the court prior to the granting of any such decree.

2.2 POSITION PRIOR TO THE FAMILY LAW (DIVORCE) ACT 1996

Since 1937, it was not possible for an individual to obtain a decree of divorce in Ireland which would permit either spouse to remarry thereafter. Article 41.3 of the Irish Constitution 1937 set out the position as follows:

> '*Article 41.3.1*
> The State pledges itself to guard with special care the institution of Marriage on which the Family is founded and to protect it against attack.
>
> *Article 41.3.2*
> No law shall be enacted providing for the grant of a dissolution of marriage.'

The Matrimonial Causes Act 1857, which created a divorce jurisdiction in England, did not extend to Ireland, and persons domiciled in Ireland could become divorced after 1857 only by way of a private Act of Parliament.

It is interesting to note that the 1922 Constitution which remained in force in Ireland until 1937, did not contain any specific prohibition on the granting of divorce decrees. The Oireachtas, which was established in 1922, could in fact have brought in legislation enabling divorce decrees to be granted but did not do so. Article 41.3.2 of the 1937 Constitution, however, removed this unused power from the Oireachtas and it is only now, with the passing of the Divorce Act, that this power has been reinstated.

2.3 THE 15TH AMENDMENT TO THE CONSTITUTION

After the referendum of the 24 November 1995, the 15th amendment of the Constitution Act 1995 was passed. An earlier attempt to delete the ban on divorce by way of referendum had failed in 1986. Even in 1995 the percentage of voters in favour of divorce was only slightly greater than those against it. Ultimately, however, Article 41.3.2 referred to above was replaced by the following Article:

> 'A Court designated by Law may grant a dissolution of marriage where, but only where, it is satisfied that:
>
> (i)   At the date of the institution of the proceedings the spouses have lived apart from one another for a period of, or periods amounting to, at least four years during the previous five years.
> (ii)   There is no reasonable prospect of reconciliation between the spouses.
> (iii) Such provision as the Court considers proper having regard to the circumstances exists or will be made for the spouses, any children of either or both of them and any other person prescribed by law, and
> (iv)   Any further conditions prescribed by Law are complied with.'

Subsequently, on 27 November 1996, the Divorce Act was passed and came into operation three months thereafter, ie on the 27 February 1997. This Act made provisions for the exercise by the courts of the jurisdiction conferred by the Constitution, pursuant to the amendment, to grant decrees of divorce and to make various other related orders.

2.4   THE GROUNDS FOR DIVORCE

Section 5(1) of the Divorce Act sets out the grounds upon which a court will grant a decree of divorce on application by either spouse. These grounds are as follows:

(a)   at the date of the institution of the proceedings, the spouses have lived apart from one another for a period of, or periods amounting to, at least four years during the previous five years;

(b)   there is no reasonable prospect of a reconciliation between the spouses; and

(c)   such provision as the court considers proper having regard to the circumstances exists or will be made for the spouses and any dependent members of the family.

2.4.1   Introduction

Absence of fault

The White Paper on marital breakdown suggested five possible approaches to a Constitutional amendment. Certain of those approaches suggested that a decree of divorce could be granted on a 'no fault' basis. Others contained detailed examples of behaviour, such as adultery, desertion, etc which could be used as a ground for the granting of a decree. The Divorce Act allows for the granting of a decree of divorce substantially on the grounds that the spouses have lived apart for a specific period of time. The question of responsibility for the break-up of the marriage is entirely irrelevant insofar as the granting of the decree itself is concerned.

When we consider the grounds on which a decree of judicial separation can be granted in Ireland pursuant to the Judicial Separation and Family Law Reform Act 1989, and indeed the grounds upon which a decree of divorce can currently be granted in England, it is perhaps surprising that the grounds for a divorce in Ireland do not include any reference to the conduct or behaviour of the parties. Section 5(1) of the Divorce Act clearly states that either spouse may apply for a divorce. A spouse therefore who has, for instance, deserted the other spouse is not barred from bringing an application for divorce which *must* be granted if the spouses have lived apart for the requisite period of four years.

Mr D Wallace TD, remarked in the course of the Dail Debates (vol 467, no 6, p 1817):

> 'there is the extremely difficult case where one partner is anxious to dissolve the marriage while his or her spouse is equally hopeful of retaining the marital links ... From being a lifelong commitment on the part of both spouses, the legislation before us clearly alters marriage to being a conditional social arrangement which may be unilaterally terminated without major difficulty by either parties ...'

2.4.2   Living apart for a period of at least four years

Definition of 'living apart'

Before a decree of divorce is granted, the applicant spouse must satisfy the court that he or she has lived apart from the other spouse for the relevant period 'at the date of the institution of the proceedings'. The four-year period, therefore, must have expired prior to the actual issuing and serving of a grounding summons. It is interesting that, under s 2 of the 1989 Act, the periods of living apart or desertion make reference to a period 'immediately preceding the date of the application' which is the date of the actual court hearing and *not* the issuing of proceedings.

There will, however, be much argument as to the interpretation of the requirement that the spouses 'have lived apart from one another'. It seems clear that an individual can be living apart from his or her spouse whilst still residing under the same roof. The Minister for Equality and Law Reform, Mervyn Taylor, who was the Minister responsible for introducing the Government's proposals with regard to divorce, stated on a number of occasions that separation could include living apart in two households but under one roof. This will lead to some uncertainty. In such circumstances, an applicant spouse will have to attempt to show that he or she has been 'living apart' from the other party either emotionally, psychologically or spiritually.

In the course of his speech on 27 September 1995, on the second stage of the Bill to amend the Constitution, Mervyn Taylor TD, stated:

> 'the term "living apart" is used in the Judicial Separation and Family Law Reform Act, 1989 and it is also a familiar term in many other jurisdictions where it has been held that this phrase will clearly cover whether the spouses have physically separated and are living in different places. The Case Law also states that where domestic life is not shared it is possible for there to be two households under the one roof.'

An effort was made to define 'living apart' in s 2(3) of the 1989 Act. This section (which deals with the various grounds for the granting of a decree of judicial separation) states that 'spouses shall be treated as living apart from each other unless they are living with each other in the same household, and references to spouses living with each other shall be construed as references to their living with each other in the same household'. Because of the use of the word 'household' instead of 'house', it is certainly arguable that, even when applying for a decree of judicial separation, the applicants can claim they are living apart whilst still actually sharing accommodation.

As Mr Taylor further remarked in the course of the Senate Debates (10 October 1996, p 1687):

> 'the crucial factor in the description is not so much whether people are living in one house but whether there are two separate households. This key provision will involve the consideration of the nature of the ties which bind people and an examination of whether there is any community of life between the spouses in a specific case. It has been stated that the practical test applied in cases where the parties are still living under the same roof, is usually whether one party continues to provide matrimonial services to the other and if there is any sharing of domestic life. Most cases will be clear, but some will require examination and determination by the Courts. It will vary from case to case.'

The granting of a decree of judicial separation does not of itself allow the couple to obtain a decree of divorce unless they satisfy the requirement to live apart for four years.

English case-law on 'living apart'

There are a number of examples in English case-law where the courts have held that a couple can be living apart from one another although residing under the same roof. These cases will be of relevance to the Irish courts when they begin to consider such fundamental matters.

The legal concept of 'living apart' does not require a change of address. It is 'not the withdrawal from a place, but from a state of things' (*Pulford v Pulford* [1923] All ER 10). Spouses would be considered to be 'living apart' when, although each is living in the family home, they have ceased 'to be one household and become two households' (*Hopes v Hopes* [1948] 2 All ER 920). See Shatter, *Family Law in the Republic of Ireland* (3rd edn) p 440.

Another case which throws some light on this issue is one which dealt with the definition of 'living apart under one roof' from an income tax point of view. The relevant case is that of *Holmes v Mitchell* [1991] STC 25.

In this case, the court held that the Revenue Commissioners were entitled to find that a couple who lived as separate households under the same roof were apparently separated for tax purposes. Since that case, the English Inspector of Taxes has been given guidelines insofar as the questions he should ask in an effort to ascertain whether or not a couple are 'living apart under the one roof', ie:

(a)   How has the house been divided up and what are the arrangements for using kitchen and bathroom facilities?
(b)   What services do the couple provide for each other, for example cooking, cleaning, etc?
(c)   What financial arrangements have been made in relation to the alleged separation?
(d)   How do the husband and the wife avoid meeting each other in the house?

These guidelines are useful in considering the meaning of 'living apart' under the Divorce Act.

Situations will arise in the future where it will be extremely difficult for a court to decide whether or not spouses have been living apart for the requisite period. An applicant husband, for example, may indicate that in his view he has psychologically removed himself from the marriage for many years while his wife may be absolutely astonished at such a suggestion.

An applicant husband may have been working abroad for, say, two years and then returned to Ireland for a number of months and thereafter travel abroad again. His wife may feel that everything is well with the marriage, but it would presumably be open to the husband eventually, after he has been abroad for the requisite period, to apply to the court for a divorce on the basis that he has been living apart from his spouse for four out of the last five years.

This is an issue which is of some importance as an applicant spouse cannot avail him- or herself of any of the powers given to the courts under the Divorce Act to make wide-ranging ancillary orders unless they are successful in obtaining a decree of dissolution of their marriage.

The courts, when deciding whether or not the parties have been 'living apart' for a period of four years, will take into account all relevant evidence when making a decision. It is therefore important when a lawyer is drawing up any matrimonial agreements such as a deed of separation, that (if the parties are actually living apart) the agreement clearly states the date on which the husband and wife commenced doing so. This will certainly be of assistance in any future application for a decree of divorce.

2.4.3 No reasonable prospect of reconciliation between the spouses

Who decides whether or not there is any prospect of a reconciliation? Is it open to a court in a particular case to say unilaterally that it feels there is a chance of reconciliation and refuse to grant a decree of divorce? The answers would appear to be 'yes'.

Section 8(1) of the Divorce Act states that:

> 'Where an application is made to the court for the grant of a decree of divorce, the court shall give consideration to the possibility of a reconciliation between the spouses concerned and, accordingly, may adjourn the proceedings at any time for the purpose of enabling attempts to be made by the spouses, if they both so wish, to effect such a reconciliation with or without the assistance of a third party'.

The important words here are 'if they both so wish'. The interpretation of this section would appear to be somewhat different from the interpretation of s 5(1)(b). There it would appear that a court can interfere of its own volition. Under s 8(1), if both the husband and the wife wish to attempt to reconcile, then the court *may* adjourn the proceedings to enable this to be done. It would be inappropriate for a court to force the hearing in such circumstances to go ahead against the wishes of the parties.

This contrasts greatly with the situation in civil cases where adjournments prior to a hearing are generally difficult to obtain and are almost unheard of during the course of a hearing once it has actually started. The legislature accepts that matrimonial cases must be dealt with in a different way from ordinary civil cases.

Section 8(1) refers to the possible assistance of a third party in effecting a reconciliation. Section 43 provides that the cost of such services 'shall be in the discretion of the court', presumably as between the parties, as certainly the State will not contribute, except in certain cases, indirectly, through the Legal Aid Scheme.

If a case is adjourned to enable parties to attempt to reconcile, a regular source of concern to both parties is the use to which any documents produced or comments made to such third parties is put thereafter. This is dealt with in s 9 of the Divorce Act which states that:

> 'An oral or written communication between either of the spouses concerned and a third party made for the purpose of seeking assistance to effect a reconciliation or to reach agreement between them on some or all of the terms of a separation or a divorce (whether or not made in the presence or with the knowledge of the other spouse), and any record of such a communication, made or caused to be made by either of the spouses concerned or such a third party, shall not be admissible as evidence in any court'.

This provision is of great importance to both spouses who are attempting to reconcile and, indeed, to the counsellor or other individual concerned.

This section also operates even if such communications were made *prior* to the issuing of proceedings. For some years, there has been doubt among lawyers as to whether or not it was possible to subpoena the records relating to such confidential communications. Now, there can be no such doubt whatsoever.

2.4.4 Proper provision for the spouse and dependent members of the family

The court must be satisfied that such provision as the court considers proper, having regard to the circumstances, exists or will be made for the spouses, any children of either or both of them, and any person prescribed by law.

Definition of 'dependent member'

In order to determine whether proper provision has been made, it is necessary to understand what is meant by 'dependent member of the family'. Section 2(1) of the Divorce Act defines such a dependent member of the family, in relation to a spouse, or the spouses concerned as meaning any child:

'(a) of both spouses or adopted by both spouses under the Adoption Acts 1952–1991 or in relation to whom both spouses are in loco parentis, or

(b) of either spouse or adopted by either spouse under those Acts or in relation to whom either spouse is in loco parentis where the other spouse being aware that he or she is not the parent of the child, has treated the child as a member of the family, who is under the age of 18 years or if the child has attained that age:

(i) is or will be or, if an order were made under this Act providing for a periodical payments order for the benefit of the child or for the provision of a lump sum for the child, would be receiving full-time education or instruction at any university, college, school or other educational establishment, and is under the age of 23 years; or

(ii) has a mental or physical disability to such extent that it is not reasonably possible for the child to maintain himself or herself fully.'

Therefore, it can be seen that a dependent member of the family includes children born to both spouses, or one spouse if adopted by both spouses or by one spouse or to whom either spouse is in loco parentis.

The age of a dependent member of the family has been increased to 23 years (while still undergoing a full-time course of education) from 21 years, which is a far more realistic age as very few children finish their tertiary education at the age of 21.

Definition of a 'spouse' and 'family'

A reference to a 'spouse' includes a reference to a person who is a party to a marriage which has been dissolved under the Divorce Act (s 2(2)(c)) and a reference to a 'family' includes a reference to a family as respects which the marriage of the spouses concerned has been dissolved under the Divorce Act (s 2(2)(d)).

Extent of enquiries by the court

The question to be asked is: how deeply will the court enquire into provisions made for the spouses and any dependent members of the family? It will be seen later that, where there are prior court orders made in relation to certain matters, the court may not be in a position to interfere at all with arrangements which have been made for the family. Where deeds of separation have been executed, s 14(1)(c) gives the court the power to vary 'for the benefit of either of the spouses and of any dependent member of the family or of any or all of those persons any ante-nuptial or post-nuptial settlement ... made on the spouses'. This clause clearly states that the courts can review existing deeds of separation if necessary, when applications for property adjustment orders are made.

If a deed of separation has been executed within a relatively short period of the court application for a divorce decree, then it is unlikely that a court would interfere with the terms of same to any great extent. In addition, if a detailed 'terms of settlement' had been executed at the same time as the application for a decree of divorce is proceeding, it is unlikely that a court would do more than briefly consider the terms, give them its approval, and make the appropriate orders by consent.

Presumably, under the provisions of s 5(1)(c), an applicant cannot simply say to a court that they will make proper provision for the dependent members of the family or the other spouse in the future at some undefined time. The provisions must have already been made or must be made by the court.

The first divorce decree granted pursuant to the provisions of Article 41.3.2 of the Constitution

Interestingly, the first decree of divorce granted in Ireland pursuant to the provisions of the Constitution was granted on the 17th day of January 1997 notwithstanding the fact that the Divorce Act had not yet come into force at that time.

The decree of divorce was granted by Barron J in the case of *RC v CC* (the High Court, unreported, 17 January 1997). The application was made by the husband, with the co-operation of the wife, as he was suffering from a terminal illness (and indeed died before the Divorce Act came into operation). In that case, the court first considered the question as to whether or not it had a jurisdiction to grant the decree. The court agreed with the submission that 'there are two instances in the Act itself which indicate that the Act is intended to regulate a jurisdiction conferred by the Constitution'. First, the long title to the Act commences: 'An Act to make provision for the exercise by the courts of the jurisdiction conferred by the Constitution to grant decrees of divorce ...', and, secondly, the power to grant a decree of dissolution contained in s 5 of the Act is stated to be an exercise of the jurisdiction conferred by Article 41.3.2 of the Constitution. The court further held that under Article 34.3.1 of the Constitution it had a full, unlimited and original jurisdiction and power to determine all matters and questions whether of law or fact, civil or criminal.

In reaching his decision, Barron J considered the various grounds for the granting of a decree of divorce. It was clear from the evidence that the parties had lived apart for a period well in excess of four years.

The court further satisfied itself that there was 'no reasonable prospect of a reconciliation' between the parties. The court then went on to consider in some detail the various provisions made for the wife and children. In this particular case there were three children of the marriage, none of whom were dependent and all of whom were in employment. Certain assets were transferred to the wife and to each of the children by the applicant husband. The court satisfied itself that these provisions were proper in the overall circumstances of the family.

It is important to note, as pointed out by Barron J, that the provisions of clause 3 of Article 41.3.2 of the Constitution differ from the corresponding statutory provision (s 5(1)(c)). The former requires: 'such provision as the court considers proper having regard to the circumstances exists or will be made for the spouses, any children or either or both of them and any other person prescribed by law'; whereas the latter provides for 'such provision as the court considers proper having regard to the circumstances exists or will be made for the spouses and *any dependent members of the family*'.

We have already discussed the definition of 'a dependent member of the family' which includes children up to a maximum age of 23 years (while still undergoing a full-time course of education). It would seem, however, that if an application is made for a decree of divorce pursuant to the provisions of the Constitution, the court will have to satisfy itself that the welfare of *all* the children of the marriage, regardless of age, is protected.

If the application for a decree of divorce is made pursuant to the Divorce Act, the court will only have to consider the welfare of children up to the maximum age of 23 years.

In the course of his judgment, Barron J stated:

> 'while I do not purport to determine that non-dependent children should necessarily have provision made for them, I am satisfied that in the particular circumstances of the present case it is proper that certainly the two daughters of the marriage should have provision made for them in the interests of the family as a whole.'

Comparison with the Judicial Separation and Family Law Reform Act 1989
It is interesting, for comparison purposes, to consider the effect of s 3(2)(a) of the 1989 Act which states as follows:

> 'Where there are in respect of the spouses concerned any dependent children of the family, the court shall not grant a decree of judicial separation unless the court:
>
> (i) is satisfied that such provision has been made, or
> (ii) intends by order upon the granting of the decree to make such a provision, for the welfare of those children as is proper in the circumstances.'

Section 3(2)(b) then goes on to define 'dependent children of the family' and 'welfare'. Under the provision of the 1989 Act, the court must satisfy itself that proper provisions have been made for the children before granting a decree of judicial separation.

Section 3(2)(a) of the 1989 Act was considered in some detail in the case of *S (V) v S (R)* [1992] 2 Fam LJ 52. The facts of this case were that the parties were married on 1 January 1972 and had two children. From early 1988, the relationship between the parties deteriorated rapidly. The plaintiff wife left the family home on about six occasions but returned in August 1990 and resided with the family again in rather abnormal circumstances with little or no communication between the spouses.

The plaintiff wife had issued proceedings pursuant to the 1989 Act and claimed a decree of judicial separation pursuant to s 2(1)(a) (adultery), s 2(1)(b) (behaviour which is of such a nature that the applicant cannot reasonably be expected to live with the respondent) and s 2(1)(f) (that a normal marital relationship has not existed between the spouses for a period of at least one year preceding the date of the application).

The circuit court refused to grant a decree of judicial separation and, as a result, no further ancillary orders could be made. The plaintiff wife appealed to the High Court and Lynch J found as a fact that she was not entitled to a decree of judicial separation pursuant to s 2(1)(a) and s 2(1)(b) of the 1989 Act, but a decree was granted under s 2(1)(f) and the reasons were given for so doing.

Lynch J then discussed s 3(2) and categorically stated that unless a court is satisfied, on the balance of probabilities, that it can make provision for the dependent children of the marriage pursuant to s 3(2) of the 1989 Act, it is precluded from granting a decree of judicial separation. In the instant case, he stated that he *was* in a position to make such provision and then proceeded to set out detailed access arrangements and granted custody of the younger child to the plaintiff wife and custody of the older child to the defendant.

This judgment is of some assistance in interpreting the provisions of s 5(1)(c) of the Divorce Act.

It is also clear that the courts can vary existing orders or agreements relating to children's custody, access or general welfare. The court can impose whatever conditions on the exercising of custody or access as it feels necessary.

2.4.5   Domicile and residence

Another condition which must be satisfied before a court can grant a decree of divorce relates to domicile or residence. A court may grant a decree of divorce only if either of the spouses concerned was *domiciled* in the State at the date of the institution of proceedings concerned *or* either of the spouses was ordinarily resident in the State throughout the period of one year ending on that date (Divorce Act, s 39(1)). The definition of 'domicile' is the same as that used in considering the validity of foreign divorces pursuant to the Domicile and Recognition of Foreign Divorces Act 1986, ie 'living in a place with the *intention* of residing in that place permanently' (author's emphasis).

2.5   THE CONTRAST WITH GROUNDS FOR JUDICIAL SEPARATION

Pursuant to the provisions of the 1989 Act, there are six grounds for the granting of a decree of judicial separation (s 2(1)). These are as follows:

(1)   *The respondent has committed adultery*
This is a difficult ground to establish. The case-law on the subject seems to require a high standard of proof that adultery actually took place. Specific proof of penetration is generally considered necessary but in some cases adultery will be assumed to have taken place in certain circumstances. The law has developed somewhat from a decision made in the case of *Goshawk v Goshawk* [1953] 109 Sol Jo 290, where it was held that it is not adultery when the sexual act relied on took place 'because of drink taken in excusable circumstances' (see also Mary O'Toole: 'An introduction to the Judicial Separation and Family Law Reform Act 1989' [1990] Fam LJ 6).

(2)   *The respondent has behaved in such a way that the applicant cannot reasonably be expected to live with the respondent*
This ground includes both mental and physical cruelty and is essentially a question of fact. The test is an objective test and it is up to a court to decide whether or not an individual can 'reasonably be expected' to put up with a particular behaviour of his or her spouse.

(3)   *There has been desertion by the respondent of the applicant for a continuous period of at least one year immediately preceding the date of the application*
There is no reference to desertion at all in the Divorce Act in relation to the granting of a decree of divorce. Desertion is considered to be a 'rejection of the marriage' and therefore one can be in desertion whilst still living under the same roof. 'Desertion' also includes 'constructive desertion' and s 3(b) of the 1989 Act defines desertion as including conduct on the part of one spouse that results in the other spouse, with just cause, leaving and living apart from that other spouse.

(4)   *The spouses have lived apart from one another for a continuous period of at least one year immediately preceding the date of the application and the respondent consents to a decree being granted*

This period is relatively short and contrasts with the four-year period required under the Divorce Act. Section 5 of the Divorce Act does not make any allowances for the fact that the spouses may be consenting to a divorce.

(5) *The spouses have lived apart from one another for a continuous period of at least three years immediately preceding the date of the application*
     This arises when one of the spouses will not consent to a decree of judicial separation and again the period is shorter than that referred to in s 5 of the Divorce Act.

(6) *The marriage has broken down to the extent that the court is satisfied in all the circumstances that a normal marital relationship has not existed between the spouses for a period of at least one year immediately preceding the date of the application*
     There is no definition of 'normal marital relationship' contained in the Act and it is on this particular ground that most of the decrees of judicial separation have been granted by the courts to date. It is sometimes thought that the reference to a 'marital relationship' is a reference solely to the sexual relationship of the parties. This is incorrect. Quite simply, this ground covers a multitude of circumstances and, indeed, it is the view of some judges that if a spouse has applied to the court for a decree of judicial separation, then this *alone* is sufficient evidence that they could not have had a 'normal marital relationship' for a period of at least one year.

2.6   THE GROUNDS FOR DIVORCE IN ENGLAND AND WALES

2.6.1   Prior to the Family Law Act 1996

The basic English legislation dealing with divorce at present is the Divorce Reform Act 1969 and the Matrimonial Causes Act 1973. (The Family Law Act 1996 is unlikely to be implemented for some years: see below.)

The Matrimonial Causes Act 1973 provides that a petition for divorce may be presented to the court by either party to a marriage on the sole ground that the marriage has broken down irretrievably. The Act, however, also provides that the court will hold that a marriage has broken down irretrievably only if the petitioner satisfies the court of one or more of five matters which are as follows:

'(a)   that the respondent has committed adultery and the petitioner finds it intolerable to live with the respondent;

(b)   that the respondent has behaved in such a way that the petitioner cannot reasonably be expected to live with the respondent;

(c)   that the respondent has deserted the petitioner for a continuous period of at least two years immediately preceding the presentation of the petition;

> (d)   that the parties to the marriage have lived apart for a continuous period of at least two years immediately preceding the presentation of the petition and the respondent consents to a decree being granted;
>
> (e)   that the parties to the marriage have lived apart for a continuous period of at least five years immediately preceding the presentation of the petition.'

It is clear that the grounds for a decree of judicial separation under the 1989 Act in Ireland are quite similar to the grounds for divorce in England and Wales. Indeed, similar phrases are used in the legislation in both jurisdictions.

Again, it is notable that the conduct and behaviour of the spouses is of relevance in deciding whether or not a decree of divorce should be granted in England, whereas under the Divorce Act in Ireland, such conduct is of no consequence in relation to the granting of a decree. It is, of course, relevant to a court when it is making ancillary orders and this will be dealt with subsequently.

In England, the Divorce Reform Act 1969 had restated the old rule that a petition for divorce could not be presented before the expiration of the period of three years from the date of the marriage unless it was shown that the case was one of extreme hardship suffered by the petitioner. This period of three years was changed to a period of one year by the Matrimonial and Family Proceedings Act 1984.

The thinking behind the imposition of such a waiting period had been to indicate the interest of the legislature in upholding the status and stability of marriage.

In reality, there is no need for any such time period to be specified in the Divorce Act as the spouses will have to have been married for at least four years before they can issue proceedings. However, it is arguable that the relevant period could commence from the first day after the marriage ceremony.

2.6.2   The Family Law Act 1996

During the late 1980s and early 1990s, the English Law Commission decided to review the grounds for divorce. It was felt that the consideration of the issue of 'fault' should be removed as far as possible from the legislation in order to reduce the bitterness between the parties and consequently minimise the harm suffered by children.

It was felt that this would also facilitate the parties in dealing properly with all financial responsibilities and obligations and, in particular, their responsibilities for their children, if they were not engrossed in arguing about who was responsible for the breakdown in the first place.

As a result the Family Law Act 1996 has been introduced in England but it encountered serious difficulties in its passage through Parliament. Although it has now been passed, its provisions have not yet been implemented and it appears unlikely that this will happen for some time.

2.6.3 'Special procedure' in England and Wales

In all undefended divorce cases there is, under English legislation, a 'special procedure' available which has become the usual procedure for dealing with the great majority of cases. This is as follows.

Following presentation of the petition, the petitioner's lawyer lodges an application for 'directions for trial' together with a standard affidavit which supports the particular ground alleged in the petition. The judge then gives 'directions for trial' by entering the case in the special procedure list and thereafter considers the evidence filed by the petitioner. If the judge is satisfied that the petitioner has sufficiently proved the contents of the petition and is entitled to the decree sought, he will make and file a certificate to that effect. The court then sends notification to the parties of the date, time and place fixed for the pronouncement of the decree nisi. The parties are notified that their attendance at the pronouncement of the decree is not necessary.

The actual process of the pronouncement of the decree is purely formal when a large number of divorces are granted at the same sitting.

2.6.4 'Consent' procedure in Ireland

Although it will be some time before a system of granting a large number of decrees of divorce together, without any of the parties being present, is introduced in Ireland, there is provision whereby a speedy application to the court for a decree of divorce can be made in certain circumstances.

Rule 11.H of the Rules of the Circuit Court (No 1) of 1997 (SI No 84 of 1997) states:

> 'In any case in which the parties are agreed in respect of all of the reliefs being sought and a defence ... has been filed and served by the respondent which reflects this agreement, the applicant or the respondent may, subject to the provisions of the following sub-rules of this rule, at any time after such defence has been filed and served, on notice to be served on the other party and, where relief pursuant to section 12 and/or 13 of the 1995 Act and section 17 of the 1996 Act is sought, on the trustees of the pension scheme concerned, not less than 14 clear days before the hearing, apply to the court for judgment, the application to be by way of motion on notice.'

Rule 11.I states that:

> 'upon the hearing of such application the court may, upon hearing such evidence, oral or otherwise, as may be adduced (i) give judgment in the terms agreed between the parties, or (ii) give such directions in relation to the service of a notice of trial/notice to fix a date for trial as to the court appears just'.

The court has the power to make whatever order it feels is just insofar as the costs of such an application are concerned (rule 11.J).

The effect of such a provision in the rules is that parties will be encouraged to settle all issues between them at an early stage and therefore speed up the entire process. In practice, with the lengthy delays which will be experienced by applicants for decrees of divorce, the parties could in fact cut down the waiting period by approximately nine to 12 months if they avail of this provision.

2.7 THE ROLE OF LAWYERS REPRESENTING APPLICANTS AND RESPONDENTS

The role of lawyers involved in matrimonial proceedings, and, in particular, divorce proceedings, is extremely important. Sometimes, the work of such lawyers can be misunderstood, but it is perhaps unfair to suggest that the main intention of matrimonial practitioners is simply to make money out of other people's problems.

Mr N Ahern expressed this view rather colourfully in the course of the Dail Debates when he stated (27 June 1996, vol 467, no 6, p 1827):

> 'this legislation will introduce divorce. What will happen then? Those with a vested interest are already out looking for their pound of flesh. The legal profession and their runners are demanding an additional £10 million funding for legal aid and the appointment of additional judges. I wonder if divorce is being introduced to give genuine people a second chance or to create another bonanza for the vultures who fly around society waiting to pick on the bones of other people's misery?'

Such comments are entirely unreasonable and the reality of the situation is reflected in the small number of practitioners in Ireland who actually specialise in matrimonial law.

Sections 6 and 7 of the Divorce Act are almost precisely the same as ss 5 and 6 of the 1989 Act. These sections impose certain duties and responsibilities on all practitioners involved in matrimonial proceedings. When the 1989 Act was passed, it was the first time, apart from the Solicitors Acts themselves, that the legislature had attempted to regulate practitioners in advising their clients. The 1989 Act and the Divorce Act do not simply give suggestions or guidelines as to how they should deal with persons involved in matrimonial disputes. The relevant sections categorically state what a practitioner 'shall' (ie must) do before making an application for a decree of judicial separation or divorce as the case may be.

Section 6 of the Divorce Act imposes certain duties and responsibilities on any family law practitioner acting on behalf of an applicant and s 7 imposes duties and responsibilities on a practitioner acting on behalf of a respondent. Both sections are almost precisely the same, apart from some minor necessary differences.

Before instituting proceedings for a divorce decree or before defending such proceedings and filing the appropriate documentation, a family law practitioner acting for both the applicant and the respondent (assuming neither of the parties are lay litigants) must:

(a) discuss the possibility of *reconciliation* and give to his or her client the names and addresses of persons qualified to help to effect a reconciliation between spouses who have become estranged;

(b) discuss the possibility of engaging in *mediation* to help to effect a separation (if the spouses are not separated already) or a divorce on a basis agreed between the spouses and give to the client spouse the names and addresses of persons qualified to provide mediation service for spouses who have become estranged;

(c) discuss the possibility (where appropriate) of effecting a separation by means of a *deed* or agreement in writing executed or made by the applicant and the other spouse and providing for their separation.

The use of the word 'discuss' in ss 6(2) and 7(2) of the Divorce Act is important. There is no obligation on spouses to actually *attend* marriage counselling or mediation prior to the issuing of proceedings. The practitioners involved merely have to talk to their clients about these matters. The discussion can be brief or lengthy depending on the parties and the practitioners involved.

Situations will arise where it is not necessary to spend any length of time discussing a possible reconciliation. There is little point in suggesting marriage counselling to a woman whose husband left her many years before and is at present living in another country with a new 'spouse' and five children.

2.7.1 Reconciliation

Presumably those qualified to help effect a reconciliation are marriage counsellors. A list of organisations which provide this service is contained in Appendix 4. Practitioners must provide their clients with such a list prior to the institution of proceedings, regardless of whether or not there is any likelihood of the client attending.

2.7.2 Mediation

A list of organisations providing a mediation service is contained in Appendix 4. Mediation is often confused with counselling and conciliation. Counselling and conciliation in effect mean the same thing, ie to assist a married couple to resolve their differences and save the marriage.

Mediation, on the other hand, assists a couple who have already made a firm and final decision to separate or divorce. The mediator should be an individual who is trained to assist both spouses to reach agreement themselves on the key issues such as custody and access, maintenance or lump sum payments, property disposals and transfers etc. The mediator does not give legal advice and sometimes leaves important issues for subsequent discussion with a lawyer (eg Succession Act rights or income tax arrangements).

The typical mediation process will involve approximately six to seven sessions with both parties attending and, if successful, heads of agreement will be drawn up by a mediator and signed by both spouses. Subsequently, a lawyer will incorporate these heads of agreement into a formal deed of separation or they will form the basis of the terms of any ancillary orders which need to be made when a decree of divorce is granted. The practitioners involved will then carry out any legal work necessary to ensure that, for instance, the family home or other property is transferred from one spouse to the other.

Some mediators are self-employed and charge an hourly rate for their work. Others are employed by the State in the Government Mediation Service and this service is free.

If the mediation process is successful, it will minimise conflict, substantially reduce legal expenses, and lead to an agreement which will to a great extent be complied with by the parties.

The parties will have, in effect, resolved the issues themselves without having solutions imposed on them by the court.

Deficiencies in the mediation process
Without attempting to detract from the usefulness of the mediation process, difficulties can arise on occasions:

(a) Mediation is most successful when both spouses are sufficiently self-confident and can present their case properly. Mediation is frequently a negotiation process where neither party is represented by lawyers. If a wife, for instance, has been confined to the matrimonial home while raising children for many years, and the husband has engaged in business activities, negotiating and dealing on a daily basis, then mediation may not be of great assistance in such circumstances. Despite the best efforts of the mediator, the wife may simply be pressurised into submission and finally agree to certain proposals which will subsequently appear to be unjust or inequitable.

(b) Sometimes, as previously stated, a number of important issues are left to be agreed between the parties and their respective lawyers. If, for example, the issue of renunciation of Succession Act rights has to be negotiated *after* the mediation process has been finalised, it can, on occasion, lead to the entire agreement falling apart. In some jurisdictions, only mediators with a legal background are permitted to act as mediators in relation to property or financial disputes. This is not the case in Ireland.

Mediators are reluctant to work with a couple if matrimonial proceedings of any description have actually been issued and are pending. Again, spouses may be reluctant therefore to attend mediation if they have to either delay the issuing of proceedings or withdraw them entirely. If the mediation process is not successful, then they will have delayed the finalisation of their affairs for many months.

2.7.3 Deeds of separation

A family law practitioner must discuss with his client the possibility of sorting out all issues by means of a deed of separation. Obviously, this is a far cheaper method of dealing with matrimonial breakdown and is to be recommended. Both the husband and the wife need to be separately represented and obtain independent legal advice before executing any such agreement. The majority of matrimonial breakdown cases are resolved by this method or by agreements entered into after the issuing of court proceedings, but before they come on for hearing.

2.7.4 Judicial separation

A practitioner acting for an applicant spouse or a respondent spouse must also ensure that his or her client is aware of judicial separation as an alternative to divorce (Divorce Act, s 6(3)). Not every party to a marriage which has broken down may wish to divorce or indeed may wish to facilitate their spouse remarrying by applying for such a decree. In addition, of course, the parties may not have lived apart for four years and may therefore not qualify for a divorce.

2.7.5 Section 6 and 7 certificates

It is important to note that not only must a practitioner acting for an applicant spouse or a respondent spouse *discuss* reconciliation, mediation, deeds of separation and judicial separation with their clients but must also *sign* a certificate which clearly states that they have done so (Divorce Act, ss 6(4)(a) and 7(4)(a)). If such a certificate is not filed, then the court may adjourn the proceedings for such period as it considers reasonable to enable the lawyer to engage in the discussions referred to above.

In addition, a copy of the relevant certificate should be served along with the originating summons on the respondent, and along with the memorandum of appearance on the applicant as the case may be.

2.8 PERSONAL LITIGANTS

Presumably, if an applicant or respondent is a personal litigant, and has not instructed a lawyer, then no certificate need be furnished to the court. In such situations the court may take it upon itself to advise a lay litigant of the possibilities of reconciliation, mediation etc.

As can be seen from the above, the role of family law practitioners is extremely important. There are many different factors to be taken into account in advising their clients. Lawyers acting in a matrimonial matter must prioritise the interests of any relevant dependent children. They should attempt to minimise conflict between the parties and, indeed, between the lawyers. They should, at all times, encourage both spouses and other family members to regard the welfare of the children as the first and paramount consideration.

The practitioner should attempt to agree as many issues as possible prior to a court hearing and attempt to minimise the areas of conflict and as a result lessen the expense which will be incurred by both spouses in any matrimonial proceedings.

A very helpful Code of Practice has been issued by the Law Society of Ireland and is reproduced in Appendix 2.

2.9 THE EFFECTS OF A DECREE OF DIVORCE

(a) Where a decree of divorce is granted, the marriage, the subject of the decree, is dissolved and either party to that marriage may remarry (Divorce Act, s 10(1)). This section contains the single most fundamental and important change in matrimonial law in Ireland since 1937.

(b) The granting of a decree of divorce shall not affect the right of the father and mother of an infant to continue to be joint guardians of any relevant children (Divorce Act, s 10(2)). The inclusion of this section clearly indicates the concern of the legislature to protect the rights and interests of children which is fundamental to all Irish Family Law legislation.
   As was pointed out by A Shatter TD, in the course of the Dail Debates (25 September 1996, p 529), the inclusion of this section in the Act was unnecessary. He stated:

   'there was never a doubt that, if a decree of divorce was granted, it could in any way affect the guardianship rights of a husband and wife. This is clear, but for comfort, because people were concerned about the impact of divorce, s 10(2) although unnecessary, is included in the Bill'.

(c) The income tax treatment of spouses in situations where payments to which s 3 of the Finance Act 1983 applies are made, shall not be affected by a divorce unless one of the spouses has entered into another marriage or is no longer resident in the State for tax purposes (Divorce Act, s 32 and Chapter 7).

(d) There will be no change in the situation relating to the payment of stamp duty and s 33 of the Divorce Act extends the stamp duty exemption provisions to a divorced couple when property is transferred pursuant to a property adjustment order. Although it is not specified in this section, the same stamp duty exemption will apply where property is transferred pursuant to the provisions of a deed of separation.

(e)   The situation relating to capital acquisitions tax, capital gains tax and probate tax is dealt with in Chapter 5.

(f)   One of the major effects of a divorce decree is, of course, the effect on the children (if any) of the first marriage and any children born to a couple in a second marriage. These effects cannot be ignored and the legislation attempts to assist in dealing with these difficulties in as much as is possible. A more detailed discussion of such issues is contained in Chapter 4.

2.10   HOW MANY DIVORCES WILL THERE BE?

Unfortunately in Ireland there is very little statistical information available concerning marital breakdown. A sociological study of marital breakdown and family law in Ireland has been carried out by Tony Fahey and Maureen Lyons ('Marital Breakdown and Family Law in Ireland – A Sociological Study' (ESRI, 1995)). Although the number of sample cases was relatively low and there were serious difficulties in obtaining proper figures from the various courts, the results of this study are quite helpful.

It included consideration given to the Census of Population completed in 1986–1991. In 1986, the number of persons who described themselves as 'separated' was 37,245. In 1991, where the definition of 'separated' was clearly stated to include those who were deserted, whose marriages were annulled, who were legally separated, who were divorced in another country, or were otherwise separated, the number of married people who so described themselves was 55,143.

It is interesting to note that in 1991, the number of women who described themselves as separated was over 12,000 more than the number of men who so described themselves. This discrepancy in the figures is a little difficult to understand and cannot be completely explained by emigration or an unwillingness among men to describe themselves as separated.

The latest Labour Force Survey undertaken in 1995 indicates that the figures for separated persons has now risen to over 85,000 which is an increase of 17,000 on 1992.

It is clear from the Census that Ireland would appear to have a relatively low rate of marriage breakdown (some 4% of the married population). The divorce rate in other European countries varies from 12% in Greece to 50% in Sweden.

According to Fahey and Lyons, Ireland, in comparison with other countries, has a breakdown rate similar to the low divorce rate in Mediterranean countries. In this regard, they are referring to the 'crude divorce rate' which is obtained by defining marital breakdown as 'those applications to courts for legal resolution of a marital breakdown situation which are successful or those attempts to achieve separation agreements between spouses where an agreement is achieved'. On this basis, the rate per 1,000 members of the population is 0.95% in Ireland. In America, which has the highest divorce rate in the world, the rate is 4.7%. In England and Wales, it is 2.9%.

As a result of the Divorce Act coming into operation in Ireland, there will be a large number of applications to court. Clearly, there will be a substantial increase in the amount of business being carried on by the courts as many who have already obtained judicial separations or executed deeds of separation will wish to obtain divorce decrees. It is estimated that approximately 10–15,000 couples may apply for divorce in the first year after the Act comes into effect.

The only valid comparison is with the coming into operation of the Judicial Separation and Family Law Reform Act 1989. Since the grounds for the old decree of divorce *a mensa et thoro* (which was the only remedy available before 1989) were very limited and since there often was nothing much to be gained by obtaining such a decree, the figures relating to such applications to court show a huge increase since October 1989 (see Fahey and Lyons, p 37). Under the 1989 Act, the courts were given extensive additional powers which could only be availed of if a decree of judicial separation were granted. This led to a large increase in the number of such applications.

It is interesting that, in Ireland and elsewhere, it would appear that women initiate proceedings in the majority of cases, ie 72% of such applications to court were initiated by women, 22% by men, 5% jointly and 1% by third parties.

In England and Wales, when the Divorce Reform Act 1969 came into operation in 1971, there were approximately 110,000 petitions for divorce during the following 12 months. In 1993, the number of petitions had increased to approximately 184,000. The divorce rate of 13.5 divorces per 1,000 married couples was one of the highest in Europe.

Chapter 3

STATUS OF SUBSISTING SEPARATION
AGREEMENTS AND COURT ORDERS

3.1 INTRODUCTION

When new legislation is enacted in the area of matrimonial law, confusion can arise as to the legal status of deeds of separation entered into prior to the passing of any such legislation.

In addition, the question now arises as to whether or not an individual can apply to court for various ancillary orders pursuant to the Divorce Act when he or she has already obtained ancillary orders under the Judicial Separation and Family Law Reform Act 1989 or the Family Law Act 1995.

Is it possible for a husband and wife to execute a deed of separation which deals with issues such as maintenance, disposal of property, custody, access and lump sums and then bring an application under the Divorce Act for a property adjustment order?

If a spouse has obtained an order for the old decree of divorce *a mensa et thoro,* can that spouse apply for ancillary orders along with an application for a divorce?

3.2 THE POWER OF THE COURT TO VARY SUBSISTING SETTLEMENTS

Difficulties have arisen and will continue to arise concerning the finality of deeds of separation. When granting a decree of divorce the court may, on application by either spouse, make a property adjustment order varying any ante-nuptial or post-nuptial settlement (including such a settlement made by will or codicil) made on the spouses (Divorce Act, s 14(1)(c)). An ante-nuptial settlement is finalised prior to the marriage ceremony, for example, a trust set up by the bride's father in order to provide funds in the future for the education of any children of the marriage or a pre-nuptial agreement entered into by the husband and wife and dealing with the division of assets in the event of a divorce. A post-nuptial settlement is entered into *after* the marriage ceremony and includes a deed of separation.

Because the definition of 'property' referred to in s 14(1)(c) of the Divorce Act is so wide, the courts would appear to be given the power, when granting a decree of divorce, to interfere with arrangements already made in relation to many matters.

The definition of 'property' is not limited simply to a family home or to real property. It includes private dwelling houses, commercial properties, furniture, jewellery, stocks and shares, horses, yachts, cattle and other animals etc. It would therefore appear on the face of this section of the Act that, despite the fact that a husband and wife may have entered into a detailed deed of separation covering all aspects of their marital situation, the courts may interfere with same as they see fit when granting a decree of divorce.

Since s 14(1)(c) of the Divorce Act is a simple repetition of s 9(1)(c) of the FLA 1995, which in turn repeats s 15(1)(c) of the 1989 Act. The case-law under those earlier provisions is directly relevant when interpreting s 14(1)(c).

3.2.1　Case-law prior to the Judicial Separation and Family Law Reform Act 1989

K v K

Prior to the coming into operation of the 1989 Act, the only relevant case dealing with this issue was *K v K* [1988] IR 161. In that case, McKenzie J, in the High Court, dealt with an application of a husband for a decree of divorce *a mensa et thoro* (the only remedy of that type then available). The husband and wife had already executed a deed of separation which did not deal with the issue of Succession Act rights. If the husband were to be successful in his application to court for a divorce then his wife would lose her Succession Act rights to his estate. This was of great importance to him as he had entered into a new long-term relationship. Judge McKenzie refused to grant the relief sought on the basis that the husband and the wife had already executed a deed of separation which relieved them of the duty to cohabit. If he was to grant a decree of divorce *a mensa et thoro*, the only effect of such a decree would be to give the husband and the wife the right to live separately and apart from each other, a right which they already had. There is no doubt that the facts of this particular case and indeed the motives of the applicant were relevant factors in the decision which was reached.

3.2.2　Case-law after the Judicial Separation and Family Law Reform Act 1989

There have been a number of circuit court judgments dealing with the question of whether or not an individual can apply for a decree of judicial separation pursuant to the 1989 Act once they have executed a deed of separation. This question is significant as the 1989 Act gave substantial additional powers to the court to make ancillary orders when granting a decree of judicial separation. An applicant cannot avail of these additional powers to make such ancillary orders unless a decree of judicial separation is granted.

N(C) v N(R)

In the case of *N(C) v N(R)* [1995] 1 Fam LJ 14, the husband and the wife were married in 1962 and at the time of the court application the children of the marriage were no longer dependent. The parties separated in 1981 and executed a deed of separation at that time. It was agreed that the husband would remain in the family home with the children and the wife would vacate the family home. It was further agreed that the family home would be sold after a period of seven years and the agreement provided for an appropriate division of the nett proceeds of sale.

Subsequently, in 1986, the parties revoked the 1981 agreement and entered into a new deed of separation. The terms of the second agreement included the wife returning to live in the family home with the youngest child of the marriage with the husband vacating the family home. The husband was to continue discharging the mortgage repayments and to pay maintenance to the wife.

Once the 1989 Act had come into operation the wife applied to the circuit court for a decree of judicial separation, a maintenance order and a property adjustment order. The husband replied that the wife's claim was barred because she had executed two deeds of separation, because both parties had already been relieved from the duty to cohabit, and therefore the wife was estopped from bringing the proceedings in the first place.

McGuinness J held that the execution of a deed of separation of itself is not a bar to the exercise of the court's discretion under the 1989 Act. She further stated that the term 'post-nuptial settlement' referred to in s 15(1)(c) of the 1989 Act includes separation agreements. Clearly, the Oireachtas intended to give the court a specific power to vary such agreements. She further stated that the existence of a separation agreement cannot through estoppel oust the jurisdiction of the court under s 15. These comments would obviously apply to s 14(1)(c) of the Divorce Act in the same way.

O'D v O'D

In the case of *O'D v O'D* (unreported 24 October 1995, Circuit Court McGuinness J), the husband and the wife married in 1961 and had two children both of whom were now adults. Over the years, the main point of dispute was the family home. In 1969, the husband transferred the family home to the wife, allegedly for tax reasons. In 1979, a deed of separation was signed by both parties which incorporated clauses clarifying the position in relation to the family home and its ownership. In 1986, the husband issued proceedings under s 12 of the Married Women's Status Act 1957 claiming an interest in the said family home. O'Hanrahan J, in the circuit court, directed that the husband was entitled to a one-fortyfifth share of the family home. Both the husband and the wife appealed this decision to the High Court which stated that the wife was entitled to the family home in its entirety and that the husband had no legal or equitable interest in the family home.

Subsequently, in 1994, the husband issued proceedings pursuant to the provisions of the 1989 Act and applied for a decree of judicial separation and a property adjustment order. The wife brought an application to dismiss the proceedings of the grounds that:

(a)   the husband was estopped from bringing proceedings because of the existence of the prior deed of separation; and
(b)   the issue was res judicata because of the application which had already been dealt with pursuant to the Married Women's Status Act; and
(c)   the proceedings of the husband were vexatious and frivolous; and
(d)   a decree of judicial separation could not be granted as both parties were already relieved of the duty to cohabit pursuant to the provisions of the deed of separation.

McGuinness J held that the husband was not estopped from issuing proceedings pursuant to the 1989 Act in looking for a property adjustment order for the same reasons as outlined in the case of *N(C) v N(R)*, above. She further stated that although the matter was res judicata insofar as an application under the Married Women's Status Act was concerned, that it was still open to the husband to obtain a property adjustment order under the 1989 Act because of the provisions of s 15(1)(c) of the Act.

Because the matter is of such importance for practitioners and individuals involved in matrimonial cases, Judge McGuinness has stated a case to the Supreme Court and asked the following questions:

(a)   Was she correct in holding that she can grant a decree of judicial separation under the 1989 Act where the parties have already signed a deed of separation?
(b)   Was she correct in stating that the existence of a separation agreement cannot through estoppel oust the jurisdiction of the court because of the provisions of s 15(1)(c)?
(c)   Was she correct in her views as to the claim that the matter was res judicata?

Since, as stated above, the court's powers under s 15(1)(c) of the 1989 Act are identical to those under s 14(1)(c) of the Divorce Act, the decision of the Supreme Court is of great relevance to divorce applications and should resolve this dilemma conclusively.

Meanwhile, it appears that at present (pending the result of the case stated to the Supreme Court) one can apply for a property adjustment order when applying for a decree of judicial separation or a decree of divorce, despite the existence of a properly executed deed of separation and the court can make whatever order it feels appropriate in the circumstances.

3.3   THE EFFECT OF SEPARATION DEEDS IN 'FULL AND FINAL SETTLEMENT'

It is important to note that in none of the judgments referred to above did the deeds of separation contain clauses stating that it was the parties' intention that the agreement was entered into in full and final settlement of all past, present and future property and financial claims which either the husband or the wife had against the other. The agreements, further, did not contain a clause (which has now become standard practice) that the husband and the wife confirmed that, apart from their rights and obligations under the provisions of the agreement, neither of them had any right, claim or entitlement in respect of any present or future property, moneys or assets of the other, whether pursuant to specific legislation or otherwise.

3.3.1 Advice to clients

McGuinness J made reference in her judgments (*N(C) v N(R)* and *OD v OD*) to the absence of such clauses in the deeds of separation. As yet, it is unclear as to their effectiveness or otherwise. It is important, however, from a practitioner's point of view, to consider in each case, when drawing up a deed of separation, whether or not such 'full and final settlement' clauses should be included. The relevance of such clauses would sometimes depend upon whether or not one is acting for a spouse who is dependent upon the other or vice versa.

A typical example of a 'full and final settlement' clause which is contained in many deeds of separation is as follows:

> 'The husband and the wife hereby agree for all the purposes and in particular for the purposes of any proceedings brought by either of them for judicial separation or divorce that it is their intention that this agreement is in full and final settlement of all present and future property and financial claims (save for periodic maintenance) which either of them may have against the other under the Constitution of Ireland and the Married Women's Status Act 1957, the Family Home Protection Act 1976, the Judicial Separation and Family Law Reform Act 1989, the Family Law Act 1995, the Family Law (Divorce) Act 1996 or under any Act of the Oireachtas amending these Acts or under the provisions of any other similar legislation of this or any jurisdiction under the Rules of the Equity, the common law or otherwise. The parties hereto agree not to issue or maintain proceedings under the leglislative provisions mentioned in this clause, save in respect of periodic maintenance.'

If a lawyer is acting on behalf of a husband who is a man of property and some wealth, the husband may wish such a clause to be included in the deed of separation. His lawyer will make every effort to prevent the wife bringing an action in the future for lump sum orders or property adjustment orders.

On the other hand, if a lawyer is acting on behalf of a dependent wife who may feel that her husband will increase his wealth substantially in the future, then she may well wish to reserve the right to bring a claim against the husband at that time and her lawyer will attempt to ensure that a 'full and final settlement' clause is *not* included in the deed of separation.

3.3.2 'Clean break' principle

Under English divorce law, it is possible to obtain court orders or reach agreements which in effect terminate once and for all the financial responsibility of one spouse to the other. It is clear from the provisions of the Divorce Act and other legislation that such an approach is not favoured by the legislature in Ireland. The issues of custody, access and maintenance can always be varied at any time by a court on application by either a husband, a wife or, in certain circumstances, a third party making such application on behalf of an infant. There is no power in Irish law for providing a lump sum to a spouse in full and final settlement of all maintenance claims either now or in the future. It is, of course, possible to obtain a lump sum order but this cannot be made conditional upon no maintenance being paid in the future. Under s 27 of the Family Law (Maintenance of Spouses and Children) Act 1976, a spouse cannot contract out of the right to claim maintenance.

It is interesting, however, that the Supreme Court has recently considered this issue of finality in the case of *F v F* (unreported, 30 November 1995, Supreme Court 377/93). Denham J in the course of her judgment in that case states that:

> 'certainty and finality of litigation are important. Some issues in family law are not capable of a final order by law, for example maintenance. However, the fact that some issues in family law courts are not capable of finality, does not deprive this area of the law of the important concepts of certainty and finality. Whereas care for dependants requires that there be no finality, in some areas the general law regarding certainty should apply unless excluded by law or justice.'

The Supreme Court may have a role to play in advancing this concept of finality before the Oireachtas takes any necessary legislative action.

Relevance of deeds of separation to the making of ancillary orders
Section 20(3) of the Divorce Act states that in deciding whether to make most types of ancillary orders:

> 'and in determining the provisions of such an order, the court shall have regard to the terms of any separation agreement which has been entered into by the spouses and is still in force.'

This provision would seem to suggest that when an application is made for a divorce the court shall not be bound by the terms of a deed of separation when making ancillary orders. This section merely states that the court shall 'have regard to' the terms of the deed of separation. The court can take into account the fact that perhaps a lump sum was paid pursuant to a deed of separation, that one spouse transferred a property to the other, or that certain other financial arrangements were made when considering the making of further ancillary orders. Presumably, therefore, it is open to the court to ignore the terms of a deed of separation if it so wishes.

The use of the words 'still in force' in this section is interesting. When does a deed of separation cease to be 'in force'. Does such a deed cease to be 'in force' if one party breaks one of its terms? Does the breach have to be a breach of a fundamental term of the agreement? If a deed of separation is held to be no longer 'in force', does it mean that the husband and the wife are no longer legally separated? If the deed contained a clause stating that it was null and void in the event of the spouses cohabiting again for a period of time, the agreement could not be said to be still 'in force' if, in fact, the couple did cohabit subsequently. These are issues which will no doubt be considered by the courts in due course.

3.4 THE POWER OF THE COURT TO VARY EARLIER COURT ORDERS

3.4.1 Case-law

The Supreme Court has, in the case of *F v F* (unreported, 30 November 1995, Supreme Court 377/93) clarified the position somewhat with regard to applications for ancillary orders under the 1989 Act (and by extension the FLA 1995) when earlier orders have already been made by the court.

In this case the wife applied for a decree of divorce *a mensa et thoro* in 1986, together with an order excluding her husband from the family home, an order for alimony and a barring order under the Family Law (Protection of Spouses and Children) Act 1981.

A written consent was entered into in 1987 which dealt with the issues of maintenance, the right of residence in the family home, custody etc. The consent also contained a term whereby both parties were given liberty to apply to the court. Proceedings were stayed on the basis of the settlement.

In February 1992, the wife issued proceedings under the 1989 Act and applied for a decree of judicial separation and various ancillary orders. She wished to make a claim under the 1989 Act in relation to the family home for a property adjustment order. The remedies available to her under the 1989 Act were far greater than those available to her under the Married Women's Status Act 1957.

In making an order under the Married Women's Status Act 1957, the courts reach a decision based largely on direct financial contributions. Under the 1989 Act (and the 1995 and 1996 Acts), there are many additional factors to be taken into consideration when making a property adjustment order (see the Divorce Act, s 20).

The Cork Circuit Court stated a case to the Supreme Court and asked the following question:

> 'Is the applicant entitled to effecitvely disregard the earlier proceedings ... and bring the second set of proceedings seeking the relief claimed?'

The answer to this question according to the Supreme Court is no. The consent which was handed into court in 1987 was a bar to further proceedings under the 1989 Act.

The Supreme Court held that the application for a decree of judicial separation was the same as an application for a decree of divorce *a mensa et thoro*. The 1989 Act simply widened the grounds for obtaining such a decree but the granting of such a decree had the same effect as the granting of a decree of divorce *a mensa et thoro*. It relieved both parties from the duty to cohabit.

The terms of the consent which was handed into court operated as a stay on the proceedings and precluded the wife from applying for a decree under the 1989 Act. If the 1989 Act had not been passed then the wife could not have applied again for a decree of divorce *a mensa et thoro*. The Supreme Court clearly stated that the wife was looking for a relief which she did not need (ie a decree of judicial separation) simply in order to obtain ancillary orders.

It is important to note that the Supreme Court in the course of this judgment did not deal at all with the issue of the relevance of deeds of separation and whether or not they operate as a bar to further proceedings under the 1989 Act (or indeed the FLA 1995 and property adjustment orders under the Divorce Act). This is a matter which still has to be dealt with by the Supreme Court in the case of *O'D v O'D* (unreported, 24 October 1995, Circuit Court, McGuinness J).

3.4.2   The situation under the Family Law (Divorce) Act 1996

The situation with regard to prior court orders has been clarified, insofar as applications for divorce are concerned, by s 26 of the Divorce Act.

Where certain orders have been made pursuant to the Family Law (Maintenance of Spouses and Children) Act 1976, the 1989 Act or the FLA 1995 and an application is subsequently made 'to the court by a spouse to whom the first mentioned order relates for an order granting a decree of divorce ... the court may by order discharge the first mentioned order as on and from such date as may be specified in the order'.

The relevant orders under the 1976 Act which can be discharged on the granting of a decree of divorce are:

(a)   a maintenance order;
(b)   a variation of a maintenance order; and
(c)   an interim maintenance order.

The relevant orders made pursuant to the 1989 Act which can be discharged on application for a decree of divorce are as follows:

(a)   periodical payments and lump sum orders;
(b)   property adjustment orders;
(c)   exclusion orders;
(d)   orders for the sale of a family home;
(e)   orders under s 12 of the Married Women's Status Act 1957;

(f) certain orders under ss 4, 5 or 9 of the Family Home Protection Act 1976;
(g) a barring order;
(h) a protection order;
(i) an order for the partition of the property under the Partition Acts 1868 and 1876;
(j) an order relating to custody of or access to children;
(k) orders for the sale of property;
(l) orders varying or discharging financial and property orders.

It is interesting to note that certain orders which have already been made under the 1989 Act, for example orders extinguishing Succession Act rights, are excluded from this section.

The orders which have been made under the FLA 1995 and which can be discharged when an application for divorce is being made are as follows:

(a) periodical payments and lump sum orders;
(b) property adjustment orders;
(c) exclusion orders;
(d) orders directing a sale of the family home;
(e) orders determining the title to or possession of any property in dispute between spouses;
(f) certain orders under the Family Home Protection Act 1976;
(g) a barring order;
(h) a protection order;
(i) an order for partition of property;
(j) orders for custody of and access to children;
(k) financial compensation orders;
(l) pension adjustment orders;
(m) orders preserving pension entitlements after judicial separation;
(n) orders extinguishing succession rights on judicial separation;
(o) orders for sale of property;
(p) variation of certain orders made under the FLA 1995.

3.4.3 Conclusions

Section 26(2) of the Divorce Act states that:

> 'where, on the grant of a decree of divorce an order specified in subsection (1) is in force, it shall, unless it is discharged by an order under subsection (1), continue in force as if it were an order made under a corresponding provision of this Act...'

It is clear therefore that a spouse may apply for a decree of divorce and ancillary orders pursuant to the Divorce Act despite the fact that he or she may have obtained a decree of judicial separation pursuant to the 1989 Act and the FLA 1995 and despite the fact that various ancillary orders may have been made under those Acts. As Mervyn Taylor TD, the Minister for Equality and Law

Reform stated in the course of the Dail debates (27 June 1996, vol 467, no 6, p 1766):

> 'provision is made ... for the situation where a couple seeking a divorce have already obtained a judicial separation. It is provided in this section that orders in relation to the separation will continue to be in force unless the court orders otherwise, notwithstanding the grant of a decree of divorce'.

Although approaching the issue from a slightly different angle the Minister clearly states that a court may interfere with earlier ancillary orders made pursuant to an application for a decree of judicial separation.

Presumably, although it is not specifically stated, spouses who have obtained the old decree of divorce *a mensa et thoro* prior to 1989 may apply for a decree of divorce and avail of all the ancillary orders which are contained in the Act. As Dr Woods TD in the course of the Dail Debates stated (27 June 1996, vol 467, no 6, p 1774):

> 'For those who obtained separation before the enactment of the Judicial Separation Act 1989, this would be of great importance because the range of reliefs available then was considerably inferior to the reliefs that became available under the Judicial Separation Act 1989 ...' (and by extension the Divorce Act).

There is no doubt that the existence of s 26 of the Divorce Act will lead to a substantial amount of additional court applications. In addition, as Dr Woods TD again points out in the Dail Debates (27 June 1996, vol 467, no 6):

> 'because there will be a four year period from separation until a divorce can be granted, it will be necessary for spouses whose marriages have broken down to continue to apply to the courts for reliefs under the Judicial Separation Act 1989 ... and it is likely that the number of applications under the Judicial Separation Act will continue, at least at the present level'.

3.5   RECOGNITION OF FOREIGN DIVORCE DECREES

Because of the decision of the Supreme Court in the case of *F v F* (unreported, 30 November 1995, Supreme Court 377/93), it is clear that if a decree of divorce has been obtained in another jurisdiction which is recognised in Ireland that a further decree of divorce cannot be applied for pursuant to the Divorce Act. The actual recognition of foreign divorce decrees themselves is discussed in Chapter 12.

The question then arises as to the status of individuals who have obtained decrees of divorce in other jurisdictions which are not recognised in Ireland as the spouses have failed to satisfy the domicile criteria laid down by the Domicile and Recognition of Foreign Divorces Act 1986.

One of the principles of law is that an applicant 'must come to equity with clean hands'. If a spouse has obtained a divorce decree in another jurisdiction which is not recognised here then it is possible that a party to the proceedings has sworn documents which are untrue. The spouse has therefore committed perjury. Can such an individual then bring an application to the Irish courts for a decree of divorce under the Divorce Act in such circumstances? The probable answer is yes but it is an issue which could cause some difficulties in particular cases before certain judges.

Quite possibly the fact that such events have occurred may well affect the type or extent of ancillary orders which would be made in a particular case when an application for divorce is before the court.

What is the position if a spouse, who has already issued proceedings pursuant to the 1989 Act or the FLA 1995 wishes to apply for a divorce decree and ancillary orders?

Since there is no specific provision in the Divorce Act permitting such a spouse to simply add on a claim for a divorce to his original pleadings, it would appear necessary for him or her to institute separate proceedings for a divorce decree and either withdraw the earlier proceedings under the 1989 Act or the FLA 1995 or continue on with them in tandem with the proceedings under the Divorce Act.

3.6   MAKING A DEED OF SEPARATION A RULE OF COURT

It is of course possible for a couple to negotiate the terms of a deed of separation and subsequently have the deed made a Rule of Court. However, it is necessary to issue proceedings in such circumstances by way of notice of motion.

The provisions contained in a deed of separation which is ruled by the court and which deal with matters such as maintenance, property transfers, custody and access have the same effect as if the same orders had been made by the court after a full hearing.

The enforceability of such an agreement which has been made an order of the court was considered, in relation to maintenance, in the case of *D v D* [1991] 9 Fam LJ 8.

A deed of separation, containing a maintenance clause had been made a Rule of Court. The applicant wife applied for a variation of the maintenance order and it was held by the court that she could make such an application without being forced to commence maintenance proceedings de novo. The maintenance clause had the same effect as a maintenance order made after a court hearing.

Chapter 4

CHILDREN

4.1 INTRODUCTION

The welfare of children is considered by all those involved in the law relating to matrimonial breakdown to be of prime importance. Nearly all matrimonial legislation makes reference to the need to protect the interests of children before any steps are taken to vindicate the rights of their parents. The main issues which come before the court on a regular basis are guardianship, custody and access.

4.2 GUARDIANSHIP

4.2.1 The nature of guardianship

When a married couple have a child, they automatically become and remain joint guardians of the child. If a child is born *outside* of marriage, the mother of the child becomes and remains the sole guardian (Guardianship of Infants Act 1964 (GIA 1964), s 6(4) as amended by the Status of Children Act 1987) unless the court decrees otherwise.

Guardianship gives a married couple the right to equal involvement in all major decisions affecting the child's welfare. Such decisions relate, for instance, to the education of the child, his or her medical treatment, the location of the child's home and the religious upbringing of the child.

4.2.2 Application to court for guardianship

In the case of a child born outside marriage, since the mother is the sole guardian of that child, that father has no rights ab initio in relation to custody, access or guardianship.

The *only* method by which a father can obtain such rights is to apply to court pursuant to the provisions of s 6 of the GIA 1964 (as amended by s 12 of the Status of Children Act 1987). This section provides that:

> 'where the father and mother of an infant have not married each other, the court may, on the application of the father, by order appoint him to be a guardian of the infant'.

Such applications to court can be quite traumatic and, indeed, where a couple have split up, are often bitterly opposed by the mother.

Even if an unmarried couple wish to have the father of a child appointed a guardian by consent, they are required by the legislation to make an application to court in this regard. They cannot arrange simply for the drawing up of a legal document appointing the father to be a guardian. The procedure for making such an application has been simplified but it is debatable whether or not requiring a couple to attend a court in such circumstances is appropriate.

It is, however, important to note that even if the father of a child has not been appointed a guardian, he is still entitled to apply for custody of, or access to, his child and appropriate orders will be made by a court which will always consider the welfare of the child to be of paramount importance (GIA 1964, s 11 as amended by s 13 of the Status of Children Act 1987).

4.2.3   The court's approach to guardianship

The court, in deciding whether or not to appoint an applicant father a guardian of his child, will make the decision solely on the basis of what is in the best interests of the child. In doing so, it considers such matters as:

(a)   the relationship of the father with the child since birth;
(b)   the day-to-day involvement (if any) of the father in caring for the child;
(c)   the financial contributions made towards the support of the child;
(d)   the relationship between the father and the mother insofar as it may affect the child, either physically or psychologically;
(e)   in certain cases, the views of the child.

4.2.4   Appointment and removal of guardians

Both the father and the mother of an infant may, by deed or will, appoint a person or persons to be guardian or guardians of the infants after his or her death (GIA 1964, s 7(1) and (2)).

A testamentary guardian shall act jointly with the surviving parent of the infant so long as the surviving parent remains alive unless the surviving parent objects to his so acting (GIA 1964, s 7(3)). If the surviving parent so objects or if a testamentary guardian considers that the surviving parent is unfit to have the custody of the infant, the testamentary guardian 'may apply to the court for an order under this section' (GIA 1964, s 7(4)) and the court may make whatever order it sees fit in the best interests of the child.

Section 8 of the GIA 1964 deals with the appointment and removal of guardians by the court where an infant has no guardian at all. The court may, on application, appoint any person or persons to be a guardian to an infant in such circumstances.

If a guardian who has been appointed by a deceased parent dies, or refuses to act, the court may appoint another person to act jointly with the surviving parent as a joint guardian.

The court also has the power to remove from office any guardian appointed by will or deed or order of court (GIA 1964, s 8(4)).

Under s 9(1) of the GIA 1964:

> 'When two or more persons are appointed to be guardians they shall act jointly and on the death of any of them the survivor or survivors shall continue to act.'

4.2.5 Powers and duties of guardians

Section 10 of the GIA 1964 provides that every guardian under the Act shall be a guardian of 'the person and the estate of the infant unless ... the terms of his appointment otherwise provides'.

A guardian appointed under the 1964 Act is entitled to issue proceedings in relation to custody or access if necesssary.

Such a guardian may also issue proceedings for the recovery of damages for the benefit of the said infant for any injury to or trespass against the person of the infant.

A guardian appointed in such circumstances 'shall be entitled to the possession and control of all property, real and personal, of the infant and shall manage all such property and receive the rents and profits on behalf and for the benefit of the infant until the infant attains the age of 18 years ... and may take such proceedings in relation thereto as may by law be brought by any guardian of the estate of an infant.'

4.2.6 Guardianship and divorce

Section 10(2) of the Divorce Act touches upon the issue of guardianship. This section states that:

> 'for the avoidance of doubt, it is hereby declared that the grant of a decree of divorce shall not affect the right of the father and mother of an infant, under section 6 of the Act 1964, to be guardians of the infant jointly'.

This section is entirely unnecessary since there is no doubt that a divorce decree cannot affect the right of guardianship.

4.3 CUSTODY

4.3.1 Introduction

It is open to both parents of a child to apply for custody whether or not they are married to each other. A genuine custody battle is the most traumatic type of case to come before the family courts.

Section 3 of the GIA 1964 states that:

> 'where in any proceedings before any court, guardianship or upbringing of an infant, or the administration of any property belonging to or held in trust for an infant, or the application of the income thereof, is in question, the court, in deciding that question shall regard the welfare of the infant as the first and paramount consideration'.

This is a vitally important section in the 1964 Act and the concept of the welfare of an infant as of primary importance is reflected in all family law legislation including the Divorce Act.

4.3.2   The welfare of the infant

Section 2 of the GIA 1964 defines 'welfare', in relation to an infant, as comprising 'the religious and moral, intellectual, physical and social welfare of the infant'.

There is no doubt, however, that it is still generally the view of many courts that the mother is a more suitable person to have custody of children than the father, unless there is very good reason to the contrary. It is still difficult, despite the comments made by courts in certain cases and despite the carefully worded legislation relating to children, for a father to obtain sole custody. It is even more difficult in situations where the relevant children are female and, in particular, females of a young age.

Such an attitude, however, is changing to a degree but such change is slow. It certainly does nothing to prevent lengthy and distressing custody battles taking place in the family courts.

It is arguable that the court system is entirely inappropriate for such cases and that they should be dealt with in a far less confrontational context, such as in some form of tribunal which has the assistance of specialist advisors.

4.3.3   Statistics as to custody

Applications to the district court in relation to guardianship, custody and access form the major part of the district family court's work. For instance, the number of such district court applications in Dublin for the year ended July 1994 were 3,365. Orders of one sort or another were made in all of these cases.

It is also interesting, but not surprising, that more men than women apply to court in relation to access and guardianship. It is clear from the statistics gathered by Fahey and Lyons ('Marital Breakdown and Family Law in Ireland—A Sociological Study' (ESRI, 1995)) that there was a large increase in such applications during the late 1980s and early 1990s partly due to a change in attitude, and partly due to the introduction of the Status of Children Act 1987.

Fahey and Lyons also attempted to ascertain the residence of children after the break-up of a marriage or relationship. They concluded that:

> 'by far the most common arrangement is for the children to live with the mother (78% of cases). In an additional small proportion of cases (6%), the parents are still sharing the same house so that the children live with both. Children live with the father in only 5% of cases, and shared arrangements where the children live equally with the father and mother are extremely unusual (only 2% of cases)' (p 93).

Effect on children of marriage breakdown

There have been a number of studies carried out concerning the effect on children of marriage breakdown. In the USA, statistics indicate that over 50% of American children would spend some time in a single parent home following divorce. There is no doubt that many of the studies of the effects of marital breakdown on children show varying degrees of behavioural difficulties occurring in children of broken marriages. It was apparent from a number of studies 'that a significant number of those children who experience their parent's divorce would enter their adolescence later under a severe handicap'.

'There is evidence from many studies that intense parental conflict poses severe threats to the psychological health of children whether the family is divorced or remains married. It is reasonable to assume that the psychological threat to a child is heightened when the parental conflict centres specifically on the child and when the parents engage in a continuing tug-of-war with the child as the object' (lecture by Dr Gerard Byrne, Consultant Child Psychiatrist on the 'effect of marriage breakdown and associated litigation on children' [1995] 2 Fam LJ at p 68).

4.3.4 Joint custody

Joint custody is not defined in any of the legislation and it is arguable that, in fact it does not exist as such. Custody is generally considered to involve one parent alone caring for a child or children and making all of the day-to-day decisions without reference to the other parent.

There are situations, however, where both parents share their children in an almost equal way from a time point of view. Dr Byrne refers to a number of studies which indicated that where a court has made orders for joint custody or greater access to both homes, the children were:

> 'significantly more depressed and more withdrawn as compared with other children in sole custody, whether that was with the father or the mother. The children in shared custody homes with a high degree of acrimony between the parents, did particularly badly. ... The implications of this is that a recommendation or an order for joint custody or frequent visitation in a situation of high conflict, is unwise'.

In other cases, however, a couple will agree that they both should have joint custody. This will be incorporated in a deed of separation or in a consent court order. The children may not actually spend an equal amount of time with both parents, but the concept of joint custody (as opposed to sole custody) may be reassuring for a parent who, for whatever reason, spends less time with the children than his or her spouse.

A positive effect of an order for joint custody is that it leads to both parents feeling (rightly or wrongly) that they have an equal say in the upbringing of the child or children. Where the couple are married, both parents remain joint guardians as has already been discussed and already have an equal say in the major issues affecting the child's upbringing. However, such an order for joint custody can act as a positive reinforcement for an individual in a difficult situation and in turn lead to greater harmony between the parents.

4.3.5   Isaac Wunder order

The court has the power, in suitable cases, to restrain a litigant from issuing further proceedings without the leave of the court (*Wunder v Hospitals Trust (1940 Ltd)*, unreported, 11 April 1967). Custody and access battles are particularly liable to lead to such situations.

It is common for a spouse to apply regularly to court for orders relating to custody or access to children. The powers of the court under the GIA 1964 are extremely wide and in effect a court can make any order it sees fit in such situations. Orders can be made in relation to the issuing of passports, holidays in Ireland or abroad, the education of children, the religious upbringing of children, and even physical activities to be undertaken by children.

On occasions, there can be abuses of the right of a parent continually to apply to court for such orders and the motivation for bringing such applications may have nothing to do with the welfare of the children. It may then be necesssary for an application to court to be made for an order preventing such regular applications.

Such an order was made by McGuinness J in the circuit court on 24 November 1994 in the case of *W (S) v W (F)* [1995] 1 Fam LJ 24. This case had come before the district court, the circuit court and the High Court on numerous occasions including a four and a half day hearing in the High Court. As McGuinness J pointed out, litigation had been virtually continuous for the previous three years. Not only that, but the parties had entered into a comprehensive deed of separation in January 1994 which had been made a Rule of Court, and which dealt in an extremely detailed manner with the issue of custody and access to the three children of the marriage.

On this particular occasion, there was a further application in relation to access with an assessment having been carried out by a Dr C. This case revolved largely around the issue of access but was also relevant to custody and guardianship applications. McGuinness J stated that she considered:

> 'that continuing litigation cannot but be damaging to the children in this case and Dr C's evidence is that the repeated applications to court had already been damaging to Mrs W. I accept this evidence absolutely. ... I am charged by the statute to put the welfare of the infants before all other considerations in deciding this matter. I am convinced that further applications to court and the endless prolongation of litigation cannot but be inimical to their welfare'.

McGuinness J pointed out that access was primarily the right of the children to enable them to maintain a relationship with the non-custodial parent. She granted the order sought by the applicant preventing Mr W from bringing any further application in regard to any of the matters referred to in the proceedings without first seeking the leave of the circuit court.

4.3.6 The court's approach to custody disputes

The welfare of the children

In practice, courts, in deciding issues of custody, will consider all the various aspects of welfare referred to in s 2 of the GIA 1964. The court will then make a decision based on the evidence presented on the assumption that the welfare of the child is of paramount importance and is of far greater relevance than any rights of a parent.

Walsh J in the case of *O S v O S* [1974] 110 ILTR 57 stated:

> 'All the ingredients which the Act stipulates are to be considered ... globally. This is not an appeal to be decided by the simple method of totting up the marks which may be awarded under each of the five headings. It is the totality of the picture presented which must be considered ... the word "welfare" must be taken in its widest sense.'

The comments of Judge Walsh in that case form the basic guidelines for any judge dealing with the issue of custody.

The views of the children

The views and wishes of children themselves are sometimes taken into account by the courts. This can occur indirectly when an assessment has been prepared by a child psychologist or child psychiatrist and produced to the court. Such a specialist interviews the parents and the children and a large amount of, what is in effect, hearsay evidence will therefore come to the attention of the court.

In these types of cases the rules of evidence are not so strictly enforced and the specialist is permitted to give evidence which specifically repeats comments made by the child to him or her.

On occasions, some judges will interview children themselves privately in their chambers in an attempt to ascertain their views and assist them in making a decision. It is almost unheard of for a child to formally give evidence in custody or access battles and be subject to cross-examination.

It is, however, not uncommon for the views of a teenage child to be taken into account by a judge in making his or her decision.

Such matters were considered by the circuit court in the case of *C(C) v C(P)* [1994] 3 Fam LJ 85 where McGuinness J followed the case of *O S v O S* referred to above.

In this case the parents were married in 1966 and had six children, two of whom were dependent at the time of the court hearing. The applicant wife left the family home in May 1993 after an alleged assault leaving her daughter aged 13 and her son then aged 11 with the respondent husband. The applicant instituted proceedings seeking, inter alia, a decree of judicial separation, custody of the two dependent children, and various other ancillary orders. The daughter left the family home at Christmas of 1993 and went to reside with her mother. A report was prepared for the court pursuant to s 40 of the Judicial Separation and Family Reform Act 1989.

It was held by the court insofar as children were concerned that:

(a)   welfare must be decided on an overall view of all the circumstances;
(b)   the wishes of a 12-year-old cannot provide the complete answer as to welfare;
(c)   a child of 15 is not at a suitable age for the making of an access order.

On appeal to the High Court, these decisions of the circuit court were affirmed in general terms.

Religious education

Where a court makes a decision that an applicant parent should not have custody of an infant child, the court shall still have the power:

> 'to make such order as it thinks fit to secure that the infant be brought up in the religion in which the parents, or a parent, have or has a legal right to require that the infant should be brought up' (GIA 1964, s 17(1)).

Section 17(2), however, emphasises that this is a situation where the wishes of a child should be taken into account and specifies that the court may 'consult the wishes of the infant in considering what order ought to be made', and specifically states that nothing in the Act shall interfere with the right of the infant to the exercise of his or her own free choice in the matter.

Relevance of conduct of spouses

Section 41 of the Divorce Act states that:

> 'where the court makes an order for the grant of a decree of divorce, it may

declare either of the spouses concerned to be unfit to have custody of any
dependent member of the family who is a minor and, if it does so and the spouse
to whom the declaration relates, is a parent of any dependent member of the
family who is a minor, that spouse shall not, on the death of the other spouse, be
entitled as of right to the custody of that minor'.

Therefore, the conduct and behaviour of spouses before, during or after the
marriage is of relevance in deciding the issue of custody.

The issue of the relevance of the conduct and behaviour of parents was
discussed by the Supreme Court in some detail in the case of *S v S* [1992] 3 Fam
LJ 84.

This case involved an extremely hard-fought custody battle. It lasted for eight
days in the High Court before being dealt with by the Supreme Court on
appeal.

The husband and the wife were married in 1973 and had three children, all
girls, aged 13, 10 and 7. The plaintiff wife had an extra-marital adulterous
relationship and in 1988 left the family home, taking the children with her. She
continued her relationship with the third party who was a married man and
intended to commence living with him as soon as the youngest child was older.
She then issued proceedings under the 1989 Act seeking, amongst other
ancillary orders, custody of the children. The defendant, in turn, sought
custody of the children for himself.

The High Court granted custody of the children to the husband with provision
for access by the wife, but not including overnight access. The plaintiff wife
appealed that decision to the Supreme Court where she was also unsuccessful.
Finlay CJ considered many issues in the course of his judgment. He referred to
the welfare of the infants as being of the first and paramount importance and
referred to Judge Griffin's comments in the case of *MacD v MacD* [1979] 114
ILTR 66 where he stated:

> 'in such (custody) proceedings, the conduct of the parent is relevant only insofar
> as it affects the welfare of the children within the definition of welfare in section 2.
> But the conduct of the parents is relevant insofar as *inferences can be drawn from it* to
> show where the priorities of the parents lie in relation to the children, as this is an
> important factor to consider in relation to their welfare' (author's emphasis).

Finlay CJ himself then went on to say in this particular case that:

> 'whilst there can be no question of custody being awarded on the basis of reward
> or punishment to either of the parents, having regard to any view of the issues
> arising with regard to the judicial separation, it is inevitable that certain of the
> facts found and also the conclusions reached by the learned trial judge in regard
> to the issues arising on the judicial separation, as distinct from the custody of the
> children, may become relevant to the welfare of the children in the manner above
> outlined.'

The Chief Justice further referred to the case of *O S v O S* [1974] 110 ILTR 57 and in particular to the comments of Walsh J in relation to the global consideration of the ingredients of welfare:

> 'This is not an appeal to be decided with the simple method of totting up the marks which may be awarded under each of the given headings. It is the totality of the picture presented which must be considered'.

Finally, Finlay CJ commented that each case is different and must be considered on the basis of its own facts. He said that whereas general principles concerning questions of custody can be gleaned from the decisions of the courts made in individual cases, such principles should be applied to the special facts of each case which vary greatly.

Social reports in custody/access cases

Section 42 of the Divorce Act states that s 47 of the Family Law Act 1995 shall apply to proceedings under the Divorce Act.

Section 47 of the FLA 1995 deals with the use of social reports in family law proceedings. It replaces s 40 of the 1989 Act, and states that the court may:

> 'of its own motion or on application to it, in that behalf by a party to the proceedings, by order give such directions as it thinks proper for the purpose of procuring a report in writing on any question affecting the welfare of the party to the proceedings or any other person to whom they relate'.

It is important to note that the court may *of its own volition* decide that such a report should be obtained. This happens regularly in cases concerning custody, access or guardianship, particularly in the district court. The orders made by a judge in such cases have such far-reaching consequences and affect people's lives to such an extent that courts regularly look for assistance or guidance from experts.

The persons who can prepare such reports are specified in s 47 as: (a) probation and welfare officers; (b) a suitably qualified person nominated by a Health Board; or (c) any other person specified in the order.

At the present time, in practice, the obtaining of a report from a probation or welfare officer attached to the court takes well over a year to obtain from the date of making of the order, largely due to lack of financial resources and the small number of probation and welfare officers who have been appointed.

It is far more common for the parties themselves to obtain the services of a child psychiatrist or child psychologist who will carry out an assessment and produce a report for the court.

The fees and expenses incurred in the preparation of a report shall be paid by the parties themselves and in such proportions as the court may determine

(FLA 1995, s 47(4)). The costs involved in obtaining such reports can be high and often the court will order that such costs be shared equally by the parties. If, however, only one party is in paid employment, he or she will have to bear the entire cost alone. If both parties are represented by the Legal Aid Board then the Board may agree to fund the cost of such a social report. If only one party is eligible for legal aid then the Board may agree to pay 50% of the costs involved.

A person who prepares such a report may be called as a witness in the proceedings to give evidence and to be available for cross-examination (FLA 1995, s 47(5)). The court itself may require the presence of such an individual in certain circumstances. Again, costs will be incurred and may be dealt with by the court as outlined above insofar as the obtaining of the report itself is concerned.

Section 47(3) of the FLA 1995 states that a copy of a report obtained in such circumstances, shall be given to the parties to the proceedings concerned and (if he or she is not a party to the proceedings) to the person to whom it relates and may be received in evidence in the proceedings. It is assumed that it is not intended by this section that copies of such reports be provided to any children who are referred to. The parties to the proceedings however have a legal right to examine the report.

The court will have regard to any submissions made by or on behalf of the party to the proceedings concerned or by any other person to whom the proceedings relate before making an order for the obtaining of a social report (FLA 1995, s 47(2)).

There is no doubt that in certain situations children run the risk of being 'over-assessed'. It is not unknown for children, and indeed, entire families to undergo a number of different processes of assessment before a final order is made. This can occur where, for instance, a plaintiff spouse is unhappy with the original report and requests the court to order a further assessment by another individual in the hope that it will be more helpful to their case.

In addition, allegations of abuse against the children of a relationship may be made by one parent against the other and this could lead to further interviews and reports by social workers or, indeed, the police. Such constant questioning and exploration of children and their parents may lead to serious psychological difficulties for the children who are themselves the subject of such investigations.

Family law practitioners should be careful when making decisions as to whether or not to apply to court under s 42 of the Divorce Act for the procuring of such a report. In most situations, if such a report is obtained, it will have a great influence on the outcome of the case and on the court's decision. If the conclusions are not in favour of the practitioner's client, there is usually little that can be done to alter this viewpoint. As has already been indicated, the practitioner may request that another assessor prepare a report, but this will only be permitted in a small number of cases.

It is open to a court to make an order relating to custody or access pursuant to s 11 of the GIA 1964 'notwithstanding that the parents are then residing together' (s 11(3)). However, such an order is unenforceable if the couple continue to reside together and the order itself shall 'cease to have effect if for a period of three months after it is made they continue to reside together'.

4.4   MAINTENANCE OF CHILDREN

4.4.1   The court's approach

The court when making, inter alia, a periodical payment order in favour of a dependent member of the family shall, under the Divorce Act, s 20(4), have regard to a number of matters when determining the provisions of such an order. These are as follows.

'The financial needs of the member' (s 20(4)(a))
In practice, an applicant parent who is looking to the court to make a periodical payments order in favour of their child or children, will set out in writing, prior to any court hearing, all expenses and outgoings relating to the dependent member(s) of the family. This is an extremely difficult task. If a mother, for instance, is residing with three children and is requesting the court to make a periodical payments order in favour of the entire family, it is almost impossible for such an individual to precisely state the costs and expenses incurred in supporting each child individually, or indeed, as a group. It is difficult to estimate the cost of, for example, the amount of food which the mother consumes and the cost of the amount of food eaten by the children. The courts, however, eventually reach a situation where they have a 'feel' for such matters and certain 'rules of thumb' are used to achieve a fair and equitable division of the family income.

'The income, earning capacity (if any), property and other financial resources of the member' (s 20(4)(b))
A very young child will rarely have any income of his or her own. There is a child benefit payable in respect of a child which would be taken into consideration by a court to a certain degree. Older children, however, may have part-time jobs, even if they are still attending a full-time course of education, and such earnings will also have some relevance to a particular case.

'Any physical or mental disability of the member' (s 20(4)(c))
Children suffering from a physical or mental disability will be more expensive to support than those who are not. In addition, maintenance payments for such children may continue for many years after they attain the age of 23.

'Any income or benefits to which the member is entitled by or under statute'
(s 20(4)(d))
An example of such a benefit is disability benefit or education grants.

'The manner in which the member was being and in which the spouses concerned anticipated that the member would be educated or trained'
(s 20(4)(e))
This is an interesting sub-section in that it indicates that a court should take into account the views of *both* parents as to the future education of their children and specifically those views which existed *prior* to the actual divorce itself. This is intended to emphasise the importance of education for children and to ensure that the court gives it priority and makes certain, insofar as is possible that the necessary funds are available for such education.

Various matters under s 20(4)(f)

The court shall also have regard to various matters which are taken into consideration when fixing maintenance for spouses, such as:

(a)   the income, earning capacity, property and other financial resources which each of the spouses concerned has, or is likely to have in the foreseeable future;

(b)   the financial needs, obligations and responsibilities which each of the spouses has, or is likely to have in the foreseeable future (whether in the case of the remarriage of the spouse or otherwise);

(c)   the standard of living enjoyed by the family concerned before the proceedings were instituted or before the spouses commenced to live apart from one another, as the case may be; or

(d)   the terms of any separation agreement which has been entered into by the spouses and is still in force.

'The accommodation needs of the member' (s 20(4)(g))

A child requires a place to reside which would usually be with one or both parents. In some cases, the dependent member of the family may have special needs if, for instance, they are incapacitated and require the use of a wheelchair. In such circumstances, additional moneys will be required to, for example, ensure that the child's home has wheelchair access.

4.4.2   Relevance of conduct of spouses on periodical payment orders for dependants

When a court is making a decision as to whether or not it should make a periodical payments order for the benefit of a dependent member of the family or when a court is deciding whether or not to vary, discharge or suspend such an order, it shall have no regard whatsoever to the conduct or behaviour of the parents involved in the proceedings (Divorce Act, s 23). This is another clear statement that in every case the welfare of children is considered by the court to be of paramount importance. A parent's bad behaviour does not mean that he or she will be refused an order for maintenance in favour of a dependent child if such an order is necessary.

It is no defence to such an application for a paying party to indicate to a court that the receiving party has committed adultery or deserted. Quite simply, any moneys available must first be used to support the dependent members of the family before consideration is given to the needs of the spouses concerned.

4.4.3   Increase in the age of the dependent child

Insofar as children are concerned, one of the most important measures contained in recent family law litigation is the increase in the age for the payment of maintenance for dependent children who are undergoing a full-time course of education to 23 years (Divorce Act, s 2; FLA, s 2). This provision has come as a shock to a number of parents who anticipated their responsibility ending at the age of 21. In many cases, however, a child commencing tertiary education would not complete it until passing the age of 21 years.

Maintenance payments therefore can now last up to the age of 23 years to assist a child in completing their course of education whereas, in earlier times it was not uncommon for children to be forced, out of economic necessity, to cease some sort of tertiary course prior to its completion and obtain paid employment.

4.5   ACCESS

4.5.1   The nature of access

As has already been suggested, access is a concept which could gradually disappear over the years and be replaced by a 'joint parenting arrangement'. The words 'custody and access' conjure up images of one spouse, usually the mother, having control of the children's lives with the other spouse, usually the father, having very limited visitation rights which take place in specific locations between specified hours. This type of arrangement is gradually being replaced by more flexible arrangements which allow the children to establish, as much as is possible, a full and worthwhile relationship with both parents, despite a decree of divorce having been granted.

It is important to note, as the courts have indicated on a number of occasions, that access is a right of the child and not of the parent.

In some situations, however, where there is a lot of friction between the parents, it may be necessary to spell out in specific detail the periods which will be spent by the children with each parent. The ideal situation is one where both parents separate or divorce in a relatively amicable fashion and agree that they shall operate an informal and flexible parenting regime for the children.

4.5.2 Refusal of access

In certain situations, one parent will refuse to agree to the other parent having access at all to the children of the marriage. This may arise in cases where the children are, in effect, being used as tools or weapons in the arguments between the parents. It is not uncommon for one parent to attempt, either consciously or sub-consciously, to turn the children against the other parent by constantly criticising that other parent and blaming him or her for the breakdown of the marriage.

It is often argued in court that access should not be granted to a non-custodial parent who has entered into a new relationship and is living with a new partner. It is contended that a new relationship may have a very confusing effect on the children and they will find it difficult to retain clear concepts of their father and mother. This view is difficult to maintain in the context of divorce.

4.5.3 Conditional access

It is open to a court under s 11 of the GIA 1964 to attach conditions to access orders. In the past, it has, for instance, been common for the court to order that a non-custodial spouse shall have access to his or her children on condition that a named third party is not present during such visits. This attitude is, however, changing to a certain degree and once the granting of divorce decrees has become more common, it is highly probable that the imposition of such a condition will become rarer. One of the basic premises for the granting of a divorce decree is that a second relationship is envisaged which will acquire the protection of law and achieve its own legal status. The very existence therefore, of a second relationship which is legally recognised could not, of itself, prevent a non-custodial spouse having access to his children in the presence of a second spouse.

4.5.4 Child abuse allegations

In some instances of marital breakdown, allegations of sexual abuse are made. It is not unknown for one spouse, in the midst of very heated and traumatic custody or access proceedings to allege, sometimes long after proceedings have commenced and been partly dealt with, that the other spouse has sexually abused one or more of the children.

In general, the making of such allegations, whether true or untrue, can cause serious difficulties for the non-custodial parent insofar as his or her relationship with the children is concerned. Even if the allegations are entirely fabricated, there will be lengthy delays in carrying out investigations and obtaining reports from experts. The entire matter may drag on for many months or indeed years and may ultimately result in the relationship between the non-custodial parent and the children becoming so damaged that it can never be revived.

A court will refuse access in only fairly exceptional circumstances and, in particular, will insist that any allegations of sexual abuse be backed up by very strong independent evidence before refusing access altogether.

It is not uncommon, however, for a judge to decide, on an interim basis, not to take an unnecessary risk in such cases, and to refuse all access whilst the appropriate investigations are being carried out. Such investigations could take a very long time and therefore further affect the relationship of the accused person with his or her children.

4.5.5   The views of the child

As a general rule of thumb, courts will take little notice of the views of children themselves in relation to access if they are under the age of 14. The views of children over that age will be taken into account, if appropriate, by a court in making an access order.

When children are in their teens, the reality is that they will 'vote with their feet'. If they wish to see the non-custodial parent, and that parent wishes to see them, then such meetings will take place. If a child of 14 years and upwards does not wish to have anything to do with the other parent, then no order of the court can force the child to do so.

4.5.6   Kidnapping children: the Hague Convention

It is not uncommon for a custodial parent to fear that the other parent will take advantage of access in order to abduct the child. The Hague Convention was introduced in order to assist custodial parents whose children have been taken abroad without that parent's permission.

HAGUE CONVENTION COUNTRIES
The following list shows the contracting States to the Convention on the Civil Aspects of International Child Abduction (The Hague, 25 October 1980), together with the territories specified under arts 39 or 40 of the Convention and the date on which the Convention came into force in each country.

Contracting State	Specified territories	Date in force
Argentina	—	1 June 1991
Australia	Australian States and mainland Territories	1 January 1987
Austria	—	1 October 1988
The Bahamas	—	1 January 1994
Belize	—	1 October 1989
Bosnia and Herzegovina	—	7 April 1992
Burkina	—	1 August 1992
Canada	Ontario	1 August 1986
	New Brunswick	1 August 1986
	British Columbia	1 August 1986
	Manitoba	1 August 1986
	Nova Scotia	1 August 1986
	Newfoundland	1 August 1986
	Prince Edward Island	1 August 1986
	Quebec	1 August 1986
	Yukon Territory	1 August 1986
	Saskatchewan	1 November 1986
	Alberta	1 February 1987
	Northwest Territories	1 April 1988
Chile	—	1 May 1994
Colombia	—	1 March 1996
Croatia	—	1 December 1991
Cyprus	—	1 February 1995
Denmark	—	1 July 1991
Ecuador	—	1 April 1992
Finland	—	1 August 1994
France	—	1 August 1986
Germany	—	1 December 1990
Greece	—	1 June 1993
Honduras	—	1 March 1994
Hungary	—	1 September 1986
Italy	—	1 May 1995
Rebublic of Ireland	—	1 October 1991
Israel	—	1 December 1991
Luxembourg	—	1 January 1987
Macedonia	—	1 December 1991
Mauritius	—	1 June 1993
Mexico	—	1 September 1991
Monaco	—	1 February 1993
Netherlands	—	1 September 1990
New Zealand	—	1 August 1991

Contracting State	Specified territories	Date in force
Norway	—	1 April 1989
Panama	—	1 May 1994
Poland	—	1 November 1992
Portugal	—	1 August 1986
Romania	—	1 February 1993
Slovenia	—	1 June 1994
Spain	—	1 September 1987
St Kitts and Nevis	—	1 August 1994
Sweden	—	1 June 1989
Switzerland	—	1 August 1986
United States	—	1 July 1988
Yugoslavia	—	1 December 1991
Zimbabwe	—	1 July 1995

The purpose of the Convention is to minimise the harmful effects on children of their wrongful removal from their country of residence to another jurisdiction and to establish procedures for their immediate return to the country where they 'habitually reside'.

The two main features of the Convention are as follows:

(a)   Where a child has been wrongfully removed from his or her country or habitual residence and retained in another Member State, that State is bound, with few exceptions, to order the immediate return of the child to the State of the child's habitual residence. Any inquiry in relation to the child's welfare must then take place in the original State from where the child was wrongfully removed. It is intended that orders for the return of the child are made automatically, except in rare circumstances. A State may not be forced to return the child if it is established:

    (i)   that the person having care of the child was not actually exercising their custody rights at the time of removal or retention, or had consented to or subsequently acquiesced in the removal or retention; or

    (ii)   there is a grave risk that his or her return would expose the child to physical or psychological harm or otherwise place the child in an intolerable situation (Art 13). Evidence of such risks must be very clear as this argument will be accepted by the courts only in exceptional circumstances.

(b)   The Convention established Central Authorities in each contracting State to facilitate co-operation with one another in this entire area. The Central Authorities in each State assist the parties to locate their children if they have been kidnapped and work with the local police force. The Central Authority will ensure that the parties are legally represented and, under the Irish Legal Aid Scheme, if an application to court is necessary, all parties may be represented by the Legal Aid Board regardless of their means.

4.5.7 Passports

It is not uncommon for difficulties to arise in relation to the issuing of passports to children of divorced or separated parents. One parent may be concerned that the other will take the children abroad and fail to return, if either a passport is issued to a particular child or, if the name of that child is inserted on the parent's passport.

It is possible for a child to have a separate passport. Only a guardian of a child may apply for the issuing of such a passport. As has already been indicated, if a child is born outside of marriage, then the mother is automatically the sole guardian of the child and the consent of the father of the child to the issuing of a passport to a child is not necessary unless he has been appointed a guardian of the child by a court (see above). Similar provisions apply in relation to the insertion of the child's name on the passport of the mother.

Where the parents of a child are married, both parents are automatically guardians and both parents must sign any forms necessary for the obtaining of a passport for the child or for the insertion of the child's name on the passport of the parents.

If one parent refuses to consent to the issuing of a passport of a child to the other parent, then that parent may apply to court for an order dispensing with the consent of the other parent to the issuing of the passport.

It is only in exceptional circumstances, where there is a real risk of kidnapping, that the court will refuse to dispense with such consent. Such an application is commonly made by a parent who wishes to take a child on holiday abroad and the other parent, out of vindictiveness or lethargy, fails to co-operate in the issuing of the passport by not completing the necessary forms.

The situation can become rather more complicated where one parent is an Irish citizen and the other parent is a non-national. In such circumstances, the child may be entitled to a passport in another jurisdiction.

In Ireland, difficulties arise in relation to Irish–American children. Indeed, the US Embassy has issued guidelines for lawyers involved in such cases.

In general terms, under US law, the issuing of a passport to a 'qualified applicant' may not be denied. Either parent may apply to obtain a passport for a child under the age of 13 years without the consent of the other parent.

However, if a court has granted sole custody of a child to one parent or made an order preventing a child being removed from the jurisdiction without the consent of the court, then the US authorities may refuse to issue a passport either to the relevant child or to the non-custodial parent on behalf of the child.

In the district court, the standard form orders for custody include a paragraph which states that the child or children shall not be removed from the jurisdiction of the courts without the consent of the other spouse or an order of the court itself.

4.6   RIGHTS OF THIRD PARTIES

4.6.1   Child Care Act 1991

The Child Care Act 1991 is of major importance in protecting the rights of children. It is the end result of the work of a taskforce on childcare set up in 1974. The taskforce produced its report in April 1981. Some ten years later, the Child Care Act 1991 was passed but it took another five years or so before the majority of the sections came into force by a Ministerial order. A major difficulty was the lack of resources available to implement the proposals contained in the report and provided for in the Act.

An interesting statistic is that, at 31 December 1992, there were 2,885 children in care. It is likely that this figure has increased since then.

4.6.2   Purpose of the Child Care Act 1991

The purpose of the Child Care Act 1991 was, according to the explanatory memorandum, 'to update the law in relation to the care of children, particularly children who have been assaulted, ill-treated, neglected or sexually abused or who are at risk'.

Prior to the coming into operation of the 1991 Act, Health Boards were responsible for children only up to the age of 16 years and could only take children under the age of 16 into care. Section 2 of the 1991 Act increased the age to 18 years.

The ethos of the Act is to promote the welfare of children insofar as is possible. The rights of children are emphasised as being of paramount importance and the rights of parents are open to limitations being imposed by the courts or interference by third parties.

The Health Boards are given the responsibility of promoting the welfare of children who are not receiving adequate care and protection. They are also given power to provide child care and family support services. The Health Board must have regard to the principle that it is generally in the best interests of children to be brought up in their own families. It is only in extreme cases that children are to be taken into care (1991 Act, s 3).

The Health Boards are given the power to receive into voluntary care orphans and abandoned children and, with the consent of the parents, children whose parents are unable to care for them (1991 Act, s 4).

The following obligations are imposed on Health Boards:

(a)   to make available accommodation for homeless children (1991 Act, s 5);
(b)   to provide or ensure the provision of an adoption service in their areas (1991 Act, s 6);
(c)   to carry out an annual review of the adequacy of the childcare services in their areas (1991 Act, s 8).

The 1991 Act further makes provisions for the protection of children in emergency situations. Section 12 of the 1991 Act empowers a Garda to remove a child to safety, without a warrant, where it would be dangerous to await the making of an emergency care order by a court. If a Garda removes a child in such circumstances, then the child must be delivered up as quickly as possible to the Health Board. The child may then be retained in the custody of the board for a maximum of three days pending the hearing of an application for an emergency care order under s 13 of the 1991 Act.

An emergency care order can provide for the placing of a child in the care of a Health Board for up to eight days where there 'is reasonable cause to believe that there is an immediate and serious risk to his safety'. The parents must be informed of the making of such an order.

The power given to the Garda to remove a child without a warrant or without a court order of any description imposes a great responsibility on the guards. There are many situations where a guard could not possibly be sure whether or not he or she should remove a child to safety and, in practice, such a decision is made only with the greatest of reluctance.

4.6.3   Care order

Part IV of the 1991 Act provides for the making of a care order where it is necessary for the child's health, development or welfare. The child is removed from the care of its parents and placed in the care and control of the Health Board.

4.6.4   Supervision order

Section 19 of the 1991 Act further provides for the making of a supervision order which authorises a Health Board to have a child visited in his home to ensure that he is being cared for properly. The child is not actually removed from the custody of his or her parents or parent as is the case when a care order has been made.

4.6.5   Legal representation of the child

Of major importance are the powers given to the court pursuant to s 25 of the 1991 Act. When proceedings have been issued for a care order, a supervision

order or an order placing a child in foster care, and the child to whom the
proceedings relate is not already a party to the said proceedings

> 'the court may, where it is satisfied having regard to the age, understanding and
> wishes of the child, and the circumstances of the case, that it is necessary in the
> interest of the child and in the interests of justice to do so, order that the child be
> joined as a party to, or shall have such of the rights of a party as may be specified by
> the court in, either the entirety of the proceedings or such issues in the
> proceedings as the court may direct' (1991 Act, s 25(1)).

The court may also, if it thinks fit, appoint a solicitor to represent the child in
the proceedings and give such directions as it sees fit as to the performance of
the duties of the said solicitor (1991 Act, s 25(2)).

Where a solicitor is appointed in such circumstances, the costs and expenses
incurred by him or her on behalf of the child shall be paid by the relevant
Health Board (1991 Act, s 25(4)). This is the first occasion where it has been
possible for a child to be separately represented in court proceedings.

It has often been argued that, in ordinary custody/access battles, it would be of
great assistance to the court if the child or children were separately legally
represented. In such cases, each lawyer involved is representing the interests of
only his or her own client, and this may not be in the best interests of the child.

Although, as has previously been indicated, lawyers acting in custody or access
cases have a duty to ensure that the welfare of the child is treated as of first and
paramount importance, in practice this is an extremely difficult goal to achieve.
The appointment of a separate legal representative for the relevant children
would be of great assistance to a court and, indeed to all parties involved in such
traumatic cases. The major difficulty in the past has been the lack of proper
financial resources to enable such a system to be set up. The provisions
contained in s 25 therefore represent a huge step forward in this area although,
at this stage, they relate only to children being taken into care.

4.6.6   Appointment of guardian ad litem

Another new provision contained in the 1991 Act is that providing for the
appointment of a guardian ad litem in proceedings for care orders, supervision
orders, or orders placing children in foster care. The court may appoint a
guardian ad litem for a child if it feels it is 'necessary in the interests of the child
and the interests of justice to do so' (1991 Act, s 26(1)).

Again, the Health Board concerned will be responsible for any costs incurred.

The guardian ad litem has the right to act, in effect, as a parent of the child and
give evidence in the course of a court hearing if appropriate. The guardian ad
litem is also entitled to arrange for other witnesses to give evidence and to act in
a full and proper sense on behalf of the child. The ISPCC will assist in providing
such a guardian ad litem.

4.7 IN CAMERA RULE

It is interesting to note that s 14(2) of the Censorship of Publications Act 1929 is repealed by s 3 of the Divorce Act.

This section of the 1929 Act prohibited the publication of reports of divorce, separation and nullity cases. The names, addresses and occupations of the parties and the witnesses could not be published. This was partly intended to protect the interests of children who would remain anonymous.

Since such proceedings cannot be reported, or published in any event, because of the 'in camera' rule, s 14(2) of the 1929 Act, was therefore unnecessary.

The 'in camera' rule means that divorce hearings take place in private with no-one present except for the parties themselves, any lawyers involved in the case, the judge and the court registrar.

It is a serious contempt of court to publish details of any matrimonial case which has been heard 'in camera'. Section 38(5) of the Divorce Act extends the provisions of s 34 of the 1989 Act to divorce proceedings. This section states that 'proceedings under this Act shall be heard otherwise than in public'.

Naturally, however, for the purposes of development and understanding matrimonial law, it is important that there is a system of reporting matrimonial cases. The printing of law reports, therefore, is not prohibited. Generally, the names, addresses and other identifying particulars of the parties are not included in the reports.

It has been argued, on occasions, that the existence of the 'in camera' rule operates as a form of disinformation. The public become aware, only to a very limited degree, of the reality of matrimonial breakdown situations and indeed of the extent of such occurrences. It is argued that if journalists were permitted to report some of the details of matrimonial hearings on a regular basis (without revealing the identity of the parties, and with the parties' consent) that it would lead to a far greater awareness of the extent of matrimonial breakdown in this country and the various problems which arise. Such coverage would also, it is argued, give the public and lawyers a greater awareness of the actual outcome of matrimonial disputes and divorce proceedings insofar as the division of property, financial arrangements and custody and access orders are concerned.

It is common in some other jurisdictions for details of divorce hearings to be published by the media. This occurs to a certain degree in the UK and to a very large degree, in the USA. It is probable that such reporting would not be beneficial to the parties involved in divorce proceedings or to their children (if any) but, in a wider context, may be of help to those who are making a decision as to whether or not they should embark upon such proceedings in the first place.

Chapter 5

THE FAMILY HOME AND CONTENTS

5.1 HISTORICAL

5.1.1 Married Women's Status Act 1957

The Married Women's Status Act 1957 consolidated the law relating to the status of married women and ensured that a married woman was in the same position as an unmarried woman in relation to the ownership and disposition of property. It also provided a mechanism for the resolution of property disputes between spouses (s 12). Section 12 has since been repealed and has been replaced by s 36 of the Family Law Act 1995.

5.1.2 Family Law Act 1995

Section 36 (and previously s 12) gives the court no discretion to award property to the more deserving spouse. Nor does the court have no power to vary or adjust the property rights of the parties. Instead, its function is limited to declaring the parties' existing rights following established legal principles.

It is useful to set out those principles here.

(a) When property is purchased by a spouse and registered in his or her name, the other spouse, does not as spouse become entitled to any share. This applies to all property including the family home.

(b) If a spouse makes a financial contribution to the purchase price of property, registered in the name of the other spouse, or to the mortgage repayments in respect of property, the owning spouse holds a share of the property on a resulting trust in favour of the other spouse. The size of that share is determined from the contributions. In calculating the share, only financial contributions are taken into account. Financial contributions can be direct (such as the payment or part payment of the deposit to purchase) or indirect (such as discharging household accounts thereby enabling the other spouse to make the mortgage repayments).

(c) If a husband buys property and registers it in the name of his wife as sole owner or as joint owner with him, a presumption of advancement applies. It is presumed that the husband intends to make a gift to his wife. The presumption of advancement only applies to gifts from husband to wife and not vice versa. This presumption can be rebutted by evidence of a contrary intention between the spouses.

(d) Spouses have a right to reside in the family home. This right exists only as against each other. Neither spouse can force the other out of the family home.

Either spouse may apply to the court for a determination of any question arising on the title to or possession of any property (FLA 1995, s 36(1)).

The court may make such order in respect of the property as it considers proper, including an order that the property be sold or partitioned and an order for enquiries and directions in relation to the property (FLA 1995, s 36(2)).

As has been stated earlier, the courts' function is limited to the ascertainment of who is entitled to the property interest. For example, a property may have been registered in the sole name of the husband. The wife may have made a direct financial contribution to the purchase price, for instance, by giving part of an inheritance she received as the deposit. Alternatively, she may have made indirect financial contributions thereby enabling the husband to discharge the mortgage repayments. In either case, the wife may apply under s 36 for an order declaring her interest in the property proportionate to the extent which her contribution to the acquisition of the property bears to the total value of the property.

Section 36 has extended the power of the court to determine disputes in relation to money or property which was previously owned or in the power or control of the other spouse and it also extends the right to apply to the court to children of a deceased spouse.

Section 36(3) allows a spouse or a child of a deceased spouse to make an application in relation to:

(a)   money which may (but does not necessarily have to) represent the proceeds of sale of property in which the plaintiff spouse had a beneficial interest; and

(b)   property (other than money) in which the spouse has a beneficial interest and in this regard where the money or property is no longer in the possession or under the control of the defendant spouse or the plaintiff spouse is uncertain if the money or property continues to be in the control of the defendant spouse.

In effect, this allows money or property to be traced through to third parties. Section 36(3) also allows a child of a deceased spouse to commence such an action or a personal representative to commence or continue an action seeking a declaration of ownership or interest in a property. This is an important extension of relief in circumstances where a wife had a beneficial interest in a property which was registered in the sole name of her husband and was at risk to the husband's creditors. The wife can now not only establish her interest, but also trace her interest to the proceeds of sale even if they are no longer in the control of the husband, for example, if the property was sold by a mortgage in possession.

EXAMPLE

Mr P was the sole legal owner of a commercial property. Mrs P made a direct financial contribution to the purchase of the property. Mr P sold the property for

£100,000 (net proceeds of sale) but did not give any portion of the proceeds of sale to Mrs P. Mrs P only became aware of the sale some months afterwards and is uncertain whether Mr P has retained the proceeds of sale. Mrs P may apply to the court for a determination as to what portion of the proceeds of sale she is entitled. In the event of the death of Mrs P, her personal representative or one of her children can make an application for such a determination.

When a spouse makes an application to the court for a determination in relation to money representing the proceeds of property or property other than money and the defendant spouse:

(a) (i) *has had* the money or other property in their possession or under their control, or
    (ii) *has* property which represents the money (either in whole or in part) in their possession or under their control; and
(b) if the defendant spouse has not made an appropriate payment to the plaintiff spouse (ie a payment representing their entitlement to the money) or made an appropriate disposition, then the court may in addition to its general power under s 36(2) or in lieu of that power make an order that the defendant spouse:
    (i) pay to the plaintiff spouse such sum of money representing the plaintiff share of the money to which the application relates, or
    (ii) pay a sum of money representing the value of the plaintiff spouse's interest in property.

EXAMPLE

Following the facts of the previous example, Mrs P may apply to the court for a determination of her interest in the property although it has already been sold. It is no defence for Mr P to say that he no longer has the proceeds of sale or that the proceeds of sale have been used to purchase another property. If the court determines that Mrs P had a 20% interest in the property, the court can order Mr P to pay the sum of £20,000 representing the value of the interest of Mrs P in the property.

Use of the word 'spouse' in s 36 includes personal representatives of a deceased spouse, parties to a void marriage, parties to a voidable marriage which has been annulled by the law of the State or the law of another State, divorced spouses and engaged couples whose agreement to marry has terminated (FLA 1995, s 36(8)).

Application by a spouse whose marriage has been annulled must be made within three years of the date of the decree and a spouse to a void marriage must make the application within three years of the date he or she ceased to reside with the other (FLA 1995, s 36(7)).

The circuit court now has jurisdiction to hear and determine proceedings for nullity and the domicile and residence requirements have also been extended (FLA 1995, ss 38(2) and 39).

5.2 FAMILY HOME PROTECTION ACT 1976

5.2.1 Purpose

The Family Home Protection Act 1976 (FHPA 1976) provides protection for a non-owning spouse in the family home.

Prior to this Act, the owning spouse (usually the husband) could sell or mortgage the family home without the knowledge or consent of his wife. It was not unusual for a wife to find a 'For Sale' sign up in the garden of her home without any prior knowledge that her husband intended to sell it. In such circumstances, there was very little that she could do.

The definition of the family home, as amended by the FLA 1995, includes a dwelling in which a married couple ordinarily reside. A dwelling includes any building or structure, vehicle or vessel or part thereof which is occupied as a separate dwelling and includes any garden or portion of ground attached to and usually occupied with the dwelling or otherwise required for the amenity or convenience of the dwelling (FLA 1995, s 54).

5.2.2 Sale of the family home

The owning spouse cannot sell or mortgage or otherwise convey the family home without the prior written consent of the non-owning spouse. Where a spouse purports to convey any interest in the home to any person except the other spouse, without the prior consent in writing of the other spouse, then the purported conveyance is void (FHPA 1976, s 3).

It is now standard conveyancing practice when a property is being purchased or mortgaged or otherwise transferred that the purchaser's solicitor should enquire about the status of the property and whether it comprises a family home. The situation must be verified by statutory declaration of one or preferably both spouses. If the property is a family home, the non-owning spouse must give a prior written consent by signing the contract. The standard form of conditions of sale includes a spousal consent at the top of the first page. The status of the spouses must be verified by production of their State marriage certificate.

If a spouse whose consent is required omits or refuses to consent then the court may, in certain circumstances, dispense with that spouse's consent. The court will not dispense with the consent of the spouse only if it considers that it is unreasonable for the spouse to withhold consent, taking into account all the circumstances such as the respective needs and resources of the spouses and the dependent children (if any) of the family, and the suitability and security of tenure of the alternative accommodation offered (FHPA 1976, s 4).

If a spouse whose consent is required has deserted and continues to desert, the court will dispense with the consent. If a spouse whose consent is required is incapable of consenting by reason of unsoundness of mind or other mental disability or has not, after reasonable enquiry been found, the court may give consent on behalf of that spouse if it thinks it is reasonable to do so (FHPA 1976, s 4).

The FHPA 1976 only gives protection against the actions of the other spouse not against actions by third parties. The Act gives minimal protection against behaviour by the owning spouse which results in placing the family home at risk, for example, by non-payment of the mortgage. In such cases, a mortgagee or lessor of a family home will bring an action against the owning spouse seeking an order for possession or sale of the home. The court may give the other spouse the opportunity (if they want it) of paying the arrears if they are capable of doing so and are capable of making the future periodical payments as they fall due (FHPA 1976, s 7).

As a matter of practice, banks and other lending institutions and judgement mortgagees or lessors seeking possession of a family home or a sale of a family home must notify both spouses by separate letter and serve the court documents separately and independently on each of the spouses. As it is standard practice for most financial institutions to address their correspondence to the first-named borrower only, the non-owning spouse or second-named borrower (usually the wife) is often unaware that the mortgage repayments are in arrears. If a husband wishes to conceal the true state of the mortgage account from his wife, it is not difficult to do so. It is only when legal proceedings are threatened or issued that a wife may become aware that a serious situation has arisen on the account.

If the non-owning spouse is worried that the owning spouse may sell or attempt to sell the family home without his or her consent, he or she can register the fact of the marriage on the title to the property. This will put any prospective purchaser of the property on notice of the fact that the owning spouse is married and that the property is a family home. A prudent solicitor acting for a purchaser will ensure that the prior written consent of the non-owning spouse is given and the usual form of statutory declaration verifying their status is obtained (FHPA 1976, s 12).

5.2.3 The family home in joint names

Most lending institutions encourage borrowers who are married to each other to register the title to the family home in joint names. However, there are still a substantial number of homes which are registered in the name of one spouse only. The family home may have been inherited by one spouse or the property may have been bought before the marriage. Section 14 of the FHPA 1976 encourages the creation of joint tenancies in the family home by providing that no stamp duty, Land Registry fee, Registry of Deeds fee or court fee shall be payable on any transaction which creates a joint tenancy between spouses in respect of a family home.

5.2.4　Occupation of the family home

It is a fundamental principle of marriage that the husband and wife will live together and establish a home together. Once a couple has chosen a home in which to live then each spouse is entitled to live there and use and occupy the property notwithstanding the fact that the property may be owned by only one of them. A spouse cannot forcibly evict or exclude the other from the family home. Nor can a spouse change the locks on the doors and effectively deny the other spouse access to the home.

If, however, a spouse behaves in a way which puts the safety and welfare of the other spouse or the dependent children at risk, an application can be made to the courts for relief under the Domestic Violence Act 1996.

5.3　DOMESTIC VIOLENCE

Violence within the home is not new. It was not until 1976 that a procedure for obtaining a barring order was introduced in the Family Law (Maintenance of Spouses and Children) Act 1976. The protection given to spouses was extended by the Family Law (Protection of Spouses and Children) Act 1981. The law is now comprehensively covered by the Domestic Violence Act 1996 which came into operation on 27 March 1996. This Act radically reformed the protection given to spouses and it broadened the classes of persons to whom that protection is available to include parents and cohabitees who suffer violence within the home.

All or some of the following persons can (depending on the relief sought) apply for safety orders, barring orders and protection orders:

(a)　A spouse of the respondent.
(b)　A cohabitee who has lived with the respondent for a continuous period of six months out of the previous twelve months.
(c)　A parent of the respondent if the respondent is of full age and not dependent or suffering from mental or physical disability.
(d)　Other persons in a non-contractual relationship, where the court will take into account the length of the residence, the nature of the duties, the absence of profit and other relevant circumstances of the relationship.

Persons in all of the above categories can apply for a safety order. A safety order directs the respondent not to use or threaten to use violence against, molest or put the applicant in fear and not to watch or beset the place where the applicant lives. The order can last up to five years.

Persons in categories (a), (b) and (c) can also apply for a barring order. If the court is satisfied that there are reasonable grounds for believing that the safety and welfare of the applicant or dependent children are at risk an order will be granted. Welfare is defined as physical as well as psychological well-being. A barring order directs the respondent to leave a property in which the applicant lives and prohibits the respondent from entering that property. The barring order may also prohibit the respondent from using or threatening to use violence against the applicant, molesting or putting the applicant in fear or attending at or near the applicant's home. A barring order can be granted for up to three years in the district court. The circuit and High Court have unlimited jurisdiction.

Where the applicant for a barring order is a cohabitee, the applicant must have (or believe that they have) an interest in the property equal to the interest of the respondent. This proviso shows the conflict between trying to provide protection for people in their homes, on the one hand, and not interfering with the property rights of the owning party on the other. Therefore, unless the cohabitee is a joint owner of the property or has made such a significant contribution to the acquisition of the property that they believe that they have an interest equivalent to that of the registered owner, then a barring order will not be made. The granting of a barring order does not prejudice the legal rights of the respondent in the property.

A protection order may be granted to ensure protection for the applicant from the date of issue of a barring or safety application to the time when the case is heard by the court. The protection order will cease to have effect on the granting of a safety order or a barring order.

The Domestic Violence Act 1996 also gives Health Boards the power to make an application on behalf of an aggrieved person if the Board believes that the person needs protection and if it also believes that the person is being deterred or prevented from pursuing an application for a safety or barring order on his or her own behalf. This provision came into operation on 1 January 1997.

5.4   THE FAMILY HOME ON SEPARATION

It is obvious that once a couple make the decision to separate they cannot continue indefinitely to reside together in the family home. A couple will often agree the principle of separation but fail to agree on the fundamental issue of who should live in the family home. The court has power when granting a decree of judicial separation to either:

(a)   permit one spouse to continue to reside in the family home to the exclusion of the other (1989 Act, s 16(9)); or
(b)   make an order for the sale of the property and a distribution of the proceeds of sale (1989 Act, s 16(6)).

The necessity of the court to ensure that spouses live separately and apart after separation was examined in the case of *K(M) v K(P)* [1991] 9 Fam LJ 10, High Court, Barron J.

In this case, the wife applied to the circuit court for and was granted a decree of judicial separation on the grounds that no normal marital relationship had existed between herself and her husband for more than 12 months from the date of the application. The court did not make an order excluding the husband from residing in the family home, nor did the court make an order for the sale of the family home. In effect, therefore, the decree of judicial separation was granted but no ancillary 'separating' order was made. The wife appealed. Section 19 of the Judicial Separation and Family Law Reform Act 1989 acknowledges that once a decree of judicial separation is granted it is not possible for the spouses to continue to reside together and that proper and secure accommodation should be provided for the dependent spouse and children of the marriage, having regard to the criteria set down to assist the court.

Barron J held that, having regard to the provisions of s 19, the court must ensure after a decree of judicial separation is granted that the spouses no longer reside together. The court may therefore make an order under s 16(e) barring a spouse from residing in the family home, or if it does not do so, then it must choose between excluding a spouse from residing in the family home pursuant to s 16(a) or making an order for sale pursuant to s 16(b).

In the case in question, Barron J did not consider that the facts warranted the making of a barring order against the husband. There were good reasons why the family home should not be sold as the youngest child was still going to school in the area and the wife had interests in the community. The family finances did not require that the family home be sold and in these circumstances an order excluding the husband from residing in the family home was made.

In practice, the options likely to be considered by the court in the context of separation are as follows:

(a)   that the wife and dependent children reside in the family home to the exclusion of the husband and the legal title to the property remains registered in the joint names of the husband and wife or vice versa;

(b)   that the wife and dependent children continue to reside in the family home to the exclusion of the husband and the husband is ordered to transfer his interest in the property into the sole name of the wife with or without payment of a consideration, or vice versa;

(c)   that the family home is sold and that the proceeds of sale are divided either equally between the husband and the wife or in some other ratio to allow both the husband and the wife the possibility of acquiring alternative accommodation.

5.5 THE FAMILY HOME ON DIVORCE

It should be remembered that there are two distinct aspects to the family home: first, the occupation of the house as a home for the family; and secondly the ownership of the house as a valuable asset.

5.5.1 Occupation of the family home

In the context of divorce, the issue of who should occupy the family home may be less difficult to deal with than it is at the time of separation.

To apply for a divorce decree the spouses must have lived apart from one another for a period of four years prior to the application. The meaning of living apart has already been examined in Chapter 2. Whilst some divorcing spouses may have continued to reside in the same house but apart from each other, most spouses will have been living separately and apart from each other in different houses.

5.5.2 The court's powers

On granting a divorce decree the court must ensure that the parties live physically separate from each other (if they are not already doing so). The court must take into account that, after a divorce decree, it is not possible for the spouses to continue to live together and consequently the court must try to ensure that the dependent spouse and family have proper and secure accommodation (Divorce Act, s 15(2)).

Depending on the circumstances of each case the court can make orders giving one spouse the right to live in the family home either for life or for a definite period or, alternatively, make an order for sale. The advantages and disadvantages of such orders and the circumstances which will influence the court in making its orders are detailed below.

Residence for life

The court may make an order giving one spouse a right to reside in the family home for life (Divorce Act, s 15(1)(a)(i)). Such an order may be made regardless of whether the home is owned by the benefiting spouse or solely owned by the excluded spouse or jointly owned by both spouses. The advantage of such an order for the benefiting spouse is that the right to reside in the home is secure for the remainder of his or her life (save for an application to vary). The disadvantage is that he or she is limited to residing in that particular property and may wish to move elsewhere at some time in the future. The disadvantage for the excluded spouse is that he or she cannot use and enjoy the property which he or she may legally own or jointly own; nor can the value of the house be converted into cash until the death of the benefiting spouse. It may also be difficult for the excluded spouse to obtain mortgage facilities to purchase a new home if there is an existing mortgage on the family home.

Such an order is less likely to be made in a case where both spouses are young and more likely to be made in a case where spouses are older.

Although the court may make an order that a spouse is entitled to reside in the property for life to the exclusion of the other spouse, the excluded spouse is entitled to apply to the court at any time after the divorce decree is granted to vary the order if the circumstances have changed. Section 15(7) of the Divorce Act specifically provides that no such application for a variation can be made if the spouse who resides in the family home has remarried and is living with their new spouse in the family home. This could become a trap for the unwary and could have very unfair consequences. If, for example, a husband is excluded from living in the family home for life, he may harbour the hope that at some time in the future his wife's circumstances may improve to such an extent that he could successfully apply for a variation of the order. The remarriage of the wife in such a case would in fact deprive the husband of the right to seek such a variation.

Residence for a period only

The court may make an order giving one spouse a right to reside in the family home for a definite period or a contingent period (Divorce Act, s 15(1)(a)(i)).

In making an order, the court must have regard to the welfare of dependent members of the family. The continuity and stability that children feel by remaining in the family home is well recognised by the courts. Therefore, a right of residence for a period of time may be set either for a specified number of years or for a contingent period, ie until such time as the youngest child completes secondary or tertiary education. The disadvantage for the benefiting spouse is that his or her security in the family home is limited and must come to an end at some time in the future when that spouse may be less able to cope with a change of residence. The disadvantage to the excluded spouse is that his or her enjoyment of the property both as to occupation and ownership is postponed. If the excluded spouse still has to pay the mortgage instalments on the property it may be difficult for him or her to obtain mortgage facilities to purchase his or her own home.

Sale of the family home

The court may make an order for the sale of the family home subject to conditions and, if necessary, can make an order dividing the proceeds of sale between the spouses (Divorce Act, s 15(1)(a)(i)). Auctioneers have estimated that approximately 10% of residential sales in recent years are as a result of marital breakdown. In the context of separation, such sales can be agreed by the spouses themselves or can be ordered by the court.

The disadvantages of a sale of the family home are obvious. The house which may have been the family home for many years is disposed of in circumstances which are upsetting for everyone. The children have to cope not only with their parents' separation but with a change of home, often a change of neighbourhood and possibly a change of school.

The advantages of a sale of the family home are that the equity in the family home is realised and can be divided between the spouses to enable one or both to purchase alternative accommodation. If the family home is subject to a mortgage, this will be discharged from the proceeds of sale and both spouses will be free of this liability and either or both can apply for new mortgage facilities to enable them to purchase alternative accommodation.

The court can direct a division of the proceeds of sale in different ratios depending on the need of each spouse. If a dependent spouse has no independent income or earning capacity, the court may direct that the proceeds of sale are split in such portions as to allow that dependent spouse to purchase an alternative property free from encumbrances. The other spouse may receive only a small portion of the proceeds of sale, perhaps enough to place a deposit on an alternative property with the shortfall coming by a loan facility.

Other miscellaneous ancillary orders

DOMESTIC VIOLENCE ORDERS
In addition to any of the orders referred to above, the court may also make a safety order, a barring order and a protection order (Divorce Act, s 15(1)(d)). These reliefs may be required if the history and circumstances of the case are such that even in the event of divorce one spouse may continue to threaten, molest, annoy or interfere with the other.

Any of the above reliefs may also be applied for on a preliminary application.

If the divorce proceedings have started, the court can, before deciding whether to grant or refuse to grant the decree of divorce, if the circumstances are serious, make an interim safety order, barring order or protection order which will remain in force until the hearing of the proceedings or such other time as the court may specify.

PARTITION
The court also retains the power to partition property (Divorce Act, s 15(1) (e)). If spouses own property jointly and they cannot agree on a sale of the property, either party may apply pursuant to the Partition Acts 1868–1876 for a division or partition of the property or for an order for sale in lieu of partition.

Partition means the physical division of the property into separate portions. This is generally impracticable and an order for sale in lieu of partition is usually sought. The court may refuse an order for a sale if there is a good reason not to sell. If the property is the family home of the spouses, the court will have regard to the circumstances which would have to be taken into account if an application was made to it under the FHPA 1976 to dispense with a spouse's consent to sale.

5.5.3 Ownership

Occupation of the home may be ordered with the ownership rights in the property remaining the same as they were prior to divorce.

Property determination

The court in the context of divorce has power to determine any question on the title to or possession of property. The jurisdiction exercised by the court previously pursuant to s 12 of the Married Women's Status Act 1957 is continued by virtue of s 36 of the FLA 1995. There will be cases where such applications are necessary particularly with property, other than the family home.

5.5.4 Property adjustment order

Section 14 of the Divorce Act provides that on granting a divorce decree the court may make one of the following orders. The application may be made by either of the spouses or by a person on behalf of a dependent member of the family.

The court may order:

(a)   The transfer of property by either of the spouses:
  (i)   to the other, or
  (ii)   to any dependent member of the family, or
  (iii) to any other specified person for the benefit of such a member.

  At its simplest, this provision allows the court to make an order that one spouse transfer his or her interest in the family home to the other. The court can also order a spouse to transfer his or her interest in the family home to any dependent member of the family: for example, if the husband and wife are joint owners of the family home, the court can order that the husband transfer his interest in the home to a dependent child over the age of 18. Alternatively, the court could order the husband to transfer his interest in the home to another person (which could include the wife) on behalf of a dependent child who, for example, may be suffering from a mental or physical disability.

(b)   The settlement of property to the satisfaction of the court for the benefit of the other spouse and of any dependent member of the family or of any or all of those persons.

  This provision allows the court to order a spouse to put the family home in trust for the benefit of the other spouse and any dependent member of the family or of all or any of them.

For example, the court could order a spouse to transfer the family home to trustees for the use of the wife for life with a remainder interest to the children. This could be ordered in circumstances where the court is satisfied that the benefiting spouse might waste the asset or put it in jeopardy due to inability to manage his or her financial affairs, mental disability or substance addiction.

The court could also make such an order if the spouses were elderly or had a marriage of short duration or both. For example, the court could order a husband to purchase a house or apartment for his wife for her life with remainder interest to him, or his estate or children on the death of his wife.

(c) The variation of any ante-nuptial or post-nuptial settlement (including such a settlement made by will or codicil) made on the spouses provided it is for the benefit of either of the spouses and of any dependent member of the family or of any or all of those persons.

This means the court can vary an ante-nuptial or post-nuptial settlement. The meaning of post-nuptial settlement was examined by McGuinness J in the case of *N(C) v N(R)* [1995] 1 Fam LJ 1995. The facts in the case were that the parties had entered into a separation agreement in 1981 and a supplemental agreement in 1986. In February 1994, the wife issued proceedings under the 1989 Act. McGuinness J, in her judgment, cited English authorities where it has long been settled law that the term 'post-nuptial settlement' is to receive a wide interpretation and includes separation agreements. *Bromleys Family Law* 8th edn (p 739) states:

> 'the terms ante-nuptial and post-nuptial settlement are used in a sense much wider than that usually given to them by conveyancers, the essential condition being that the benefit must be conferred on either or both of the spouses in the character of spouse or spouses. It is immaterial whether it comes from one of the spouses or from a third person, provided that this condition is satisfied ... A separation agreement comes within the section even if it is not in writing'.

In the case in point, McGuinness J stated:

> 'it seems to me that the separation agreement made between the parties in the instant case comes squarely within this established definition of a post-nuptial settlement. It must be assumed that those who drafted s 15 of the 1989 Act were aware of this broad definition of a post-nuptial settlement and that therefore the intention of the Oireachtas must have been to give the court the specific power to vary separation agreements. Had this not been so one would have expected a specific provision to exclude separation agreements from the operation of the sub-section'.

Section 15(1)(c) of the 1989 Act is in the same terms as s 12(1)(c) of the Divorce Act.

Trusts and settlements are discussed further in Chapter 6.

(d) The extinguishment or reduction of the interest of either of the spouses under any such settlement.

If a spouse is a beneficiary under a settlement, the court could direct that that spouse ceases to have an interest in the trust assets. If a spouse is a settlor of a settlement, the court may direct that a certain beneficiary cease to have an interest. This was done in the case of *F(R) v F(J)* [1995] 3 Fam LJ where the court directed that the name of the mother of the respondent husband be removed from the list of beneficiaries of a trust created by him.

5.5.5   Criteria for making orders

As has already been discussed, s 20 of the Divorce Act sets out all the circumstances which must be taken into account by the court before deciding to make an ancillary relief order and in deciding the exact provision of such an order. In general, the court must be satisfied that proper provision is made for the spouses and any dependent member of the family. The term 'proper provision' is not defined and it is therefore at the discretion of the court to define it in each individual case (Divorce Act, s 20(1)).

In the context of a property adjustment order in relation to the family home the court is likely to focus on the following.

Section 20(2)(a)

> 'the income, earning capacity, property and other financial resources which each of the spouses concerned has or is likely to have in the foreseeable future,'

The court will have regard to all income and all property from whatever source. If a spouse has inherited property or had received damages from an accident claim, the court will take account of the availability of those funds. In deciding whether to allow a wife and dependent children to remain in the family home or whether it should be sold, the court will take into account the fact that the husband owns property other than the family home or has income and an earning capacity which would enable him to obtain a mortgage facility to purchase a home for himself. If a husband has significant property or other financial resources, a transfer of the family home to the wife may be appropriate. If a wife has capital available to her as a result of a redundancy or inheritance or whatever, the court may only consider making a property adjustment order in her favour if a payment is made to the husband in respect of any interest he may have in the family home.

Section 20(2)(b)

> 'the financial needs, obligations and responsibilities which each of the spouses has or is likely to have in the foreseeable future (whether in the case of the remarriage of the spouse or otherwise),'

The primary financial need that each spouse has is to support and maintain themselves and the dependent members of the family. A spouse may have a moral obligation and responsibility to another member of that spouse's family, such as an elderly parent or disabled brother or sister, and the court may take these obligations into account provided they are reasonable. In the Senate debates, Professor Lee (Parliamentary Debates Seanad Eireann 24.10.96, vol 149, no 1, p 26) moved an amendment to include the contribution made by a spouse not only to the welfare of the family but also to any dependent parent. Minister Taylor, referred to the provision whereby the court can take into account the financial needs, obligations and responsibilities of the spouses. In particular, he stated:

> 'Maintenance of children must be a priority, but infirm parents or other members of an extended family to whom it is reasonable to expect either party to look after in the circumstances, are also included. Not all these obligations are legally enforceable. In the context, though, a moral obligation and the voluntary assumption of a responsibility, provided it is reasonable, may be as relevant as a legal obligation' (Parliamentary Debates Seanad Eireann 24.10.96, vol 149, no 1, p 27).

It is inevitable on separation or divorce that there is a diminution in the living standards of the spouses. The financial needs must be reasonable and what is reasonable will depend on the circumstances of each case. What is reasonable for one situation may be unreasonable in another. The court must make difficult decisions and divide out the available assets and income as fairly as possible. If, for example, the financial needs of a wife with custody of a number of dependent children are such that after the payment by the husband of the mortgage repayments for the family home, it is simply not possible for those reasonable needs to be met, the court may consider it more prudent to sell the family home and order that a smaller property be purchased free from encumbrances, thereby ensuring that a greater portion of income is available for the day-to-day needs of the wife and children.

Section 20(2)(c)

> 'the standard of living enjoyed by the family concerned before the proceedings were instituted or before the spouses commenced to live apart from one another, as the case may be,'

This is probably most relevant in cases where there are substantial assets. For most couples, there is an inevitable diminution in living standards after separation and divorce. While the court shall have regard to the standard of living prior to separation, this does not necessarily mean that a spouse is entitled to be kept in a manner to which they have become accustomed. It can, however, be used to support an application by a wife to allow her to remain living in the family home in a neighbourhood and community where she is known and has interests and where the needs of the dependent children in relation to educational and recreational facilities can be met.

Section 20(2)(f)

> 'the contributions which each of the spouses has made or is likely in the forseeable future to make to the welfare of the family, including any contribution made by each of them to the income, earning capacity, property and financial resources of the other spouse and any contribution made by either of them by looking after the home or caring for the family,'

This allows the court to take into account the contribution that a spouse had made to the welfare of the family but also includes any contribution made by a spouse to the income, earning capacity, property and financial resources of the other spouse. For example, a wife may work unpaid in the husband's business thereby making a financial contribution to the family's financial well-being.

In the case of *Preston v Preston* [1982] Fam 17, [1982] 1 All ER 41, Ormrod LJ illustrated two ways in which the contribution of a spouse could be made. First, 'active participation by the wife either by working in the business or by providing finance, will greatly enhance her contribution to the welfare of the family ... this, in effect recognises that she has "earned" a share of the total assets, and should be able to realise it and use it as she chooses.' Secondly, 'the acceptance by the wife of a frugal standard of living throughout the marriage, enabling the husband to plough back into the business a large proportion of the profits and so develop it into a considerable enterprise, is a factor.'

Section 20(2)(j)

> 'the accommodation needs of either of the spouses,'

In the case of *O'L v O'L* [1996] 2 Fam LJ, the wife sought a transfer of the family home into her sole name. McGuinness J in her judgment stated:

> 'When approaching the making of an order pursuant to s 15 of the 1989 Act, the court must consider all the factors which are set out in s 20 of the Act. In this case virtually all of the financial contributions towards the acquisition of the family home came from the husband. The wife has made some indirect contributions to the home from her savings. She gave up her career in order to care for R and for the home generally. It is also important, and I am so directed by s 20, that I should bear in mind the future needs of the parties and of the wife and R. This includes not only the future need of the wife and R for accommodation, but also the future need of the husband for accommodation. As far as the conduct of the parties are concerned, I do not feel that it is really such that it would be unjust to ignore it, particularly as it is clear that there were faults on both sides. In considering this question, I have been referred by counsel for the husband to the unreported judgement of Mr Justice Lynch in the High Court in the case of *JD v PD* (unreported, 9 August 1994). In that case, a somewhat similar situation arose in

regard to the possibility of sale of the family home and the purchase of a new house for the wife and child. In considering that position, the learned High Court judge said as follows: "The family home is in the joint names of the husband and the wife. The husband wants it sold and wife objects ... The practicalities and common sense indicate a sale as soon as possible rather than having the wife and two young children occupying a large five bedroomed house standing on three-quarters of an acre of grounds and worth at least £200,000. The only basis on which a sale was really opposed by the wife was a suggestion by her, tentatively supported by the clinical psychologist, that the added stress of moving house might adversely affect the daughter. However the daughter moved house from London to Ireland in 1990 at the age of 2 years without any adverse affects. Moving house can be portrayed as an adventure to a young child and it is up to the wife so to portray it to the daughter ... In all the circumstances I am satisfied that common sense and justice require that the family home be sold and that the proceeds of sale be divided so as to provide as far as possible for the purchase by the wife of a smaller house in a more convenient location for schools and generally and to provide for the husband something towards a deposit on the purchase by him of suitable accommodation for himself. In the present case I do not really accept that the child will be harmed to a very great extent by a move of house particularly if such a move is handled properly".'

The court will generally go through each of the provisions of s 20 and give them whatever weight it feels is appropriate to the circumstances of the particular case and on looking at the totality of factors and circumstances make an appropriate order.

5.5.6 Conveyancing matters

If the court orders one spouse to transfer the family home to the other, it is essential that all documents necessary to give effect to the transfer are prepared, signed and registered.

If the family home is subject to a mortgage, the consent of the relevant lending institution must be obtained because a transfer without consent is in breach of the covenant against assignment contained in the mortgage.

Consent is not always forthcoming particularly if the transferor spouse wishes to be released from all liability on the mortgage.

Most mortgagees take the view that it is preferable to have two borrowers jointly and severally liable for the loan rather than one. However, mortgagees must also deal with the practical realities and if they are satisfied that the transferee spouse can meet the repayments on the mortgage as they fall due, they will consent to the transfer and release the transferor spouse from liability on the mortgage. The mortgagees will take into account the size of the mortgage, the balance of the term of years to run, the value of the property and the manner in which the account has been operated by the borrowers in the past. If the transferee spouse, the wife for example, has no independent income, the mortgagee may require the husband (or some other appropriate person) to guarantee the payments. Practitioners should be familiar with the circumstances in which a consent to transfer may or may not be forthcoming so that they can use this knowledge in presenting the application to court.

Mortgagees have their own particular legal requirements and will have to be joined as a party to the deed for the purposes of consenting to the transfer and releasing the transferor spouse.

If an order for transfer is made by the court, many mortgagees believe they cannot refuse to consent to the transfer although they may refuse to release the transferor spouse from liability for his obligations under the mortgage.

5.5.7   Signing the documents

Any deed of conveyance, assignment or transfer ordered by the court must be signed by the transferor spouse in order to give a full effect to the order.

There is no general agreement amongst practitioners as to whether full requisitions on title or a shortened version of requisitions should be raised to deal with matters within the knowledge of the transferor spouse, or, if such requisitions are raised, whether the transferor spouse is required to reply to them.

If, for example, a wife knows or advises her solicitor of a planning problem or a boundary difficulty can she insist that the matter is regularised by the husband? The answer is probably no. This may be an issue that can be agreed between the parties. It does not appear to be within the power of the court to order that the transfer take place on terms and conditions. If the transferee's solicitor identifies problems at the time of transfer, they should be dealt with. It is the practice of the mortgagee's solicitors to raise a short form of requisitions to ascertain whether any extensions have been built to the property or whether the freehold of the property has been purchased, so as to ensure that the title is in order at the time of the transfer.

The other documents that are required to be signed by the transferor spouse are a declaration pursuant to the FHPA 1976 and a deed of waiver in respect of a sale of the property in the future.

If the transferor spouse refuses or neglects to sign the deed or other instrument or if the court believes that there is any other reason (eg the transferor spouse lives out of the jurisdiction) preventing execution by the transferor, the court can direct another person to sign the deed on behalf of the transferor (Divorce Act, s 14(5)).

In the past the court under its general powers has made directions that the deed of waiver be signed by the County Registrar. The transferor spouse was named as a party and the order of the court was recited, directing the county registrar to execute the requisite documents to give effect to the transfer, and the document was signed, sealed and delivered by (name) the County Registrar for and on behalf of the transferor spouse.

Section 14(5) of the Divorce Act envisages the transferor spouse being given an opportunity to sign the relevant documents but the scope is broad enough to allow the court to make the order at the time of granting the divorce decree if, for example, the transferor spouse was unlikely to sign the documents when requested.

In addition, when a property adjustment order has been made, the registrar or clerk of the court must send a certified copy of it to either the Land Registry or the Registry of Deeds, as appropriate, for registration (Divorce Act, s 14(4)). To assist the registrar or clerk, practitioners should state in the pleadings if the property is registered in the Registry of Deeds or the Land Registry, and, if the latter, the registered owners, the folio number and the county.

The cost of giving effect to a property adjustment order shall be borne entirely by one spouse or by both in proportions as determined by the court (Divorce Act, s 14(6)).

5.5.8 Taxation

Stamp duty

No stamp duty or registration fee is payable when a joint tenancy in the family home is created between spouses (FHPA 1976, s 14).

The Finance Act 1990 relieves all transfers of property between spouses from stamp duty (s 114). In order to qualify for this exemption, the following certificate should be inserted in the relevant deed:

> 'It is hereby certified by the transferor and the transferee that they are related to each other as lawful husband and wife and that the exemption from stamp duty is claimed in respect of the within transfer under the provisions of section 114 of the Finance Act 1990.'

In the context of divorce, if property passes from one spouse to the other by order of the court, it is important that this relief from stamp duty is maintained. Section 33 of the Divorce Act provides that transfers of property between former spouses by order of the court are not chargeable to stamp duty. This relief is limited to transfers which are made pursuant to an ancillary relief application under Part III of the Divorce Act. For example, if a divorced man voluntarily transfers property to his ex-wife, the deed of transfer is stampable at full ad valorem rate because the relief from stamp duty is limited to spouses and to transfers made pursuant to an order of the court. If the court orders property to be transferred to a dependent member or other specified person then the transfer deed is chargeable to stamp duty as there is no stamp duty relief. If the order is made in favour of a child of the transferor spouse, stamp duty is payable at half the ad valorem rate of the market value of the property (Stamp Act 1891).

Capital acquisitions tax

Capital acquisitions tax is a tax on gifts and inheritances received by any person. The tax is payable by the recipient. There are exempt thresholds based on the relationship between the disponer and donee or successor, ie parent and child, brother, sister, uncle, aunt, nephew, niece. The amount of the threshold limit is raised each year in line with the consumer price index.

There is no capital acquisitions tax payable on gifts (since 1 January 1990) or inheritances (since 30 January 1985) taken by one spouse from the other nor are such gifts or inheritances aggregated for the purposes of computing the tax on gifts or inheritances from other disposers. This relief continues to apply even if the spouses are separated from each other.

This relief is maintained in the context of divorce in respect of property passing either by gift or by inheritance between spouses by order of the court pursuant to the provisions of the Divorce Act (s 34). If, therefore, a wife receives the family home from her husband by property adjustment order, this will not constitute a gift from her husband and it will not be taxable, nor shall its value be taken into account in computing any liability the wife may have on other gifts or inheritances received by her. The situation is the same if she receives an inheritance from the husband's estate pursuant to s 18 of the Divorce Act.

But it must be stressed that this relief will apply only if the gift or inheritance is taken by virtue or in consequence of an ancillary relief order made by the court. If, by contrast, a divorced man makes provision for his ex-wife in his will, the value of the devise or bequeath or legacy is taxable in the hands of the ex-wife, and will only have the benefit of the lowest of the three class thresholds.

Capital gains tax

The Capital Gains Tax Act 1975 provides for the taxation of gains realised on the disposal of assets. The word 'disposal' has a broad meaning and includes disposal of assets by sale, exchange and by gift. The tax is payable by the person who disposes of the asset. The level of gain is generally calculated as the difference between the acquisition cost of the asset and the value when disposed of less the costs of disposal. Certain other deductions are also allowable in computing the level of the gain.

An individual is entitled to an annual exemption of £1,000 and married persons living together to £2,000.

Any gain that arises on the disposal of a principal private residence is exempt from capital gains tax.

There is no capital gains tax chargeable on a disposal of property from one spouse to the other while they are living together. The spouse who receives the asset is deemed to have acquired it at the date on and the cost at which the other spouse acquired it. In the event of the receiving spouse disposing of the property, the original base date and cost are used. For example, a husband bought shares in Bravo Bank plc on 27 March 1991 at a price of £2.15 per share.

On 5 June 1994, he gifts the shares to his wife on which date the shares are each worth £2.80. The wife sells the shares on 23 September 1996 for a price of £3.50 per share. The wife will be deemed to have acquired the shares at the same date and at the same price as the husband and the calculation of the gain or loss will be so made. The gain on the disposal is, therefore, £1.35 per share (£3.50–£2.15).

In the context of separation, it is important that this relief is continued and s 52 of the FLA 1995 provides that property which passes from one spouse to the other by deed of separation or by order of the court is not liable to capital gains tax. This relief only applies to disposals made after 1 August 1996.

Section 35 of the Divorce Act preserves this relief in the context of divorce. The transfer of assets between spouses must be by virtue of or in consequence of an order of the court. A spouse who receives the asset is deemed to have acquired it at the date and at the cost at which the other spouse acquired it, as the example above illustrates.

Practitioners should be aware of the implications of the capital gains tax provisions when negotiating or presenting applications to the court. If, for example, a husband offers to transfer or is ordered by the court to transfer shares he owns to his wife, the value of the shares to her on a specified date may not represent the real value to her if the disposal by her gives rise to a chargeable gain and a liability to tax. A calculation of the likely capital gains tax payable should be made to ascertain the net value for the wife in the event that she disposes of the shares.

The relief provided in s 35 applies only to disposals between spouses. If the court makes a property adjustment order by which property is transferred by one spouse to trustees for a dependent member of the family, this may give rise to a liability to tax by the transferor spouse.

Residential property tax
Residential property tax is an annual tax chargeable on the excess market value of residential property owned and occupied on 5 April in the tax year where the total gross household income exceeds a specified limit.

If one spouse has ceased to live in the house then only the income of the spouse in occupation (and any children) will be taken into account in calculating the household income. The spouse in occupation is the accountable person for the tax and even if that person is below the income threshold, an RPT form must be filed on 11 October each year if the value of the house is over the general market value level.

As the tax or any under-payment of the tax or interest due remains a charge on property for 12 years (Finance Act 1983, s 110A(a)) it is essential that a clearance certificate is obtained from the Revenue Commissioners when a property is being transferred from one spouse to the other. Application is made on form RP54. Provided that the tax has been fully discharged, a certificate will be issued promptly by the Revenue Commissioners.

The Minister for Finance in his budget speech on 22 January 1997 announced the abolition of Residential Property Tax. The procedures referred to above in relation to obtaining clearance certificates will, however, apply for all tax due and payable prior to that time.

5.5.9   The family home at risk

General

In many cases of marital breakdown, the financial issues are not so much about sharing the assets as paying the debts.

The stresses caused by financial worries can often be the cause of marital disharmony. If spouses are not communicating with each other, they often cannot or do not take the necessary steps to prepare a budget plan for the family and adhere to it. In other cases, the pain of coping with the break-up of a marital relationship is anaesthetised by heavy personal spending on entertainment or holidays. If a spouse is having an affair, it will undoubtedly have a financial impact. In other cases, the difficulties caused by marital breakdown impact on a spouse's ability to work or run a business effectively and for those who are self-employed there can be a diminution in the income that is generated from a practice or a business.

Debts

Neither spouse is automatically responsible for the debts of the other. If the family home is registered in the joint names of the husband and wife and there is a mortgage on the property, the responsibility for the payment of the mortgage is the joint and severable liability of both spouses. The standard form of mortgage used by most banks and building societies covers not only the home loan that was advanced to purchase the property but also covers 'all sums due' by the borrowers. 'All sums due' means precisely that and includes an overdraft on a current account, term loans, credit card liabilities or any debt guaranteed as surety either by the spouses jointly or by one spouse alone.

Repossession

It is the policy of many banks and building societies to address their correspondence to the first-named borrower only. If, however, a bank or building society take any steps to repossess the family home or seek an order for sale on foot of the mortgage, separate letters are sent to both the husband and the wife. Where a mortgagee or lessor of the family home brings an action against a spouse in which the claims possession or sale of the home by virtue of the mortgage or lease because of non-payment, the court can give the non-owning spouse an opportunity to rectify the situation by allowing the other spouse (if desired and if the spouse is financially capable) to pay the arrears of money due within a reasonable time and to pay the future periodical payments as they fall due.

If the court believes that it is in the interests of all parties, it may adjourn the proceedings for such period as would allow the non-owning spouse time to address the problem.

In particular, the court will have regard to whether the spouse of the mortgagor or lessee has been informed (by or on behalf of the mortgagee or lessor or otherwise) of the non-payment of the sums in question or of any of them.

Judgment mortgages

The registration of a judgment mortgage on the title of a property which is registered in the joint names of a husband and wife automatically severs the joint tenancy. This can have very serious consequences as the spouses may be relying on the property passing by survivorship. When a judgment is obtained against a debtor, many financial institutions, as a matter of policy, proceed to register the judgment as a judgment mortgage on the title to any property that the debtor may own. The judgment creditor may or may not make an application for an order that the judgment mortgage is well charged and an order for sale. Many creditors, particularly if the amount is not substantial, are content to leave the judgment registered against the property in the hope that it may eventually be paid if the property is sold.

In other cases, the judgment mortgagee may seek a well charging order over the interest of the debtor in the family home and an order for sale in lieu of partition pursuant to the Partition Act 1868. The court has discretion to refuse an order for sale if there are good and sufficient reasons to the contrary (Partition Act 1868, s 4).

These issues were dealt with in the case of *First National Building Society v ER and AR* [1992] 3 Fam LJ 74.

The facts were that the plaintiff obtained a judgment against Eamonn Ring and registered the judgment as a judgment mortgage over the interest of Eamonn Ring in the family home which he owned jointly with his wife Adrienne Ring. The plaintiff sought a well charging order and an order for sale in lieu of partition. The wife was joined as a party and she opposed the application. The wife was not in any way responsible for the debt to the plaintiff. The wife had two dependent children residing with her in the family home and she contended that the home was central to the life of the family and if it was sold the disruption would be very detrimental. It was unlikely that the wife would have sufficient money to purchase alternative accommodation with her share of the proceeds and her family would be homeless and destitute. The plaintiff wanted a well charging order and an order for sale. The net issue to be determined by the court was whether or not there was good and sufficient reason to the contrary to direct a sale of the property.

Having reviewed the authorities, Denham J held that the wife was a co-owner of the property and an innocent party to the judgment mortgage. As she would undoubtedly suffer if the family home was sold, she did not believe it was appropriate to make an order for sale. A well charging order was made and an order that enquiries be made of the persons interested in the property, their shares and proportions, the current market value, the feasibility of sale and whether there was any possibility of the wife buying out the interest of the husband at an agreed price. The balance of the proceedings were then adjourned.

Bankruptcy

Where a person has been adjudged bankrupt then all property belonging to that person vests in the official assignee in bankruptcy for the benefit of creditors (Bankruptcy Act 1988, s 44).

If a bankrupt is the owner of the family home either solely or jointly with the other spouse, the interest of the bankrupt in the family home vests in the official assignee. The official assignee has power to sell all property of the bankrupt, but in the case of a property which comprises the family home no sale can take place without the prior permission of the court. If such an application is made, the court may postpone any such sale, have a regard to the interests of the spouse and dependants of the bankrupt as against the interests of the creditors and look at all the circumstances of the case.

This issue was examined in the case of *Rubotham v Young* [1996] 1 Fam LJ 14.

The plaintiff was the official assignee in bankruptcy in the estate of John Young (the bankrupt), who was the husband of the defendant. The bankrupt was so adjudicated in August 1988. Among his assets was a half share in the family home which was held in joint names with the defendant. The plaintiff sought an order for sale either under the Partition Acts or under s 61 of the Bankruptcy Act 1988, and the application of the bankrupt's half share of the proceeds of sale in discharging some of the liabilities of the bankrupt. The defendant asked that the court exercise its discretion and either refuse an order for sale in lieu of partition or postpone the sale of the family home. The court held that:

(a) As the Bankruptcy Act 1988 deals specifically with the family home, it was appropriate to make whatever order was necessary under that Act rather than under the Partition Acts.
(b) Under s 61(5) of the Bankruptcy Act 1988, the court is given specific guidelines as to the matters to be taken into account in exercising a discretion to postpone a sale.

(c)   The bankrupt was adjudicated almost seven years before and the creditors had been paid nothing, and would be paid nothing until the family home was sold.

(d)   The spouse and dependants had lived in the house at the expense of the creditors for almost seven years and all of the children were of full age.

(e)   In view of the length of time that the defendant and her family had been in the house since the adjudication, there were no real grounds for postponing the sale any longer. The court postponed the sale for a period of four months from the date of the order.

HOUSEHOLD CHATTELS

A person adjudged bankrupt is entitled to retain articles of clothing, household furniture, bedding, tools or equipment of his trade or occupation or other necessaries for himself and his wife and children up to a value of £2,500 (Bankruptcy Act 1988, s 45).

VOLUNTARY CONVEYANCES

If a bankrupt within six months of being adjudicated a bankrupt has conveyed or transferred or mortgaged property or made payments in favour of a creditor with a view to giving that creditor preference, such a conveyance, transfer or payment is void as against the official assignee. This does not apply to transfers to a person who acts in good faith and purchases for valuable consideration (Bankruptcy Act 1988, s 57).

This provision may be critical in the context of a transfer of assets on separation or divorce. If, for example, a husband is in debt and has creditors and as part of a settlement of separation or divorce proceedings transfers the family home to his wife, is this a voluntary transfer? The wife may not be making a cash transfer to the husband in respect of his interest in the property; however she may be giving valuable consideration by perhaps taking over the liability for an existing mortgage, renouncing her rights under the Succession Act or not making any claim in respect of maintenance for herself. If an order for the transfer of the family home is made by the court, this could not be construed as a voluntary conveyance and in this example it would be more prudent for the wife to seek relief from the court.

5.5.10   Local authority housing

As adequate housing is a basic requirement for all, the public policy response to this social need has traditionally consisted almost entirely of the provision of housing by local authorities for renting to households on approved waiting lists. New strategies have however been introduced to widen the approach of local authorities and to encourage home ownership especially for younger couples.

Tenancy

It is the policy of most housing authorities to ensure that rented local authority housing is placed in the joint names of the husband and the wife. The tenancy agreement with the local authority has the usual clauses in relation to occupancy, payment of rent and keeping the property in good repair. In the event of separation and/or divorce, if one spouse ceases to reside in the property, the occupying spouse can seek to have the tenancy transferred into his or her sole name on the basis that the other spouse is not in occupation of the property (as required by the tenancy agreement). It is appropriate to obtain an order from the court that the spouse who continues to reside in the property is entitled to reside there to the exclusion of the other.

Tenant purchase

From time to time, local authorities offer to sell houses to existing tenants and many tenants find very attractive the possibility of becoming owners of their homes at reasonable cost. If the spouses are tenant purchasers of their homes from the local authority, a property adjustment order must be sought. If the order is made, the practitioner must ensure that the legal title is transferred into the sole name of the benefiting spouse. The local authority does not necessarily need to join in the transfer deed although a letter from the local authority consenting to the transfer may be necessary to comply with s 90(6) of the Housing Act 1966. The local authority is generally favourably disposed to consenting if there are no arrears of payments.

Shared ownership system

In order to assist couples, a shared ownership system operates. Under this scheme the approved applicant will initially acquire at least 50% of the equity in the house of their choice and 'rent' the remaining equity from the local authority giving an undertaking to buy out the rented share of the equity within 25 years. It is envisaged that the occupier would normally fund the purchase of their share of the equity by means of an annuity mortgage loan from a bank or building society. The rented share of the dwelling will be financed by the local authority by means of an indexed-linked loan from the housing finance agency under which the repayments will be structured to match the local authority's income from rent and subsidy, if any, from the dwelling.

While undoubtedly this system allows couples who might otherwise be unable to own their own home to do so, the framework is complicated and tends to lock the couple into remaining in the particular property. In the context of a divorce, a property adjustment order must be obtained to transfer the title into the sole name of a benefiting spouse.

Mortgage allowance for tenants

Some householders who are tenants or tenant purchasers of local authority houses wish to become owner-occupiers of other houses. In order to assist such households, there is a scheme of financial assistance by way of an allowance towards the mortgage repayments for tenants who return their dwellings to the local authority. The allowance is paid over a period of five years so as to ease the transition to full mortgage repayments. The allowance is paid directly by the Department of the Environment to the lending agency. The subsidy in effect results in a low start mortgage arrangement, thereby reducing the burden of the repayments in the early years.

Local authority housing loans
Local authorities continue to lend to those who cannot obtain a suitable mortgage from a commercial lending agency. They charge a variable interest rate which is the same as the lowest building society rate. There are maximum loan limits and income limits are adjusted from time to time.

Private rented sector (rental subsidy)
The private rented sector is very important in the overall housing system. Investment in private rented accommodation has been encouraged by successive governments to ensure that a supply of rented accommodation continues to be available and that rents are not driven up by excess demand. Since 1988, an attractive incentive (often known as s 23 relief (from s 23 of the Finance Act 1981)) has been available so that the cost of acquiring a property is allowable in full against the rental income for income tax purposes. In addition, local authorities often use property in the private sector to provide accommodation for qualifying applicants for housing. The local authority will either pay a subsidy to the tenant or pay the rent directly to the landlord. Tenants do not have any real security of tenure in such properties and if the landlord wants the house back they are so entitled.

5.5.11   Contents
The most bitter disputes can arise over an item of furniture of insignificant or questionable value. Furniture and effects are property and can be the subject of a property adjustment order. If a court makes a property adjustment order in respect of the family home in favour of the wife, it will usually also include an order in respect of the contents with a proviso that the husband keep as his own certain specified items.

The FHPA 1976 provides specific relief in relation to household chattels. Household chattels are defined in s 9(7) of the FHPA 1976 as furniture, bedding, linen, china, earthenware, glass, books and other chattels of ordinary household use or ornament and also consumerable stores, garden effects and domestic animals but does not include any chattels used by either spouse for business or professional purposes or money or security for money. Under s 9 of the FHPA 1976, if it appears to the court that there are reasonable grounds for believing that the other spouse intends to sell, lease, pledge, charge or otherwise dispose or remove from the family home such a number or proportion of household chattels as would be likely to make it difficult for the applicant spouse or dependent child of the family to reside in the family home without undue hardship, the court may by order prohibit the other spouse from making such intended disposal or removal.

Section 15 of the Divorce Act allows the court on granting a decree of divorce to make orders pursuant to s 9 of the FHPA 1976. In addition, where matrimonial proceedings have been instituted by either spouse, neither spouse is entitled to sell, lease, pledge or charge or otherwise dispose or remove any of the household chattels in the family home until the proceedings have been finally determined unless the other spouse consents or unless the court permits that spouse to do so. It should be noted that paintings and other objets d'art are not specifically included in the definition of household chattels and in the event that a spouse was seeking to dispose of a valuable painting which could not be classified as a household chattel, relief could be obtained under s 36 of the Divorce Act.

While there have been no reported judgments on this issue, the existence of s 9 and s 36 are useful deterrents to a spouse who attempts to take items of furniture away from the family home before the case has been heard by the court or agreement has been reached between the spouses.

Chapter 6

PROPERTY AND OTHER ASSETS

6.1 INTRODUCTION

In many cases, the assets of the family comprise the family home and contents, the family car, the income of one or both spouses and possibly a small level of savings. In other cases, there is property, businesses, shares in private and in publicly quoted companies, investments and substantial savings, some of which may be located outside Ireland. All that has been said in Chapter 5 in relation to property adjustment orders, the powers of the court, the criteria for granting relief, property determination and partition, conveyancing and taxation matters, apply to other property and assets.

Particular assets can give rise to their own problems and it is worth examining these difficulties.

6.2 FARMS

Where the assets of the spouses comprise a family farm, farmhouse outbuildings and farming equipment, the court has a particular difficulty in trying to achieve a fair distribution between the spouses on divorce. The simple approach of selling everything and dividing the proceeds of sale is usually not appropriate. The farm may have been inherited by one spouse from a parent or relative and have been in the family for generations.

Since the court has power to make a property adjustment order in respect of all property, it can do so in respect of the family farm or any part of it. It is essential that the court has all relevant information. The court should be presented with the following:

(a) details as to the nature of the farming carried on;
(b) the value of any milk quota;
(c) a recent valuation by an auctioneer;
(d) a map of the farm showing the location of the various holdings, if more than one, the location of the family home, out-offices and farm buildings;
(e) details of access to various holdings and rights of way;
(f) details of any additional land leased or rented and their location;
(g) the level of borrowings on the farm and what further borrowings the farm could comfortably service;
(h) the farm's accounts for the previous two or three years.

With the above and any other information relevant to the case, the court may consider the following as possible solutions:

(i)   The court may refuse a property adjustment order in favour of the applicant spouse. Instead, the court may make a substantial periodical payment order in favour of the spouse who is being excluded. This may be considered appropriate in a case where the husband owns the farm and the wife has not made any financial contribution and/or has contributed for only a short period.

(ii)   The court may make an order that the owning spouse pays a lump sum to the other spouse to provide alternative accommodation. This may be considered appropriate in a case where the husband owns the farm but the wife needs adequate and secure accommodation for herself and the dependent members of the family. The lump sum could be raised by borrowings if the farm is not already heavily mortgaged or if other family members are anxious that the property stays within the family and can assist in the raising of the necessary finance.

(iii)   The court may partition the farm if part of the farm can be easily severed from the main holding and the essential buildings.

(iv)   The court may order a sale of part of the land to enable a lump sum to be paid to the spouse to provide alternative accommodation.

(v)   The court may order a combination of options (iii) and (iv) above. The court may order a transfer of a portion of the farm land and a sale of another portion to raise funds to build alternative residence.

Despite the importance of the family farm in rural Ireland, the courts, when considering the positions of separating spouses, have not been ideologically opposed to forcing farmers to sell a portion of the farm or to mortgage the farm to provide capital for the other spouse. Bearing in mind the fact that the spouses cannot continue to reside together after divorce, the court must make a 'separating' order. The court will take all the circumstances of the case into account, including how the farm was acquired and the contribution made by the spouses to its development. The modern family farm, even if it is registered in the sole name of one spouse, is very much a family business with both spouses and often the children of the family working hard to make it a viable proposition.

EXAMPLE

> Mr F became owner of the family farm and farmhouse and outbuildings when his father retired and transferred it to him. The transfer was subject to a right of residence in the farmhouse in favour of the father. Mr F and his wife had effectively been running the farm for some years prior to that. Mrs F actively assisted in the farming in the early years of the marriage 12 years previously but has been less actively involved in recent years as there are three children of the marriage and her father-in-law required her care and attention. The marriage of Mr and Mrs F has irretrievably broken down. Mrs F would like to remain residing in the family farmhouse and to exclude Mr F from residing there. Mrs F does not want to disturb the children in their home. The out-offices and farm buildings and farm equipment that are essential for the workings of the farm are adjacent to the family home so that, even if excluded, Mr F would continue to require access

to the area immediately adjacent to the family farmhouse. In addition, since Mr F's father still resides in the farmhouse, Mr F would need the right to visit and be with his father. The force of practical considerations make it unrealistic for Mrs F to remain living in the family farmhouse. Instead, the court is more likely to make an order providing her with alternative accommodation and maintenance.

In presenting applications and counterclaims, practitioners should try to assist the court by suggesting arrangements which are practical and viable and which are based on accurate information. In the example above, the court should be given evidence on the cost of adequate alternative accommodation for Mrs F and the children, whether a bank or other financial institution would make further borrowings available to Mr F on the security of the farm and whether any portion of the land could be sold to raise funds without interfering with the viability of the farm itself.

6.3   RESIDENTIAL BUSINESSES

Many of the points made in relation to the family farm apply to residential businesses such as licensed premises or retail shops. However, if the property is one single unit, the option of selling part will not be feasible and the court may be limited to ascertaining the extent to which property can be used to raise capital by borrowings or the income which can be generated to provide maintenance for the dependent spouse.

6.4   SHARES IN PRIVATE COMPANIES

6.4.1   General

If a spouse owns shares in a private company, the value of the shares can be a source of great argument between the spouses and their advisors, often to no practical effect. A spouse may be a shareholder in a private company with others or the spouses may have shares in a company owned by one or both of them.

The following considerations should always be borne in mind.

(a)   The courts are reluctant to interfere with a spouse's ability to generate an income and earn a livelihood.

(b)   The courts realise that the presence of divorced spouses as shareholders in the same company could destabilise the company and jeopardise the source of income of the spouse who provides for the financial needs of the family.

(c)   The value of the shares owned by a spouse as assessed by an accountant does not always mean that the shares are readily realisable at that value.

(d) The transfer of shares in a company is subject to the provisions of the memorandum and articles of association.

6.4.2 Valuation

The words of Mrs Justice Booth in the English case of *Evans v Evans* [1990] All ER 147 must be the starting point of any consideration of share valuation:

> 'While it may be necessary to obtain a broad assessment of the value of a shareholding in a private company, it is inappropriate to undertake an expensive and meaningless exercise to achieve a precise valuation of a private company which will not be sold.'

The valuation of shares in private companies is difficult and complex and accountancy advice will be needed. Accountants, however, will themselves often disagree on the value and the basis of the valuation, be it assets based or earnings based or the extent to which goodwill should be taken into account. The accountant should be instructed to carry out a broad assessment of the value of the company and where it is clear that the company will not be sold they should be asked to direct their attention to the company's liquidity to ascertain if there are reserves of cash which could be paid out to a shareholder spouse and also to find out the true extent of the benefits received by the shareholder spouse from the company including costs of motoring expenses, travel, health insurance, telephone accounts, etc.

The words of Dunn LJ in the English case of *Potter v Potter* (1983) 4 FLR 331 should act as a warning to practitioners:

> 'No fewer than four accountants were instructed to value this comparatively small business. Three of them were called to give evidence; none of them agreed as to their conclusions, which were hotly contested ... We were told that the total cost of this enquiry amounted to £12,000.... At the end of the day the exercise, namely the *detailed* valuation of the business, is an almost wholly irrelevant consideration' (author's emphasis).

Anthony Lincoln J in *P v P (Financial Provision)* [1989] 2 FLR 241 echoed these warnings when he stated:

> 'Once again I am confronted with the fact that the total realisable funds of the family have been severely reduced by incurring of vast costs by both sides in order to resolve an issue as to the value of their respective shareholding. In the outcome that issue provided to be of little or no importance. In my view legal advisers in cases such as this should strain to adopt any viable alternative, compatible with the interests of their clients, in order to avoid costly valuations detrimental to both parties and particularly to the children.'

6.4.3 Share transfer

If a spouse owns a minority shareholding in a company and the other spouse owns the remaining shares, the court is likely to order the minority shareholder to transfer his or her shares to the other. It is usually accepted that the spouses cannot both continue as shareholders of a company after separation. If a spouse does continue as a minority shareholder, there is a real risk of applications for suppression of minority pursuant to s 205 of the Companies Act 1964. The court may order that one spouse purchases the shares from the other, or the value of the shares may be taken into account in other ways in distributing other family assets.

Criteria for granting relief

All the criteria in s 20 of the Divorce Act will be taken into account by the court in deciding whether to make a transfer order in respect of shares in a private company. The court will try and achieve a fair distribution of family assets bearing in mind that the value of the shares in a private company may represent a significant portion of those assets but are not readily realisable. The court will have regard to the contribution which a wife, for example, may have made to the establishment of a business, working without remuneration, accepting a frugal standard of living, or making sacrifices to ensure the financial stability and viability of the business. The court may also take into account the fact that if the company in the past was the primary source of the family assets, it should be capable of continuing to do so in the future.

The following examples illustrate a number of typical situations that can arise.

EXAMPLE 1

Mr W was made redundant seven years ago and he and three colleagues set up a company manufacturing and supplying parts to their former employer. They each contributed equally using their redundancy payments and each has a 25% holding in the company. The company has expanded over the years and is now very successful. The company owns its factory and warehouse, subject to a bank loan. The company's shares have recently been valued at £1m.

The court may take the view that it is not appropriate for the Mrs W to obtain part of the shareholding of Mr W for operational reasons. This would impose an additional shareholder on the other shareholders of the company and diminish the husband's shareholding, possibly weakening and jeopardising his position within the company. Neither is the court likely to order a sale of all or part of the shareholding. The articles of association will limit the right to transfer shares and often the other directors have rights to purchase the shares at first instance.

EXAMPLE 2

Mr X always had the ambition of establishing his own business in the importation and supply of safety and health equipment to factories and offices. With the agreement of Mrs X, Mr X gave up work and with a bank loan and various government grants set up Safety Supplies Limited. This is a private company with 100 shares, 90 issued to Mr X and 10 to Mrs X. Initially, Mr X used the garage of the family home to hold stock and the spare bedroom as an office. Mrs X did the accounts, invoicing and administration in the evenings. The family relied on Mrs X's earnings for the first few years of the business. After a few lean years the business started to take off and it has now established a good customer base, it employs one person for the secretarial and administrative work, another to do deliveries and a sales representative to take orders and develop new customers.

The court in this case is likely to order Mrs X to transfer her share to Mr X. However, the court may take into account the contribution made by Mrs X to the establishment and development of the company in distributing the other family assets. If the company was subsequently sold, Mrs X could make an application to the court for a lump sum payment in respect of the value of her shares.

EXAMPLE 3

Mr E and Mrs E are each 50% shareholders in a company which owns a furniture and household retail shop. Mr and Mrs E are both directors and Mrs E is also the company secretary. Prior to setting up the business both had worked in similar retail outlets. They both worked equally hard to develop the business and the drawings from the company in the early years were very modest as they both wanted to put back into the company any profits earned. Both Mr E and Mrs E may make an application for a property adjustment order in respect of the shareholding of the other.

As they have an equal number of shares, they must give compelling reasons why the transfer should be made in their favour. Relevant information should be presented to the court such as the attitude of the bankers to the company, suppliers, employees and customers. In these circumstances the court may order that the transfer be at a fair value for the shares, possibly as fixed by the company's auditors.

6.4.4   Share options

If a spouse is a director/shareholder of a company, enquiry should be made as to whether they have the option to purchase shares in the company at a discounted value at certain dates. The difference between the option price and the market value could represent a valuable interest although the gain achieved is liable to capital gains tax.

6.4.5   Business Expansion Scheme

The Finance Act 1984 introduced tax relief for investment in certain indigenous companies and industries. The relief applies only to qualifying companies and the tax payer must retain the shares for a period of at least five years. Investment is very popular with high rate tax payers and even couples with relatively modest incomes have invested in such schemes. The ownership of BES shares and whether they should be the subject matter of a property adjustment order needs to be addressed in the context of divorce. It should be noted that if the shares are disposed of within this period (other than to a spouse who is living with the tax payer) then the relief is withdrawn or reduced.

6.4.6 Company assets

A company is an independent legal person from its shareholders. The court cannot make a property adjustment order against a company or order the company, to transfer assets or sell assets to generate cash for one of its shareholders to enable them to make a lump sum payment to their spouse. However, if for example the husband has a substantial shareholding in a company with healthy cash reserves, the court may order him to make a lump sum payment to his wife, confident that the husband can raise the capital by borrowings.

6.5 SHARES IN PUBLICLY QUOTED COMPANIES

If a spouse has shares in a publicly quoted company, the value is easily ascertainable either from a stockbroker or simply by checking the share price index in the newspaper where the closing prices of all shares are given each day. The court can make a property adjustment order in respect of such shares or, alternatively, the court can order their sale and payment of a lump sum from the proceeds. The capital gain tax implications of a transfer or a sale should be examined prior to the hearing.

6.6 SUBSTANTIAL ASSETS

In most family law cases the court must make difficult choices on the distribution of the family's assets to provide adequately for everyone. Invariably the needs of the parties exceed the income and assets available. Some cases, however, involve substantial assets and the court takes a broader view than it might otherwise do when constrained by the limitation of assets. Contrary to public perception, spouses are not automatically entitled to a particular percentage share of the assets of the other. If a husband is the sole owner of assets worth £2m, the wife has no automatic entitlement to half of those assets. There have unfortunately been no recorded cases giving detailed analysis of how the court might interpret the criteria set out in s 20 of the Divorce Act in cases of substantial wealth. Whilst there have been such cases before the courts, many cases settle prior to the hearing or, if heard by the court, have not been the subject matter of a written judgment. In cases involving substantial assets, the dependent spouse will seek provision in each of the categories of ancillary relief, ie accommodation, maintenance, both as to periodic payment and lump sum payment, property transfer, pension adjustment orders and financial compensation orders.

The criteria of s 20 of the Divorce Act takes on a different emphasis when examined against the backdrop of substantial assets. The 'needs' of a dependent spouse in such a case will be entirely different from an ordinary case with limited assets. Reasonable needs may include a quality residence free from encumbrances, indoor and outdoor staff, a holiday home, regular holidays abroad and generous household and entertainment allowances. The court will also look at the standard of living enjoyed by the family before the proceedings were instituted or before the spouses commenced to live apart from one another. The court will also take into account the age of the spouses and the duration of the marriage and the length of time during which the spouses lived with one another. If a dependent spouse had a very comfortable lifestyle in an expensive residence with access to funds for personal expenditure and entertainment during a marriage of 20 years and, if the financial circumstances of the other spouse are such that this provision can continue after divorce, the court may be disposed to make the appropriate orders in favour of the dependent spouse.

This issue was examined in the case of *L B v H B* (unreported, July 1980, High Court), in the context of a wife's application for maintenance under the Family Law (Maintenance) Act 1976. In this case, Mr B was a man of substantial wealth. Barrington J stated:

> 'I am also satisfied that he has not maintained his wife in the style to which the wife of so wealthy a man may reasonably aspire and which she formally enjoyed . . . I am satisfied therefore that the defendant has not maintained the plaintiff in the manner which is proper in the circumstances. I accept the evidence of the plaintiff that she cannot live with any measure of comfort in a house the size of the family home without at least the services of a housekeeper and a gardener.'

In the case of *Preston v Preston* [1982] Fam 17, Ormrod LJ stated:

> 'If the money is there, people are entitled to be kept in broadly the manner to which they have become accustomed. Not so as to indulge in profligate over spending but at least to enjoy a very comfortable standard of living.'

As in all cases, the court will also take into account the contributions which each of the spouses has made or is likely in the foreseeable future to make to the welfare of the family, including any contribution made by each of them to the income, earning capacity, property and financial resources of the other spouse. It is open to the court in cases involving substantial assets to take into account the fact that a dependent spouse could be said to have 'earned' a share in the total assets of the family. If a wife has either by working in the business of the husband or by providing finance and making a direct financial contribution, contributed towards the financial welfare of the family this will be taken into account. If a wife has accepted a modest standard of living, thereby enabling a husband to establish and develop a business this will also be taken into account. In cases of this kind the court will examine all the criteria listed in s 20 of the Divorce Act and then exercise its discretion to make provision as is appropriate in all the circumstances of the case.

The court may be more likely to use their property adjustment powers to create settlements in cases of substantial wealth if appropriate in the circumstances.

EXAMPLE

> Mr W and his family have lived in a mansion house for generations. Mrs W has lived there for all 35 years of her married life. The court may order Mr W to settle the property for the benefit of Mrs W for her life and remainder interest to his children.

In England and Wales, it is a commonly held view that there is need for a fundamental reassessment of ancillary relief and many lawyers question whether the interpretation of the criteria (similar to those described above) adequately protects dependent spouses and children. In the vast majority of cases, there is simply not enough money to go around, but in cases of substantial assets, the division is based on the 'needs' of the dependent spouse rather than an equal division of what is available. The debate of 'needs versus equality' continues. The factors which the court takes into account in theory allow the court to divide fairly the assets between the husband and the wife. However, the interpretation of the criteria to date does not appear to have given the same significance and weight to the emotional support of a spouse, home-making and child rearing responsibilities as successful business practice or wealth accumulation.

It is to be hoped that the Irish courts in the context of divorce will, in those cases where the assets allow, use their discretion not only to meet the needs of the dependent spouse, but make a fair division of the property that has been accumulated during the course of the marriage.

6.7 TRUSTS AND SETTLEMENTS

In some cases, assets are owned not by the spouses but by trustees either for the benefit of one spouse alone or for the benefit of a class of beneficiaries which may include (among others) the spouses or one of them and their children. To what extent can the court take the value of the trust assets into account, particularly in relation to a discretionary trust where a beneficiary merely has an expectation to be considered and has no actual entitlement to any particular share of the assets of the trust?

There are two distinct aspects to this problem. The first is what impact the existence of a trust will have on a court in exercising its discretion to grant ancillary relief, and the second is whether the trust comes within the definition of ante-nuptial or post-nuptial settlement and is therefore capable of being varied by a property adjustment order.

The fact that a trust exists and that a spouse is a beneficiary or a potential beneficiary will be a factor that the court will, at the very least, have to examine and give due consideration to depending on the circumstances of each case.

EXAMPLE 1

> Mr T has a life interest (with remainder to his children) in a trust fund valued at £150,000 which is invested in marketable securities. Mr T receives the dividend income each year. The court will take this income into account in assessing maintenance, however, the court cannot make a property adjustment order in relation to the trust unless it comes within the definition of ante-nuptial or post-nuptial settlement.

EXAMPLE 2

> Mrs A, Mrs B and Mrs C and their children form the class of beneficiaries of a discretionary trust. In the past the trustees have exercised their discretion in favour of Mrs C who is in poor financial circumstances. Mrs A has never received anything from the trustees. Mrs A is now divorcing her husband. What significance will the court put on the fact that Mrs A is in the class of beneficiaries of this trust with the potential of receiving financial assistance from the trustees? The court cannot force the trustees to exercise their discretion in favour of a particular beneficiary. This point was examined by Carroll J in the case of *Crowe Engineering Limited v Lynch and Others* [1992] 2 Fam LJ, which will be discussed later in the context of pension trustees. Would the court take a different view if in the past Mrs A had received money from the trustees?

The second aspect to this problem is whether the trust can be the subject matter of a property adjustment order. Can *any* trust or settlement be varied. The definition of ante-nuptial and post-nuptial settlement must be carefully examined.

An obvious ante-nuptial settlement is a pre-marriage contract which the spouses make with each other in contemplation of their marriage. A less obvious example is if a parent or grandparent of one of the spouses settles property in anticipation of the marriage on the spouses and/or any children of the marriage.

The term post-nuptial settlement also has a broad meaning. In the case of *Brooks v Brooks* [1995] 3 All ER 257, it was held that a pension scheme of which Mr Brooks was a beneficiary was a post-nuptial settlement. As discussed earlier at **5.5.4**, a separation agreement comes within the meaning of the term. Use of words '(including such a settlement by will or codicil)' suggests that the post-nuptial settlement can be made by a third party, for example the father of a wife, who may by will leave assets on trust for his daughter with remainder interest to his grandchildren.

The court can vary any settlement made *on the spouses*. As discussed earlier, the term post-nuptial settlement has received a wide interpretation by the English courts. The critical ingredient is that a benefit must be conferred on either or both of the spouses in their character of spouse or spouses and the benefit can come from one of the spouses themselves or from a third party.

In the case of *F(R) v F(J)* [1995] 3 Fam LJ (discussed in detail below), the husband transferred £52,700 into a trust where the trustee was a trust company and the beneficiaries were the two children of the marriage and his mother. McGuinness J made a property adjustment order varying the terms of the trust by directing the removal of the husband's mother from the list of beneficiaries.

In the case of *E v E (Financial Provision)* [1990] 2 FLR 233, the court accepted that property purchased by the husband's father (during the course of his son's marriage), which was placed on discretionary trust, the beneficiaries of which were the husband, the wife and the husband's children, was held to be a post-nuptial settlement.

It is questionable, however, whether a discretionary trust can be considered a post-nuptial settlement solely on account of the fact that a spouse comes within the class of possible beneficiaries, as EXAMPLE 2 above illustrates.

The issue of variation of a post-nuptial settlement was examined by McGuinness J in the case *F(R) v F(J)* [1995] 3 Fam LJ. The facts were that the parties had lived together since 1984 but had only married in 1990. There were two dependent children of the marriage. The applicant wife instituted proceedings in 1993 seeking a decree of judicial separation and ancillary relief. In 1994, the respondent husband transferred all of the then remaining off-shore funds, approximately £52,700, into a trust. The trustee of the trust was a trustee company and the beneficiaries were the two children of the marriage and the husband's mother. McGuinness J stated in her judgment:

> 'the trust deed and a letter of wishes by the husband were handed into court but oddly enough were not opened to me in any detail at the trial. On reading the deed I find that it is subject to the law of Guernsey. No evidence as to the law of Guernsey was brought before the court and no submissions were made as to the effectiveness or otherwise of any order that might be made by this court concerning moneys held in an irrevocable trust under the law of Guernsey. On 18 October 1994 an order was sought and obtained joining Haven Trustees Limited as a notice party to these proceedings and providing for service of the pleadings on them. This was a most proper order to seek given the amount of money in the trust funds. However, no proof of service appears on the court file nor was evidence of service given in court nor was any evidence given as to what response if any to the proceedings were made by Haven Trustees Limited. One would have thought that this too was essential evidence. The husband is not legally advised and since in any case it is the wife who wishes to challenge this trust, it lay with the wife to bring this evidence before the court. Instead the wife's case seems to have sailed happily along, confident that an order of the Dublin Circuit Court would be binding on the Alderney domiciled trustees of a trust governed by the law of Guernsey. I am far from being sure that this is so and I do not intend to embark upon making any order directed to Haven Trustees Limited – and indeed it would be most improper for me to do so given the absence of evidence of service.

> However, on the trust deed the husband occupies a role described as protector. This role and its powers are described in clauses 21 and 22 of the trust deed. Clause 21 states that the first protector shall be J F (the husband) and gives his then address in Guernsey. Clause 22 states "notwithstanding anything herein contained and in particular anything conferring an absolute or uncontrolled discretion on the trustees all and every power and discretion vested in the trustees by clauses 5, 6, 9 and 10 and regulations 8 and 10 of the first schedule shall only be exercisable by them with the prior or simultaneous written consent of the protector". The role of the protector therefore seems to me to be decisive and powerful one and I propose to make an order in personam directing the husband to take certain actions in regard to the trust. I hope this will be effective as a method of dealing with the matter. I will give liberty to apply in the event that such an order proves to be ineffective.'

McGuinness J went on to direct that from the trust moneys in Guernsey, the husband shall pay the sum of £25,000 to the wife. With regard to the remainder of the money in the trust fund, the judge directed that it should be left in trust for the benefit of the education of the children, however, she further directed that the husband's mother be removed from the list of beneficiaries of the trust. This was done pursuant to s 15 of the Judicial Separation and Family Law Reform Act 1989 (property adjustment order section) permitting her to make an order altering the terms of settlement.

6.8   VARIATION

Section 22 of the Divorce Act gives the court power to vary every type of ancillary relief order except:

(a)   a property adjustment order by way of transfer;
(b)   a pension adjustment order in respect of a retirement benefit where the right to vary has been excluded by s 17(26); or
(c)   an order precluding an application for provision from the estate of a deceased spouse.

Every other order may be the subject matter of a review by the court and application can be made by:

(i)   the spouses or either of them;
(ii)   if one of the spouses is dead, by any person who has sufficient interest in the matter;
(iii) by a person on behalf of the dependent member of the family; or
(iv)   in the case of remarriage of either spouse, his or her spouse.

The court will take into account all the matters set out in the criteria of s 20 of the Divorce Act and if there is a change in circumstances or if there is any new evidence the court can:

(a)   vary or discharge an order;
(b)   suspend any provision temporarily;

(c) revive the operation of an order or provision so suspended;
(d) further vary an order previously varied;
(e) further suspend or revive any provisions previously suspended or revived; or
(f) divest any property vested.

Section 22(5) of the Divorce Act specifically states that the court's powers to vary shall not prejudice the rights of a third party.

6.9 TAXATION

All that has been stated on stamp duty, capital acquisition tax and capital gains tax in Chapter 5 are equally relevant to the issues considered in this chapter.

When a case involves property other than the family home, company shares or other assets, there are two aspects to consider. The first is to distribute the assets in terms of value as fairly as appropriate in the circumstances of the case. The second is to do so in a tax-effective manner. An arrangement which on its face seems sensible can have negative consequences. Accordingly, the parties' solicitors should analyse the situation carefully and always consider taking the advice of an accountant. The role of the accountant/tax advisor is discussed further in Chapter 12.

EXAMPLE

Mrs P wants the family home transferred to her free from encumbrances. The balance due on the mortgage is £40,000. Mr P has shares in XY plc which he bought three years ago and which have substantially increased in value since then. Mrs P wants Mr P to sell his shares and discharge the mortgage on the family home from the proceeds of sale. If, however, Mr P sells the shares he will trigger an immediate charge to capital gains tax which will deplete the net proceeds of sale by approximately 40%.

6.9.1 Business relief

The Finance Act 1994 introduced a business relief to reduce the taxable value of qualifying business assets. The purpose of the relief is to reduce the liability to capital acquisitions tax when business assets are passed by gift or inheritance from, for example, a parent to a child. One of the conditions which must be complied with is that the relevant property, be it land or buildings or shares, must be in the ownership of the disponer for a continuous period of five years in respect of gifts and for a continuous period of two years in respect of inheritances. There is no provision in the Divorce Act which states that a period of ownership by one spouse can be carried over as a period of ownership by the other spouse. This is a problem which may have to be rectified in future finance legislation.

Chapter 7

MAINTENANCE AND LUMP SUM ORDERS

7.1 THE FAMILY LAW (MAINTENANCE OF SPOUSES AND CHILDREN) ACT 1976

The basic legislation dealing with maintenance is the Family Law (Maintenance of Spouses and Children) Act 1976. Section 5(1)(a) of this Act states that:

> 'where it appears to the court, on application to it by a spouse, that the other spouse has failed to provide such maintenance for the applicant spouse and any dependent children of the family as is proper in the circumstances, the court may make an order ... that the other spouse make to the applicant spouse, periodical payments, for the support of the applicant spouse and of each of the dependent children of the family for such period during the lifetime of the applicant spouse, of such amount and at such times as the court may consider proper'.

For the first time, a statutory obligation was placed on both spouses to support and maintain the other.

7.2 PHILOSOPHY BEHIND SUPPORT OBLIGATIONS

Paul O'Connor in *Key Issues in Irish Family Law* (The Round Hall Press Ltd, 1988) discusses some of the principles and concepts inherent in the maintenance regime.

The 1937 Constitution emphasises, in Article 41, the role of the mother in the matrimonial home and states clearly that she should not be forced to work if at all possible because of economic necessity.

In addition, children have the right to the provision of religious and moral, intellectual, physical and social education. All of this costs money.

It is interesting that under s 11 of the Guardianship of Infants Act 1964, a court is empowered to make maintenance orders in favour of an infant regardless of whether or not a separate maintenance application is made under this section, or under the 1976 Act, or indeed, under the Family Law Act 1995 or the Divorce Act.

7.3 STATISTICS OF MAINTENANCE APPLICATIONS

Most maintenance applications are made in all courts along with applications for other types of relief. In the district court, such applications may be made together with requests for custody and access orders or barring orders.

In the circuit and High Courts, they may be made by way of application for ancillary reliefs along with applications for decrees of judicial separation or divorce. It is, however, possible (and not uncommon) to simply apply for a maintenance order on its own under the 1976 Act and for no other relief whatsoever.

It is clear from some of the statistics available that the number of maintenance applications made to the court in any one year are very substantial.

For example, from August 1993 to July 1994, there were 2,943 maintenance applications made in the district court in Dublin. The bulk of these applications were made under the 1976 Act and maintenance orders were made in approximately 2,241 of these cases. This represents 76% of all applications. Only a few of those maintenance orders were made under the Maintenance Act 1994 which allows for reciprocal enforcement of maintenance orders between Ireland and the UK (Fahey and Lyons, 'Marital Breakdown and Family Law in Ireland – A Sociological Study' (ESRI, 1995 at p 26)).

These figures relate only to the district court in Dublin and, in addition to these applications, there would be numerous maintenance orders made in the circuit court on a daily basis both in Dublin and in other court areas. Maintenance orders are also made in the High Court and in the various sittings of the district, circuit and High Courts around the country.

In the year ended July 1994, 97% of the maintenance applications were made under the 1976 Act (Fahey and Lyons, p 26).

Maintenance for spouses and children is the second most common ancillary order applied for in the circuit court when applications are being made for decrees of judicial separation (Fahey and Lyons, p 27).

7.4   MAINTENANCE IN PRACTICE

7.4.1   Definition of 'dependent children'

A dependent child of the family is defined in s 3 of the 1976 Act as a child of both spouses, or adopted by both spouses or in relation to whom both spouses are in loco parentis or a child of either spouse, or adopted by either spouse, or in relation to whom either spouse is in loco parentis. In addition, the child must be aged under 16 or, if over that age, still be receiving full-time education or instruction at any university, college, school, or other educational establishment, and is under the age of 21 or is suffering from mental or physical disability to such extent that it is not reasonably possible for him to maintain himself fully. These age limits have been increased by the Family Law Act 1995 and the Divorce Act and the definition of 'dependent member of the family' is widened to include children under the age of 18, or if a child has attained that age and is still undergoing a full-time course of education under the age of 23.

This increase in the qualifying age is important as, these days, it would be rare for a child entering tertiary education to complete his or her course until they have at least attained the age of 23.

7.4.2 Definition of 'full-time education'

One of the difficulties which arises in maintenance applications is the definition of 'full-time education or instruction'. What is the definition of 'other educational establishment'? A child does not have to attend at a school or college five days per week, 50 weeks of the year, to come within the definition of a child for whom maintenance can be paid. A child, for example, could be attending the Open University, and studying at home on a regular basis and still qualify. There are certain educational courses where a child is paid moneys (largely for subsistence purposes). Presumably, these courses could be considered to be 'full-time education or instruction'. It is unlikely, however, that a child can simply sign on for a particular course, pay a deposit or fees of some sort, and then fail to attend at the said educational establishment or carry on any study at all and still, if over the age of 18, come within the definition of 'dependent member of the family'. The majority of situations will be quite clear but there will always be a minority of unusual circumstances which will lead to disputes and confusion.

7.4.3 Limits on orders

The present limits on maintenance orders in the district court are £200 for a spouse and £60 for a child (Courts Act 1991).

Maintenance applications can also be made at first instance to the circuit court or the High Court. There are no limits on the amounts which can be awarded in these courts. If a spouse is particularly wealthy and has a relatively large income, then proceedings will be issued in the circuit court or the High Court.

Since there are no limits in either the circuit court or the High Court, it is sometimes difficult to make a decision as to which of these two courts is the more appropriate. There are a number of factors to be taken into consideration before making a decision in this connection, including the extent and value of the other assets in the case (excluding income) and also the complexity of the financial affairs of the particular spouse.

If, for instance, a husband is a director of a major corporation and has many property interests and financial investments, it may be wiser to issue proceedings in the High Court which would be more used to dealing with complicated commercial cases.

7.4.4 Children outside marriage

Initially, until the passing of the Illegitimate Children (Affiliation Orders) Act 1930, it was not possible to obtain maintenance for a child born outside of marriage. This entire Act has since been repealed by s 25 of the Status of Children Act 1987 which greatly expanded the rights of children born outside marriage, particularly in relation to maintenance.

Section 28 of the 1976 Act had already improved the position of children born outside marriage somewhat, but a basic concept behind the enactment of the Status of Children Act 1987 was to ensure that extra-marital children were treated in exactly the same way as children born within wedlock as far as financial support and inheritance is concerned.

7.4.5   Bars to relief

The usual bars to relief have traditionally been desertion and adultery. However, the effect of desertion or adultery on maintenance orders has changed over the years.

Desertion

Section 5(2) of the 1976 Act states that 'the court shall not make a maintenance order for the support of a spouse where the spouse has deserted and continues to desert the other spouse'.

This section of the 1976 Act, however, was amended by s 38(2)(b) of the Judicial Separation and Family Law Reform Act 1989 which stated that a maintenance order could not be made for the support of a spouse where that spouse has deserted 'unless having regard to all the circumstances (including the conduct of the other spouse), the court is of the opinion that it would be repugnant to justice not to make a maintenance order'.

The insertion of such a provision in the 1989 Act is clearly an attempt by the legislature to ensure that children do not suffer as a result of the behaviour of one or both parents. If a mother of young children is refused maintenance of any realistic amount because of her desertion, this would clearly impact on the children (if any) who could not be properly supported by the mother if she was in receipt of only a limited amount of money from her husband and was not employed. It was not unknown for judges in the district and indeed the higher courts to refuse a maintenance order in favour of a 'deserting spouse' but to make a very substantial order for the support of the children which, in effect, negated the relevance of the desertion in the first place.

Constructive desertion

Section 2(3)(b) of the 1989 Act states that: 'desertion includes conduct on the part of one spouse that results in the other spouse with just cause, leaving and living apart from that other spouse'. These are precisely the same words as are used in the 1976 Act when dealing with desertion as a bar to maintenance.

The courts use the same criteria to define 'constructive desertion' when dealing with desertion as a ground for the granting of a decree of judicial separation or divorce as when deciding whether or not there has been 'constructive desertion' in a maintenance application.

'Habitual drunkenness, violence, adultery and mental cruelty have in practice all been regarded as sufficient grounds for a spouse's departure' (A Shatter, *Family Law in the Republic of Ireland* (3rd edn) p 444).

In the case of *J C v J H C* (unreported, August 1982, High Court), Keane J stated that 'the wife was justified in leaving the family home because of the husband's occasional outbursts of violence'.

The first detailed judgment dealing with the whole question of constructive desertion was that of Kenny J in the case of *Counihan v Counihan* (unreported July 1973, High Court). Kenny J stated that:

> 'an intention to disrupt the marriage or bring the co-habitation to an end must be shown in such a situation. However, the probable consequences of the conduct of a spouse can give rise to a presumption of such an intention, even if the spouse says he or she never wanted his or her spouse to leave'.

In this case, Kenny J held that the husband's irresponsibility in financial matters, his recklessness in contracting large debts, and his taking a job which meant he could be at home only at week-ends, did *not* constitute cruelty or conduct which 'a reasonable man would know would have the consequences that the marriage would be disrupted' and, therefore, did not justify the wife in telling the husband to leave. Therefore the husband was not guilty of constructive desertion.

Adultery

Under s 5(3) of the 1976 Act, it is clear that adultery was intended to be a *discretionary bar* to maintenance. If, however, the other spouse had condoned or connived at, or by wilful neglect or misconduct, conduced to the adultery, it could not be a ground for refusing maintenance. In addition, s 5(3)(b) stated that even if there was no condonation or connivance, the court could still make a maintenance order if adultery had taken place where 'having regard to all the circumstances (including the conduct of the other spouse), the court considers it proper to do so'.

However, this section was deleted by the 1989 Act (s 38(2)(b)) which inserted an additional sub-section to s 5(4).

Section 5(4) of the 1976 Act now states:

> 'that the court, in deciding whether to make a maintenance order and in determining the amount of such order, shall have regard to all the circumstances of the case and in particular to the following matters:
> (a) the income, earning capacity, property, and other financial resources of the spouses and of any dependent children of the family;
> (b) the financial and other responsibilities of the spouses towards each other and any dependent children of the family and the needs of any such dependent children including the need for care and attention;

(c)   *the conduct of each of the spouses, if that conduct is such that in the opinion of the court, it would in all the circumstances be repugnant to justice, to disregard it.'*
       (author's emphasis).

This amendment to the 1976 Act has the effect of watering down the concept of adultery as a serious discretionary bar to maintenance. The effect of the behaviour or 'fault' of the applicant spouse is therefore of far less importance than in the past.

7.4.6   Amount of maintenance awards

It is extremely difficult to anticipate with any degree of accuracy the amounts of maintenance which may be awarded by a court or ultimately agreed. There are no clear guidelines which can be referred to.

When applying for periodical payment orders, or maintenance pending suit orders, the criteria to be used are set out in s 20 of the Divorce Act. There are some general principles to be taken into consideration when fixing the amount of maintenance but awards of maintenance continue to be made of varying amounts, depending upon the circumstances of each case and the courts which actually make the orders.

Research by Peter Ward BL in 1990 (*The financial consequences of marital breakdown,* Combat Poverty Agency, 1990) showed that the amounts ordered to be paid by way of maintenance in the district court were extremely low, ie 60% of the orders were for amounts less than the rate of supplementary welfare, which is the lowest social welfare payment available.

In addition, default rates were extremely high and approximately 75% of maintenance orders made in the district court were in arrears of six months or more when examined in 1990 and only 13% were up to date.

The above-mentioned statistics, whilst helpful, are somewhat misleading in that they do not include situations where maintenance is agreed between parties either informally or through a deed of separation. The figures also do not include maintenance orders made in the circuit court or the High Court.

Fahey and Lyons in 'Marital Breakdown and Family Law in Ireland – A Sociological Study' (ESRI, 1995), investigated the figures for maintenance awards in the district court *and* circuit court, insofar as possible. The samples examined, however, were relatively small. An attempt was made to provide the median amounts of maintenance payable per week among concluded cases by court level. Obviously, the higher the court, the higher the award.

Statistics help us little in the long run and the reality is that each case depends on its own facts. In each case, consideration must be given to the income and assets of *both* spouses and the dependants and also the outgoings of both spouses and the dependent children.

An attempt was made by Finlay C J to suggest an approach to be adopted by the courts when determining a claim for maintenance in the case of *R H v N H* [1986] 1 LRM. Judge Finlay stated in that case that:

> 'certain broad principles are . . . applicable to the fixing of maintenance pursuant to s 5 of the Act of 1976, arising from the terms of that section as well as from general principles of law. The court . . . in carrying out that task must first have regard to the somewhat pathetic fact that upon the separation of a husband and wife, particularly a husband and wife with children, it is inevitable that all the parties will suffer a significant diminution in the overall standard of living. The necessity for two separate residences to be maintained and two separate households to be provided for makes this an inescapable consequence of the separation. Subject to that overriding consideration the court must . . . ascertain the minimum reasonable requirements of . . . the wife and the children for whose upkeep she is responsible; it must then ascertain the income earned or capable of being earned by the wife, apart from the maintenance for which the husband is responsible; its next task is to ascertain the true net take-home pay and income of the husband and lastly it must ascertain the reasonable living expenses of the husband, bearing in mind the general consideration of economy affecting all the parties concerned, but leaving him with a reasonable standard of living'.

In effect, this judgment indicates that a court must take all circumstances into account when making a maintenance order. Not only will a court take into account present income, and possible future income, but would also consider any capital assets which belong to either spouse.

The commonly held belief that a wife is entitled to enjoy a similar lifestyle *after* a separation or divorce to that enjoyed before, is untrue. That is only possible if there are sufficient assets or income to provide such a lifestyle. The courts tend, in most cases, to look at the reality of the financial situation and generally take into account the needs of both spouses and the children. Only in exceptional cases is a spouse 'punished' by a court for inappropriate marital behaviour by way of an excessive maintenance award.

7.4.7 Apportionment of maintenance orders

Apportionment

When making a maintenance order, the court must apportion maintenance between the applicant spouse and the children of the marriage (if any). Such apportionment generally does not take place when interim awards of maintenance are being made. It is also, of course, possible to obtain a maintenance order for a child alone without any order for maintenance being made in favour of the custodial spouse. This may occur in situations where both the husband and the wife are employed and in receipt of roughly the same income. In the alternative, a court may decide that a spouse is not entitled to maintenance for himself or herself because of their conduct or behaviour, for example, adultery or desertion.

Tax implications

The tax implications of the apportionment of a maintenance order are important and are considered later in this chapter. The general position is that, where spouses are separately assessed for income tax purposes, maintenance payments to a spouse are taxable in the hands of the receiver and tax deductible in the hands of the paying party. Maintenance payments made for a child are neither taxable nor tax deductible.

How is apportionment achieved?

There are no specific guidelines as to how to apportion a maintenance order. It is almost impossible to decide what proportion of a maintenance order will be spent on a child as opposed to a parent. Who knows how much food a seven-year-old child will eat?

It is common to apportion a larger proportion of the maintenance payment to the applicant spouse than to the children of the marriage. A typical case would be where Mrs A had four children and obtained a maintenance order against her husband in the amount of £200 per week. This sum may be apportioned as to £100 for Mrs A and £25 for each of the four children.

Attempts have been made in other jurisdictions, particularly in the US, to provide guidelines in such circumstances. O'Connor discusses these in *Key Issues in Irish Family Law* at p 128, and refers in particular to the Delaware Child Support Formula which is extremely stringent. He lists the features of the formula as follows.

(a)   Parents are entitled to keep sufficient income to meet their most basic needs in order to encourage continued employment.
(b)   Until the basic needs of children are met, parents should not be permitted to retain any more income than that required to provide the bare necessities for their own self-support.
(c)   Where income is sufficient to cover the basic needs of the parents and all dependants, children are entitled to share in any additional income so that they can benefit from the absent parent's higher standard of living.

It is clear that similar guidelines would be of assistance in Ireland when dealing with the amount of maintenance payments awarded to children, as the apportionment of payments as between the spouse and children is often purely arbitrary.

7.4.8   Earnings of third parties

One of the questions which is regularly asked is whether or not the earnings of a second 'partner' are of any relevance in deciding what maintenance payments should be made to another spouse. Where a spouse, for example, the husband, has commenced living with another person on a full-time basis as if they were husband and wife, and where that new partner is employed and earning a reasonable income, should such earnings be added to the husband's income when assessing the extent of his wealth and making a maintenance order for the benefit of his first family unit?

Up to the passing of the Divorce Act, the courts have held that such earnings were not to be considered in assessing maintenance amounts.

In the case of *O K v O K* (unreported, 16 November 1982) the court stated that:

> 'neither the fact that the husband is living in an adulterous association nor the fact that the third party is earning or not earning, is a consideration which should be taken into account. The wife should not be entitled to any greater maintenance from her husband because he has the benefit of earnings of a third party with whom he is living, nor should the wife suffer because the third party with whom her husband is living is not earning and has to be supported by him.'

However, one of the effects of the Divorce Act is to give proper legal status to second marriages. It is most unlikely, therefore, that a court would ignore the income of a second wife, or the obligation to maintain her if she is not working, when assessing the amount of maintenance to be paid by a husband to his first family unit. 'The right to re-marry and start a new family implies a duty to provide maintenance and support for that family' (O'Connor, *Key Issues in Irish Family Law*, p 139). The duty to provide maintenance and support for a second family unit makes no sense if prior maintenance orders could not be varied by the courts on remarriage or because of the cost of raising any children born in that marriage. The Divorce Act specifically states that such responsibilities and obligations are one of the criteria to be taken into account when assessing the amount of maintenance orders and it is clear that in the future such matters will have to be considered by the court in attempting to deal with such orders in a realistic and practical fashion. Further, the interpretation of s 20(2) (b) and (l) of the Divorce Act supports such an argument as reference is made in these subsections (dealing with the criteria for the making of ancillary orders) to the financial needs, obligations and responsibilities which may arise in the event of remarriage, and to the rights of such second spouses.

7.4.9 'Final break' concept

Under Irish legislation, there is no possibility of a 'final break' from a financial point of view from one's spouse, unless of course, he or she remarries. Even then, if there are dependent children, maintenance obligations will continue.

Section 27 of the 1976 Act states: 'An agreement shall be void in so far as it would have the effect of excluding or limiting the operation of any provision of this act'. Therefore, the insertion of a clause in a deed of separation which states that neither party shall look for or receive maintenance from the other, either now or in the future, is unenforceable. Such clauses are none the less often included in agreements but, in the event of future court applications for maintenance, would only be of limited evidential use.

In England and other jurisdictions there are provisions for a court to make maintenance orders for a specific period only, for example ten years. Often the intention behind such time-limits is to ensure that children have grown up and are adequately maintained during their early years. In addition, in certain jurisdictions it is possible to 'buy-out' one's maintenance obligations by means of a payment of a lump sum.

Under Irish legislation it is, of course, possible to obtain lump sum orders but such orders cannot be made conditional upon the non-payment of maintenance by one spouse to the other. Regardless of the payment of a lump sum, either by agreement or by means of a court order, a receiving spouse can still apply for maintenance at any stage and cannot be prevented from doing so.

7.5   MAINTENANCE ON DIVORCE

Generally speaking, the provisions in the Divorce Act relating to maintenance pending suit orders and periodical payments and lump sum orders are similar to those provisions contained in the 1989 Act which were repealed by the FLA 1995. There are, however, additional provisions to cover the situation where parties have obtained a valid decree of divorce and have remarried. In addition, the position concerning attachment of earnings orders has been radically altered.

7.5.1   Definitions

Before examining this area, it is important to note the various definitions contained in s 2 of the Divorce Act. The most important definition contained therein is that of 'dependent member of the family' which has already been discussed. Unfortunately, 'lump sum orders' or 'secured periodical payment orders' are not clearly defined in the Act. The relevant sections dealing with these matters are examined later.

7.5.2   Maintenance pending suit orders

The powers of the court

Section 12 of the Divorce Act gives very wide powers to the courts to make orders for maintenance pending suit, ie an order requiring either of the spouses concerned, to make to the other spouse such periodical payments or lump sum payments for his or her support, and also for the benefit of any dependent member of the family. The period of payment shall begin not earlier than the date of the application to court and end not later than the date of its determination. In other words, the court can specify a precise period in which interim maintenance has to be paid. It is important to note that maintenance pending suit orders can commence only from the date of the application to court, ie the court hearing, and not the date of issuing of the summonses.

The court may also attach certain terms and conditions to such interim payments as it considers appropriate. An example of this would be where, for instance, a judge orders that a sum of £50 per week is paid by a husband to a wife subject to the condition that she uses it for the payment of school fees for the children. An order could be also be made for a weekly sum to be paid by a husband to a wife out of a lump sum which he has obtained until a certain proportion of that lump sum has been used up.

The court can, in addition, order that a lump sum payment be made on an interim basis pending a full hearing of the action. Such an order could be made where it was clear to a court that one of the spouses has such a lump sum, or the means of obtaining one, and the other spouse will, almost certainly, eventually obtain from the court at least part of this asset.

In what circumstances should an application be made?

If one spouse, for example, the husband, is in gainful employment, and is not paying any maintenance to his wife for her support or that of any children of the marriage, it is necessary to make an application for maintenance pending suit when the full hearing of the case may not be dealt with for some time.

In certain circumstances, however, it can be difficult to decide whether or not such an application should be made. In some cases, one spouse may be paying a certain amount of maintenance and the other spouse may feel that he or she needs more. In other cases, both spouses may be working and earning roughly equivalent sums of money and one spouse may simply require maintenance towards the support of the children.

In these situations, an applicant spouse should be aware that a maintenance pending suit order will often be made despite a lack of financial information and discovery. The fixing of a maintenance figure by a court can be arbitrary and may be relatively low. When the matter eventually comes on for full hearing, the figure in everyone's mind is that amount which was awarded at the interim hearing. It is sometimes difficult to persuade a court to move away from that figure or to obtain an increase at a full hearing regardless of the production of additional evidence and information.

7.5.3 Periodical payment orders

When granting a decree of divorce or at any time thereafter, the court may make a periodical payments order which, under s 13 of the Divorce Act is defined as:

> '(i) an order that either of the spouses shall make to the other spouse such periodical payments of such amount during such a period and at such times as may be specified in the order, or

(ii)   an order that either of the spouses shall make to such a person as may be so
       specified for the benefit of such (if any) dependent member of the family
       such periodical payments of such amount during such period, and at such
       times as may be so specified.'

An application for a periodical payments order can be made by either of the
spouses concerned or by a person on behalf of a dependent member of the
family. A 'dependent member of the family' is defined in s 2 of the Divorce Act.
Therefore, not only parents may apply, but also persons who are actually
looking after and raising a child, for example, grandparents, in circumstances
where one or both parents are not contributing financially.

It is interesting that both s 5(1)(a) of the 1976 Act and s 13(1)(a)(i) of the
Divorce Act make reference to periodical payments orders being made for
certain periods. This would seem to suggest that a court can order that
maintenance payments only be made for, say, five years or some other similar
period. The court can, of course, order that maintenance payments be made
for the lifetime of one or other of the spouses.

It is, however, very unusual for the court to state that periodical payments
should last only for a particular specified period. Usually an order remains in
force until it is varied by the court when there is a change in circumstances.

In certain situations, under English legislation, it is common for courts to make
maintenance awards for a specified period in order to facilitate and assist the
dependent spouse (usually the wife) in her attempts to make herself financially
independent after a divorce. The concept of a 'final break' is prevalent in
England where the court has a duty to see if matters can be dealt with on a clean
break basis.

7.5.4   Orders for payments to cover expenses incurred prior to application to court

Since there can be lengthy delays in obtaining a hearing date for applications
for a periodical payments order from the court, it is important that the power is
available to a court to make orders that a spouse:

'pay a lump sum to the other spouse to meet any liabilities or expenses reasonably
incurred by that other spouse before the making of an application by that other
spouse for an order under subsection (1) in maintaining himself or herself or any
dependent member of the family' (Divorce Act, s 13(2)(a)).

In addition, the court is given the power to award a lump sum to third parties
who may have incurred liabilities or expenses for the benefit of a dependent
member of the family before the making of an application on behalf of the
member for an order under s 13(1) of the Divorce Act.

It would appear, therefore, that where an application for a periodical payments
order is being made, the court may add up all money reasonably spent by the

applicant spouse or third party in either supporting themselves, or a dependent member of the family, as the case may be, during the entire period which has elapsed since the date of actual separation and then award such total amount to the applicant.

Such orders will be made only in very exceptional circumstances and only in cases where there are substantial funds available to facilitate the making of such payments.

In order to lessen the impact of such orders to a certain degree, s 13(3) of the Divorce Act allows the payment of the lump sum to be made by way of instalments with such amounts as may be specified in the order. The court can therefore make an order that the lump sum be paid off by way of instalments over a relatively lengthy period.

It is important to note that any such liabilities or expenses which have been incurred must be 'reasonable' (Divorce Act, s 13(2)(a)). An applicant spouse cannot simply present a list of money actually expended on many and various items and expect to be fully recompensed. The court may feel that a spouse was justified in, for example, borrowing moneys to pay school fees and expenses, but not to pay for a holiday in Barbados.

The liabilities and expenses must have been incurred by way of maintenance for the applicant and/or the children or incurred for the benefit of a child, for example educational fees or medical expenses.

It would appear, therefore, that a lump sum order in such circumstances would not be made to cover legal fees incurred by a spouse or borrowings raised to pay such fees which are necessary to pursue an application for divorce.

From a practical point of view, it would be wise for a practitioner to advise his or her clients to keep careful records of all necessary expenses incurred prior to any court hearing.

Loans obtained by an applicant spouse from his or her own immediate family should also be noted and recorded. Such loans are not, however, given the same status by the court as loans obtained from a financial institution such as a bank or building society, but may still be relevant.

In practice, the courts have only rarely made such orders to cover expenses incurred prior to applications being made to court. The general approach at the time of a court hearing is to deal with all financial issues as they exist at the time of such hearing and to make the appropriate orders.

It can be difficult to persuade a court, after making such orders, to attempt to compensate the applicant spouse for events which have taken place in the past when he or she is about to receive a reasonable share of the family assets and a reasonable maintenance payment for the future.

7.5.5   Secured periodical payments orders

The court can order that once it makes a periodical payments order, it should be secured in some way to the satisfaction of the court. Section 13(1)(b) of the Divorce Act states that such secured periodical payments orders may be made in favour of spouses or for the benefit of a third party who is caring for a dependent member of the family. The amounts of such payments, the period of payment and the times of payment are also to be specified by the court.

An example of a secured periodical payments order would be where a court directs an employer to deduct a certain sum from the employee's pay cheque and forward it to a dependent spouse (attachment of earnings orders are discussed at **7.10.2**).

Another example could occur where the husband perhaps owns an investment property with a regular flow of income and the court directs that the payment of maintenance be deducted from that income and paid directly to the wife. This would have the effect of ensuring that the payments continue even if the spouse, who is responsible for such payments, leaves the jurisdiction or loses his job and has no other income.

A third example could arise where the husband has a bad maintenance record and, for instance, the family assets consist of a house, gardens and, say, 40 acres of agricultural land.

In such circumstances, a court may order that the house and gardens be transferred into the sole name of the wife, the remaining lands to become and remain the sole property of the husband, a maintenance order be made in favour of the wife for her support and that of the children *and* the maintenance order to be secured on the lands belonging to the husband.

This would protect the wife in the event of the husband failing to comply with the terms of the maintenance order, and if he fell into arrears, she could make an application to court seeking an order for sale of a portion of the land in order to facilitate the discharging of any arrears of maintenance due.

In such a case, it is probable that the husband could sell only a portion or all of the land himself in the future with the prior approval of the court.

This power was originally given to the courts by s 14 of the 1989 Act but has been rarely used.

7.5.6   Lump sum orders

The powers of the court

On granting a decree of divorce, the court may order either of the spouses to make to the other spouse, a lump sum payment or payments of such amount and at such time as may be so specified. Alternatively, the court may make such an order in favour of a 'dependent member' of the family (Divorce Act, s 13(1)(c)).

It is arguable that a court cannot order a lump sum payment for *both* a spouse and a 'dependent member' of a family. Under the Family Law Act 1995, it was clearly possible for the court to make lump sum orders in favour of spouses *and* 'dependent members' of the family (s (8)(1)(c)). However, the word 'or' was inserted by s 52 of the Divorce Act in between the references to lump sum payments to spouses and the references to lump sum payments for dependants.

The courts have had the power to make such lump sum payments since the coming into operation of the 1989 Act and have used this power widely. It is important to note that an application can now be made in the district court for a lump sum order to a maximum amount of £5,000 (FLA 1995, s 42(4)). There is no limit to the amount which can be awarded in the circuit or the High Court.

In circumstances where the family assets consists of the family home and perhaps some other properties, or substantial cash assets, the court would, after considering all relevant factors, including the valuation of the various properties, etc make an order transferring, for example, the family home into the sole name of the wife, leaving all other properties in the sole name of the husband and awarding a compensating lump sum to be a paid by the husband to the wife within a certain period. This would be done in an effort to divide fairly the various family assets. The needs of the children would also be taken into consideration.

The amount actually awarded by way of a lump sum is sometimes a purely arbitrary figure and is very difficult to predict in advance of a court hearing.

General principles in English law relating to lump sum payments
The courts in Ireland have the widest possible discretion to order payments of lump sum amounts. This power has existed in England and Wales for some years and has been used widely.

It is worthwhile noting that the above-mentioned lump sum provision is similar to that contained in the English Matrimonial Proceedings and Property Act 1970. Such orders have been made in many cases and there are some general principles which can be drawn:

(a)   The court will only order that a lump sum payment be made if the paying spouse has capital assets which are of sufficient value to enable such a lump sum to be paid.

(b)   The courts will order a lump sum payment if the paying spouse has sufficient income to enable him or her to arrange the necessary loan facilities comfortably.

(c)   If a substantial lump sum award is made in favour of a wife, then this may lead to a reduction in the amount of periodical payments awarded to her as she will, in theory, be entitled to an income from any such lump sum.

(d)   If a lump sum is awarded, it is generally made outright. Although the
       courts have the power to attach conditions to the awarding of such a lump
       sum, they generally do not do so (see Bird and Cretney, *Divorce The New
       Law* (Jordans, 1996)).

These general guidelines will be of much assistance to the courts in Ireland
when making similar lump sum orders.

Instalments

It is common, however, for a court to provide for the payment of a lump sum by
way of instalments, particularly if the amount awarded is large (Divorce Act,
s 13(3)). Such a payment by instalments may be secured by the court, ie
registered as a charge against property owned by the paying spouse.

Lump sum and periodical payments orders

It is important to note that a lump sum order may be made *in addition to* a
periodical payments order but not instead of such a periodical payments order.
It is, of course, open to a court to award a lump sum and refuse to make a
maintenance order. However, an applicant cannot be prevented from
reapplying to court for a maintenance order in the future if there is any change
in circumstances, or new evidence comes to light.

It is also not possible to renounce one's right to claim maintenance in a
separation agreement when receiving a lump sum payment. Section 27 of the
1976 Act is still applicable and states that: 'an agreement shall be void insofar as
it would have the effect of excluding or limiting the operation of any provision
of this Act'.

In other jurisdictions, it is possible for a husband, for example, to provide a
lump sum to his wife in lieu of maintenance payments for her lifetime. This can
be done by agreement or by court order. In Ireland, a spouse has a right to be
maintained for his or her lifetime unless there is good reason why he or she
should not be so maintained. Section 13(4) of the Divorce Act states that
periodical payment orders: 'shall begin not earlier than the date of the
application for the order and shall end not later than the death of the spouse,
or any dependent member of the family, in whose favour the order is made or
the other spouse concerned'.

7.5.7   Retrospective periodical payments orders

Section 21 of the Divorce Act permits the court to make periodical payments
orders retrospective to the date of issuing of proceedings for the grant of
decree of divorce or such later date as may be specified.

This provision is intended to encourage the parties to negotiate a reasonable
level of interim maintenance in order to provide for day-to-day expenses which
arise from the date of the issue of the proceedings to the date of the hearing of
the case.

If this provision were implemented on a regular basis, then it would encourage the paying spouse, prior to any court order being made, to ensure that the maintenance being paid was reasonable so that they would not be faced with an order for substantial arrears of maintenance at the time of making the final order. In practice, however, this provision is used quite rarely in the context of applications for judicial separation. The negative aspects of applying for interim maintenance orders have already been dealt with.

The court can also order that such retrospective payments be discharged in one sum and before a specified date (Divorce Act, s 21(1)(b)). The court can direct from where the money to discharge the sum is to be obtained. In deciding the extent of the lump sum to be paid in such circumstances, the court may order that certain payments or amounts discharged by the paying spouse during the period between the issuing of proceedings and the making of the order for the grant of the decree, be deducted from the said lump sum (Divorce Act, s 21(1)(c)).

7.5.8 Cessation of periodical payments orders

In general terms, periodical payment orders last for the lifetime of a dependent spouse, or, where children are concerned, until they commence working or attain the age of 23 (while still undergoing a full-time course of education), whichever is earlier.

However, periodical payments orders shall cease to have effect in the following circumstances:

(a) upon the remarriage of the spouse in whose favour an order is made (Divorce Act, s 13(5)(a)). Any payments made to children shall continue to have effect even after the remarriage of a spouse. Any arrears due to the dependent spouse up to the date of the remarriage shall also remain the liability of the paying spouse. If no periodical payments order is made at the time of the granting of a decree of divorce, then, if a spouse remarries, subsequently, the court shall not make a periodical payments order in favour of that spouse (Divorce Act, s 13(5)(b));
(b) the death of either spouse;
(c) where a fundamental change in circumstances leads to the discharging of a maintenance order, for example, due to a paying spouse being made redundant or the receiving spouse aquiring a substantial unexpected lump sum or taking up full-time employment.

7.6 CRITERIA FOR DETERMINING APPLICATIONS

It is quite difficult, as has already been stated to estimate in advance what amount the court will award under a periodical payments or a lump sum order.

However, s 20 of the Divorce Act, which is broadly similar to s 16 of the FLA 1995, lists factors which should be taken into account by the court when making periodical payments orders, maintenance pending suit orders, attachment of earnings orders or lump sum orders. These factors are set out below.

7.6.1 Family Law (Divorce) Act 1996, s 20

Section 20(2)(a)

> 'the income, earning capacity, property and other financial resources which each of the spouses concerned has or is likely to have in the foreseeable future,'

The court must taken into account all financial aspects of the particular case including not only present income and resources, but also possible future income. Reference is clearly made to 'earning capacity'. When applications for periodical payment orders are being made, the court will often state that it must only deal with the 'here and now' situation. Section 20, however, envisages a court taking into account the ability of the spouse to earn money, even if they are not actually employed at the time of the making of the order. All property owned by either spouse is also highly relevant when making such orders. The property may consist of houses, stocks, shares, moneys on deposit, jewellery, cattle, etc. All these assets are capable of being used to create an income. For a periodical payments order to be made, it is not absolutely essential to show that there is any income in existence at all. A court will not, of course, make a periodical payments order against a spouse who is collecting social welfare and has no other assets. However, if there are sufficient valuable assets available, and no regular income, such an order may be made.

Section 20(2)(b)

> 'the financial needs, obligations and responsibilities which each of the spouses has, or is likely to have in the foreseeable future (whether in the case of the remarriage of the spouse or otherwise),'

Prior to the coming into operation of the FLA 1995 when making a decision as regards a periodical payments order or lump sum order, the court was not expected to take into consideration the obligation on one spouse to support a third party who was not a child, for example, a new partner. Now, however, if an individual remarries after obtaining a divorce, then the fact that he or she has a financial obligation and responsibility towards that new spouse or children must be considered by the court as a relevant factor. Similarly the earnings of the new spouse will be taken into consideration when estimating what moneys are available to a liable spouse to enable him or her make such payments.

In addition, the court will consider the financial needs of each of the spouses. Both spouses are entitled to a certain minimum standard of living insofar as is possible, and both spouses are entitled to ensure that they have sufficient moneys to pay for basic essentials such as housing, food and clothes.

In practice, it is important clearly to set out in writing a full and detailed statement of outgoings, both for the present and as estimated for the future. When preparing such lists for a court hearing, it is important to cover every possible expense. The list should include the cost of food, clothes, educational fees and expenses, extra-curricular school activities, school uniforms, travel expenses to and from school and work, lunches and meals outside the home, medical expenses, dental expenses, chemist bills, health insurance, holidays, entertainment, presents, church donations, newspapers, toiletries, life insurance premiums, house insurance premiums, house repairs, mortgage repayments, rent, electricity, gas, telephone, TV licence, loan repayments, cable TV, haircuts, charitable donations, legal fees, etc.

In cases of substantial wealth, the list may include the cost of gardeners, home helps, personal bodyguards, PE instructors, etc.

Section 20(2)(c)

'the standard of living enjoyed by the family concerned before the proceedings were instituted or before the spouses commenced to live apart from one another as the case may be,'

It is a commonly held belief that there is a legal obligation imposed on a husband to provide for his wife after separation or divorce the same standard of living which was provided for her prior to such an event. This is not, in fact, the position. The court can take into account the standard of living enjoyed by the family prior to separation but, in reality, this carries little weight except in cases of substantial wealth. The courts feel that the reality of the financial situation must be addressed and, as the Supreme Court has remarked in a separation situation: 'it is inevitable that all the parties will suffer a significant diminution in their overall standard of living', particularly where there are children involved (*R H v N H*) [1986] ILRM 352).

Section 20(2)(d)

'the age of each of the spouses, the duration of their marriage and the length of time during which the spouses lived with one another,'

If, for example, a wife is elderly at the time of divorce, then the court will attempt to ensure that she is as financially secure as is possible in the circumstances. There is no doubt that the older the applicant, the higher the maintenance award. An older applicant has a greater need for security of a financial nature for his or her future. A court will often feel that a younger applicant has greater opportunities to obtain a reasonable income or amass savings in the future and that as a result a periodical payments order or a lump sum order may be less than that which would be awarded to an older applicant.

The time spent together during the marriage is also of relevance. In effect, an applicant spouse may be rewarded for staying in the marriage for a lengthy period, and penalised for leaving the marriage at an early stage.

Section 20(2)(e)

'any physical or mental disability of either of the spouses,'

Physical and mental disability are factors which will certainly affect the decision of a court. If an applicant is suffering from a physical or mental disability which prevents them from working, a periodical payments order may be higher than normal. A court could not possibily take into account the fact that such an applicant could obtain employment in the future if the disability is severe. The court would further have to assume that such an applicant will require maintenance or a lump sum for their lifetime. In situations such as this, it is possible that a court would, in certain circumstances, order that a lump sum be invested in some type of pension or investment policy to provide an income for such an applicant in later life.

Section 20(2)(f)

'the contributions which each of the spouses has made or is likely in the foreseeable future to make to the welfare of the family, including any contribution made by each of them to the income, earning capacity, property and financial resources of the other spouse and any contribution made by either of them by looking after the home or caring for the family,'

The first reference to placing a value on caring for a family or looking after a home was made in the 1989 Act (s 20(2)(f)). This was a major development in the area of family law as up to then such a contribution was entirely disregarded despite the provisions of the 1937 Constitution. It is, of course, virtually impossible to place a financial value on such contributions but there is no doubt that the courts, in assessing periodical payment orders or lump sum payments, will take such contributions into account.

In addition, specific reference is made to contributions by either spouse to the others' 'income, earning capacity, property and financial resources'. An example of such a situation is where a wife looks after young children and also works to support the family unit while the husband continues his study which leads in turn to greater career prospects. The fact that the wife supported the family during that period (which could last for several years) is of great relevance to the parties' divorce and to the court in deciding the extent of periodical payments orders or lump sum orders to be made. The wife will receive substantial credit for her role in contributing to her husband's 'earning capacity'.

Section 20(2)(g)

'the effect on the earning capacity of each of the spouses of the marital responsibilities assumed by each during the period when they lived with one another and in particular, the degree to which the future earning capacity of a spouse is impaired by reason of that spouse having relinquished or forgone the opportunity of remunerative activity in order to look after the home or care for the family.'

This section attempts to, in some way, assist the court in placing a value on the fact that a spouse, usually a wife, gave up her job or possible promotion prospects in order to have children and care for the home. It is virtually impossible to place a financial value on this contribution. The courts still find it difficult to financially compensate a spouse in such circumstances and, in practice, rarely take this factor into account at all. There is no doubt that, in reality, many spouses are at a serious financial loss as a result of engrossing themselves in the home and caring for the family. Despite the inclusion of such clauses in the 1989 Act, the FLA 1995 and the Divorce Act, it will be some time before this particular criterion is given the importance it perhaps deserves.

Such a situation was of much more relevance in Ireland in the 1960s and 1970s when women were forced to give up their employment as civil servants, teachers, air hostesses, etc immediately they got married. In the 1990s, the effect of marriage on a woman's career is not so immediately drastic.

Section 20(2)(h)

> 'any income or benefits to which either of the spouses is entitled by or under statute,'

When a court is attempting to fix a sum to be paid by one spouse to the other by way of maintenance or by way of lump sum, they will take into consideration all income received by both parties from all sources. This includes income from employment, income from interest on deposits, social welfare payments, children's allowance, regular gifts from third parties such as parents, rental income, income from lodgers and income from all other sources, whether taxed or otherwise.

This section extends the criteria to be taken into consideration by including all social welfare payments and payments to which either the spouse is entitled by statute, for example, old age pensions, disability benefits, child benefit etc.

Section 20(2)(i)

> 'the conduct of each of the spouses, if that conduct is such that in the opinion of the court it would in all the circumstances of the case be unjust to disregard it,'

Prior to the coming into operation of the 1989 Act, the conduct or behaviour of one spouse was extremely relevant in deciding the issue of maintenance.

Section 5(2) of the 1976 Act specifically states that: 'the court shall not make a maintenance order for the support of a spouse where the spouse has deserted and continues to desert the other spouse'. However, this section was amended by the 1989 Act (s 38(2)) and the position since then (and repeated in the FLA 1995 and the Divorce Act) is that desertion is a bar to a periodical payments order or a lump sum order unless having regard to all the circumstances of the case (including the conduct of the other spouse) the court is of the opinion that it would be unjust not to make the order. In effect, desertion is now a *discretionary* bar to maintenance and not an *absolute* bar as it was prior to 1989.

Adultery has always been a discretionary bar to the making of a maintenance order (1976 Act, s 5(3)). The 1989 Act lessened the impact of adultery on the making of a maintenance order even further by deleting s 5(3) of the 1976 Act and expanding on s 5(4) and, as a result, ensured that there was no specific reference to adultery per se. The section merely stated that it was included in the 'conduct' which was to be considered when making a maintenance order or refusing to do so.

It is intended that, when making lump sum orders, the court will also take into account the conduct or behaviour of both spouses. Although, therefore, the concept of 'fault' has nothing to do with the actual granting of a decree of divorce, it may be taken into account when a court is making ancillary orders once the decree itself has been granted. On the other hand, the conduct of the parties is only one of 12 criteria to be considered by a court when making such orders and its effect is therefore diluted.

CONSTRUCTIVE DESERTION
The whole area of constructive desertion is relevant to s 20(2)(i).

Section 16(3)(b) of the FLA 1995 states that: 'a spouse who, with just cause, leaves and lives apart from the other spouse because of conduct on the part of the other spouse shall not be regarded for the purposes of paragraph (a) as having deserted that spouse'.

'Habitual drunkenness, violence, adultery and mental cruelty have, in practice, all been regarded as sufficient grounds for a spouse's departure' (A Shatter, *Family Law in the Republic of Ireland* (3rd edn) p 444).

In the case of *J C v J H C* (unreported, August 1982, High Court), Keane J stated that a wife was justified in leaving the family home because of the husband's 'occasional outbursts of violence'.

In the case of *Counihan v Counihan* (unreported, July 1972, High Court), Kenny J stated that there must be 'an intention to disrupt the marriage or bring it to an end'. However, the probable consequences of the conduct of a spouse can give rise to a presumption of such an intention, even if the spouse says that he or she never wanted his or her spouse to leave and never had any intention of ending the marriage.

In practice, in the majority of cases which are dealt with by the courts, very little time is spent on examining the reasons for the breakdown or the behaviour of either of the spouses. The courts lists are full and there is little to be gained by exploring who did what to whom and when. In general terms, courts tend to concentrate primarily on the financial aspects of a case and the welfare of the children.

Although there are six separate grounds for the granting of a decree of judicial separation under the 1989 Act, there is rarely any argument at a hearing of an action as to the precise ground for the granting of a decree. The majority of decrees are granted under s 2(1)(f), which states that: 'the marriage has broken down to the extent that the court is satisfied in all the circumstances that a normal marital relationship has not existed between the spouses for a period of at least one year, immediately preceding the date of the application'.

'Irretrievable breakdown' is becoming the major ground for the granting of a decree of judicial separation and is, in effect, the only ground for the granting of a decree of divorce. It is important to note, however, that, under s 2(1)(f) of the 1989 Act, it is necessary to give oral evidence at the hearing of the action as to the reasons why the marriage has broken down, even in circumstances where all the terms of a separation have been agreed. A decree of judicial separation under s 2(1)(f) cannot be granted simply by consent without the formal giving of evidence. In practice, this rule is enforced by some judges and not by others.

Section 20(2)(j)

> 'the accommodation needs of either of the spouses,'

When assessing the amount of a periodical payments order or the amount of a lump sum to be paid, the court acknowledges that the spouses must live separate and apart from each other and will, therefore, have to be allowed a reasonable sum to provide for rent or mortgage repayments, as the case may be. A court would not consider it reasonable, for example, to order that a husband continue to make repayments on a mortgage of, for example, £150,000 on a family home so that the wife may continue residing there, whilst he can afford to pay rent only on a small bedsit. If the family home is of a substantial nature and the wife wishes to continue residing there (if it is possible financially), the inclination of the court would be to ensure that the husband also has sufficient funds to pay a reasonable rent or mortgage to enable him to enjoy acceptable living accommodation. Such accommodation will facilitate a non-custodial parent having regular overnight access to any children of the marriage.

On the other hand, when there are children who will be residing generally with one parent, the court will naturally accept that the spouse with children requires larger living accomodation than the other spouse who only has to provide for himself. The existence of children also has an impact on the making of property adjustment orders.

Section 20(2)(k)

> 'the value to each of the spouses of any benefit, (for example a benefit under a pension scheme), which by reason of the decree of divorce concerned, that spouse will forfeit the opportunity or possibilty of acquiring,'

This is an entirely new provision which was first contained in the FLA 1995, s 16(2)(k) insofar as decrees of judicial separation were concerned.

As can be seen from Chapter 10, when dealing with pension adjustment orders, on the granting of a decree of divorce, a spouse may lose certain entitlements entirely, or have certain entitlements reduced substantially. As a result therefore, this is yet another factor to be taken into account by a court when deciding on the amount of a periodical payments order or the amount of a lump sum order which should be paid to an applicant spouse. In effect, the court will compensate a spouse for the loss of such possible benefits. A court will be greatly assisted by evidence given by an actuary in order to attempt to estimate the possible value of such a loss and the possible compensatory amount to be provided for an applicant spouse.

As a result of this section and the provisions relating to pension adjustment orders (Divorce Act, s 17), there are a growing number of 'pension specialists' setting up who are attempting to provide specialist services in this area. In some cases, such services may be of great assistance.

Section 20(2)(l)

> 'the rights of any person other than the spouses but including a person to whom either spouse is remarried.'

Again, this is an entirely new concept which was first referred to in the FLA 1995 (s 16(2)(1)).

For the first time, since the FLA 1995, the court will take into consideration the fact that a second spouse has a right to be maintained by his or her spouse. Presumably, as has already been stated, if a second spouse is employed and earning an income, that will also be taken into consideration in assessing the amount of a periodical payments order or the amount of a lump sum to be awarded in favour of the first spouse.

Prior to the implementation of the FLA 1995, the earnings of such new partners or the fact that they may have needed to be supported, was held to be irrelevant in assessing the amount of maintenance to be paid. In the case of *O K v O K* (unreported, 16 November 1982, High Court), it was held that:

> 'neither the fact that the husband is living in an adulterous association nor the fact that the third party is earning or not earning, is a consideration which should be taken into account. The wife should not be entitled to any greater maintenance from her husband because he has the benefit of earnings from a third party with whom he is living, nor should the wife suffer because the third party with whom her husband is living is not earning and has to be supported by him.'

Obviously this judgment only dealt with situations where a spouse was residing with someone to whom he or she was not married. However, the fact that because of the Divorce Act second marriages are legally recognised, the second spouse's income or dependency cannot be ignored.

This is a major development in the law relating to marital breakdown and in many cases will impact to a negative degree on the amount of maintenance awarded to a first spouse, and the amount of lump sums awarded to such a spouse.

7.6.2 Members of the defence forces

It is interesting to note that under the Defence Act 1954, s 98(1)(h), an attachment of earnings order could be made in relation to earnings of a member of the defence forces without necessarily having to prove any default in maintenance payments. The relevant provisions are extended to include reference to maintenance pending suit orders and periodical payments orders and secured periodical payments orders (Divorce Act, s 29). In such situations, for many years, an attachment of earnings order has been made automtically.

7.6.3 Income tax

Section 31 of the Divorce Act states that: 'payments of money pursuant to an order under this Act ... shall be made without deduction of income tax'. This matter is discussed later in this chapter at **7.12**.

7.6.4 Evidential nature of prior separation agreements

In deciding whether to make a periodical payments order or maintenance pending suit orders, or in assessing the amount of those orders, the court shall have regard to the terms of any separation agreement which has been entered into by the spouses and is still in force at the time of making the orders (Divorce Act, s 20(3)). In such situations, the court shall merely 'have regard to the terms of such an agreement'. The court is not bound by this and, in practice, the weight given to the terms of such an agreement will vary from case to case.

What may be of more relevance is that there may be provisions in the deed of separation for the payments of lump sums which have already been made by one spouse to the other. In addition, transfers of property may have taken place. A court is bound to take such transactions into account in assessing amounts of future maintenance.

Once the parties have lived apart for four years, a decree of divorce will be granted and, pursuant to s 14(1)(c) of the Divorce Act, the court may vary the terms of the deed of separation and order that, for example, the family home remain the sole property of the wife whilst also making a periodical payments order in her favour. It is now common practice to insert in deeds of separation and terms of settlement of judicial separation proceedings a clause which states that the agreement entered into is to form the basis for any ancillary orders which may be made on the granting of a decree of divorce in the future, and is also to be considered as a reasonable settlement for the purposes of the granting of a decree of divorce. It is not known how effective such clauses will be as they have not yet been tested by the courts.

7.6.5   Case-law

C(C) v C(J)

The case of *C(C) v C(J)* [1994] 1 Fam LJ 22 considered the making of ancillary orders pursuant to the granting of a decree of judicial separation under the 1989 Act. This case does, however, help to demonstrate how the courts operate in a typical matrimonial situation insofar as ancillary orders are concerned and how they will deal with such applications in divorce proceedings in the future.

The husband and wife were married in 1972 and at the time of the court hearing there were two children aged 17 and 15 years, both of whom resided with the mother. The attended a non fee-paying school but had substantial fees and expenses in relation to extra-curricular activities and basic needs for the school. One of the children suffered from asthma and required expensive orthodontic treatment. The other child had a slight problem with dyslexia.

The family home was registered in the sole name of the husband who had purchased it prior to the marriage and made all the mortgage repayments, etc.

In 1982, the husband and the wife agreed to separate but did not actually do so at that time. The husband went away for a period to work and made substantial savings out of high earnings during that period.

Ultimately, the husband and the wife separated in 1985 and the husband moved to a different county and spent substantial sums of money on renovating an old mill and turning it into a fine home.

The court accepted that all of the husband's available financial assets had been eaten up in this enterprise. The court further accepted that the value of the renovated house was the same as the value of the family home.

Remedial work on the family home required a sum of approximately £10,000. The wife had also spent about £5,000 on the property over the years, since the breakdown of the marriage.

The wife resigned from her job on becoming married and received a gratuity of £1,450, which was placed in a joint deposit account in the Educational Building Society. These moneys were eventually used by the husband when he was renovating his new home.

At the time of the court hearing, the husband was paying the wife a sum of £14,753 per annum for her maintenance and that of the children. In addition, he paid a sum of £1,321 by way of mortgage and insurance on the family home.

The wife derived a small income from the sale of paintings and from occasional private art classes. These earnings amounted to approximately £2,500 per annum. The wife was also a qualified Montessori teacher. She had a liability to income tax and Barr J indicated that: 'it must be borne in mind that if she is awarded any increase in maintenance, approximately half of it would be payable by her in income tax at the present rates'.

The husband's net annual pay after deductions was £35,339. In addition, he had a telephone and car allowance as well as expenses for meals and overnight stopovers in connection with his work. He paid a total of approximately £16,000 for the benefit of his wife and children leaving him with a net balance of approximately £19,000.

The court granted a decree of judicial separation without any difficulty and also made orders in relation to custody and access which were not disputed.

Barr J considered all of the evidence given in relation to the issue of maintenance and dealt with it on a global basis firstly, and then sub-divided the maintenance as between the wife and children.

He felt that the wife's claim for an additional sum by way of maintenance was reasonable in the circumstances, but stated that she would not have too much difficulty in making up at least a significant part of that increased amount herself by utilising her qualifications as a Montessori teacher. 'Such employment would seem to be suited to her present circumstances and would not interfere with her duties as a mother'. Barr J also indicated that the wife's expertise as an artist was likely to be an additional advantage in obtaining such employment. He increased the maintenance by a lesser amount than that requested by the wife and ordered that the husband continue to make the mortgage repayments.

Barr J accepted the wife's evidence that she had spent approximately £5,000 on the family home since the breakdown of the marriage and further substantial amounts on other matters. He made a lump sum order of £10,000 in respect of such items and also stated that the wife was entitled to a sum of £500 by way of a refund of the amount expended by her on orthodontic treatment for one of the children.

The court then estimated what the present-day value of the sum lodged in the Educational Building Society account would be and made a further lump sum order of £5,000 in this regard. Accordingly, the wife was entitled to a total lump sum of £15,500.

A property adjustment order was also made in this case. The purpose of discussing this case in some detail here is to show how a court will, in a given case, reach its decisions. The figures which were eventually ordered were relatively arbitrary but do have some logic to them. It is a typical case where neither the husband nor the wife would have been 100% happy with the outcome of the hearing but would have managed to live with it.

7.7   CRITERIA FOR ASSESSING THE AMOUNTS PAYABLE FOR DEPENDANTS

The criteria are listed in s 20(4) of the Divorce Act. They include the financial needs of the dependent member, the income, earning capacity, property and other financial resources of the member, any physical or mental disability of the member and any income or benefits to which the member is entitled to by or under statute.

It is also stated that the court should consider the type of education which has been received and is intended to be received by the dependent member in the future. This issue is often one which causes great conflict in matrimonial breakdown. The intention is that courts will have regard to the cost of any necessary education for a dependent member and will respect the wishes of one or both parents, regarding future education. The reality, however, is that, in many cases, there are simply insufficient funds to, for instance, enable a child to remain in an expensive fee-paying school, once the parents have separated. In a number of cases, the courts have queried the ability of parents to continue to send their children to private fee-paying schools. The court looks at the overall financial situation in a realistic and practical fashion and realises that once a couple separate, the money available to fund expensive education is often no longer available.

The court will also take into consideration the income and earning capacity of both spouses, their needs and obligations and responsibilities and also the standard of living enjoyed by the family prior to the institution of proceedings. In addition, the court will consider the accommodation needs of the dependent member of the family. If the child has any physical or mental disabilities which lead to special accommodation needs then the cost will be reflected in any periodical payments order or lump sum order.

These criteria have been discussed in some detail in Chapter 4.

7.8   RELEVANCE OF CONDUCT

When a court is deciding whether or not to make a maintenance pending suit order, periodical payments order or a lump sum order for the benefit of a dependent member of the family, it shall *not*, under any circumstances, have regard to the conduct of the spouses concerned when deciding whether or not such an order should be made or in deciding the amount of such order. The behaviour of a dependent member's parent is therefore, irrelevant (Divorce Act, s 23).

Section 23 of the Divorce Act is in line with the general view of the legislature that the interests of children are paramount in all situations and should be considered as the utmost priority. It would be entirely unreasonable to interfere with maintenance payments for children simply because one of their parents had behaved badly. It is open to a court to refuse to make a maintenance order in favour of children for a number of reasons, but most usually because of lack of means. The court, however, cannot refuse to make a maintenance order for a dependent member of a family simply because one of the parents has acted improperly, committed adultery, or been violent.

7.9 PAYMENTS OF MAINTENANCE

When a periodical payments order is made, it is common practice, particularly in the district court, for such payments to be directed to be made through the district court clerk. The District Court Family Law Office deals with the receipt of weekly or monthly maintenance payments and forwards them to the appropriate receiving parties (Divorce Act, s 28 and 1976 Act, s 9).

In fact, in all cases where a periodical payments order is being made, the court shall direct that the payments shall be made to the district court clerk, unless the recipient requests the court not to do so and the court considers that it would be proper not to do so. In such cases, the payments may be made by standing order into a bank account or directly to the receiving spouse.

The intention behind directing such payments to be made through the district court clerk is that there will always be a clear record of payments. The order originally made is therefore relatively easy to enforce as long as the maintenance debtor remains in employment.

The district court clerk is given power under s 9(2) of the 1976 Act to take all necessary steps to recover any arrears of maintenance that may arise, by proceeding in his own name for an attachment of earnings order, or otherwise.

It is important to note that, where a maintenance or periodical payments order is made in the circuit court or the High Court, it can be enforced in the district court if the order originally made directs that the maintenance payments be made through the district court clerk. If, however, the circuit court order or the High Court order directs that maintenance payments are to be made by way of standing order into a maintenance creditor's bank account, or directly in some other fashion, then such orders are only enforceable in the court in which they were originally made and are not simply enforceable through the district court. It would obviously be far cheaper from a legal fees point of view to enforce a periodical payments order in the district court rather than the High Court.

In practice, it is often extremely difficult for an individual who has an obligation to pay maintenance, to make such payments into the district court office. As yet, there is no system whereby one can pay by standing order or direct debit into the district court office and, if a paying party wishes the maintenance payment to arrive on time to his or her spouse, then he or she will have to call down in person to the appropriate district court office in order to make the payment. This can, of course, be quite time-consuming and, indeed, interfere with the paying party's employment.

An individual who is required to make such a payment through the district court clerk may also find the whole process somewhat embarrassing and humiliating. It is not unknown for an applicant spouse to insist upon payments being made through the district court simply to cause the maximum amount of difficulty to the paying party.

7.10   ENFORCEMENT OF PERIODICAL PAYMENTS ORDERS

Research carried out has shown, not only that the amounts of maintenance awarded in district court cases was extremely low, but also showed that default rates were extremely high (P Ward, 1990).

The figures were taken from the district court files and therefore do not include maintenance orders made in the circuit court or the High Court. Neither do the statistics include figures relating to compliance with maintenance terms in deeds of separation.

Mr Ward found that in 1990, approximately three-quarters of maintenance orders made were in arrears of six months or more. Only a small percentage of the orders made were up to date, insofar as regular payments were concerned.

The study by Fahey and Lyons pertaining to figures for the year 1993/1994 also included statistics relating to the higher courts and settlements reached outside court. It is clear from these figures that the default rate was extremely high at that time.

There are basically four methods of enforcing a periodical payments order (see also the discussion by O'Connor, in *Key Issues in Irish Family Law*).

7.10.1   Imprisonment

Imprisonment as a method of enforcement can be used where the paying party is either in employment or self-employed. Application is made under s 8 of the Enforcement of Court Orders Act 1940, as amended by s 29 of the 1976 Act, s 22 of the FLA 1995 and s 26 of the Divorce Act. The defaulter can receive a sentence of up to three months' imprisonment.

Further, under s 20 of the 1976 Act, if an employer or maintenance debtor, where an attachment of earnings order has been made, gives false or misleading information or fails to operate the order correctly, then he or she will be liable to a sentence of six months in jail.

In practice, it is most unusual for maintenance debtors to be imprisoned for failing to make payments unless the failure to do so is clearly contemptuous and deliberate. The court would also have to be quite satisfied that the maintenance debtor has sufficient funds to make the payments.

7.10.2 Attachment of earnings orders

The Family Law Act 1995 and the Divorce Act have substantially changed the law in regard to attachment of earnings orders. Section 8(6) of the FLA 1995 abolished the need to establish that there had been default in maintenance payments pursuant to a court order prior to the making of an attachment of earnings order. This is a major development insofar as periodical payments orders are concerned and a similar provision is contained in s 13(6) of the Divorce Act.

If a court is satisfied that the person against whom the periodical payments order is made is a person to whom earnings fall to be paid, the court *shall* 'in the same proceedings' make an attachment of earnings order.

An attachment of earnings order can only be made in cases where a paying spouse is employed by another person or organisation and is not working for themselves. The earnings have to be paid by a third party.

The provisions of s 13(6) of the Divorce Act would seem to suggest that in the majority of the cases the court should make an attachment of earnings order at the same time as the making a periodical payments order.

The onus appears to be placed on the paying spouse to show the court why such an order should *not* be made rather than on the applicant spouse to show *why* such an order should be made in the first place.

The spouse against whom the order might be made has to be given an opportunity by the court to make the following representations to which the court shall have regard:

(a) whether the spouse concerned is a person to whom such earnings as aforesaid fall to be paid; and

(b) whether he or she would make the payments to which the relevant order under s 13(1)(a) relates (Divorce Act, s 13(6)(b)).

Presumably, therefore, the court will consider some of the history of the financial affairs of the parties and listen to evidence relating to the financial recklessness or rectitude of one or both of the spouses, before finally deciding to make an attachment of earnings order.

DIFFICULTIES RELATING TO ATTACHMENT OF EARNINGS ORDERS

It would appear to be an extremely difficult task for a spouse against whom a periodical payments order is made to prove that he or she would make the payments in the future, particularly if payments have been irregular in the past.

Many spouses would find it very embarrassing for their employers to know, either that they are separated in the first place or, if they are already aware of this, the amount of maintenance which is being paid.

In addition, the making of an attachment of earnings order can sometimes lead to difficulties with promotion at work whether consciously or unconsciously on the part of employers. The making of such an order generally implies that the paying party either has defaulted or will default in supporting his or her spouse and infants. An attachment of earnings order should not be made lightly and, indeed, should not be sought by practitioners on their clients' behalf without first considering the long-term effects of the order.

As has already been stated, where a paying spouse is self-employed it is not possible for an attachment of earnings order to be made. It is possible where a spouse is in receipt of a pension or, indeed, should be possible where a paying spouse is in receipt of a regular income from some State agency (eg a builder who on occasion carries out work for the State on a contract basis).

The provisions of the 1976 Act (ss 10–20) still apply. The major change, as previously stated, is that the court no longer needs to be satisfied that there has been a 'default' in the making of any payment.

Normal deduction rate

An attachment of earnings order must specify 'the normal deduction rate'. The 'normal deduction rate' is the amount required to be deducted from the earnings of the paying spouse to satisfy the regular maintenance payments and also to satisfy any arrears of maintenance due. The 1976 Act states that a reasonable period must be given to discharge such arrears where appropriate.

Protected earnings rate

An attachment of earnings order shall also specify the 'protected earnings rate'. The 'protected earnings rate' is the minimum amount which must be received by the paying spouse where any payment out is made on the basis of an attachment of earnings order. This is relevant where, for instance, a periodical payments order may have been based, to a large degree, on overtime earned or bonuses granted. If such overtime cannot be obtained or bonuses are not paid, then obviously the net income of the paying party will be reduced. If this would in turn lead to a reduction in the amount fixed as the protected earnings rate, then this would not be permitted to occur and the maintenance payment itself would have to be reduced.

This gives quite a bit of scope to a paying spouse to cut down voluntarily his or her overtime or fail to make any effort to obtain bonuses.

The attachment of earnings order is served on the employer of the paying party and the employer is under a legal obligation to comply with same after the expiry of 10 days from the date of service of the order (s 11 of the 1976 Act).

Difficulties arise where a paying spouse changes employment, possibly on a regular basis. If a paying spouse is in the type of employment which is in great demand such as, for example, a plasterer during a building boom, he or she can generally change jobs at will. It is only where an employer is aware that there is an attachment of earnings order in existence that the employer is liable to discharge same. If the employer is not aware, because the employee chooses not to tell him or her, then the employer does not have to deduct any payments whatsoever from the salary of the paying spouse. The debtor spouse would then have to apply to the court for a further attachment of earnings order and such an exercise may have to be repeated on a number of occasions.

There is also no doubt that some employers would allow, either consciously or unconsciously, the making of an attachment of earnings order to interfere with the promotion or advancement of the paying spouse. An employer may feel that an employee who is involved in serious matrimonial difficulties is unable to devote himself fully to his job. If indeed the situation has advanced to the stage of the making of an attachment of earnings order then an employer may be concerned that there will be numerous future applications to the court which will seriously interfere with the time spent by an employee at his place of work.

7.10.3 Obtaining judgment

It is also possible for a spouse to enforce either a maintenance order or an agreement to pay maintenance contained in a deed of separation, by suing by way of contract debt in a summary fashion. Judgment against the maintenance debtor can then be obtained and, if possible, registered as a charge against any property owned by the maintenance debtor. This method of pursuing an individual who is refusing to make maintenance payments is of particular use insofar as deeds of separation are concerned.

7.10.4 Distraint

This method of enforcing maintenance orders is rarely used. The courts have the power pursuant to s 8 of the Enforcement of Court Orders Act 1940 (as amended by the 1976 Act) to order that arrears of maintenance be discharged by the seizing of goods belonging to the paying spouse and the disposal of same to provide the necessary funds to discharge the arrears. This method can sometimes be used when substantial arrears have built up and the matter is pursued by way of a simple contract debt. However, such a remedy is of little assistance in providing for the weekly or monthly needs of a dependent spouse and children.

7.10.5   Orders for sale of property

One method of enforcing secured periodical payment orders or lump sum orders is contained in s 19 of the Divorce Act. Where such orders are made, at that time or at any time thereafter, a court may make an order directing the sale of such a property as may be specified in the order to ensure that the appropriate payments are made under a secured periodical payments order or a lump sum order. The relevant property must be property 'which, or in the proceeds of sale of which, either or both of the spouses concerned has or have a beneficial interest either in possession or reversion' (s 19(1)). This power of the court shall not be used so as 'to affect the right to occupy the family home of the spouse concerned that is enjoyed by virtue of an order under this part'.

7.11   WORLDWIDE ASSETS

A difficulty which regularly arises in practice, particularly in relation to wealthier spouses, is that a husband may have assets in various jurisdictions or income streams in a number of different countries.

An example of such a situation is where a husband resides with his wife and children in Ireland. The husband is a best-selling author/scriptwriter/ songwriter. He is domiciled in England for tax purposes and has a substantial income stream in America, France, the UK and Ireland. There is a holding company registered in Panama, which ultimately receives the income from all the various jurisdictions and disposes of same pursuant to certain trust documents.

The question to be asked is where does the wife issue proceedings? It is clear that she cannot apply for a divorce in more than one jurisdiction. She may feel that since the bulk of the income is earned in America, that she should issue proceedings there. However, she may have difficulty satisfying the necessary domicile or residency requirements in order to justify issuing an application for divorce in America.

She may then consider issuing proceedings for divorce in England since the husband is domiciled there for tax purposes. However, an English court could not make orders which would be enforceable against, say, the trustees of the Panama company or collectors of income for the husband in America or France.

One option for the wife would be to issue proceedings in Ireland for a decree of judicial separation pursuant to the 1989 Act and 1995 Act and obtain as many orders as is possible thereunder. The Irish courts could make any relevant orders concerning Irish property or assets. At the same time, she could issue proceedings for divorce in England and obtain orders in relation to the English income or assets.

It would appear clear that the Irish courts cannot make orders directed towards foreign domiciled trustees, companies or individuals.

In certain situations, in Ireland, it has occurred pursuant to applications made under the 1989 Act that orders have been made *in personam* directing a spouse to take certain actions and carry out certain steps in relation to a trust or foreign-based company.

An example of such an order occurred in the case of *(FR) v (FJ)* [1995] 3 Fam LJ at p 90.

In this case, the husband and wife had lived together since 1984 and married in 1990. There were two dependent children of the marriage and judicial separation proceedings were instituted in 1993.

The respondent husband had worked abroad and earned substantial monies which had been lodged in offshore accounts. Monies from these accounts had been used over the years to provide for the purchase of the family home and for general living expenses. In 1994 (after the wife issued proceedings), the respondent husband transferred the remaining offshore funds into a trust fund subject to the Law of Guernsey. The beneficiaries were the two children and the respondent husband's mother. An order was obtained joining the trustees of the trust fund to proceedings in October 1994, but there was no actual evidence of the service of this order.

The wife applied for various ancillary orders including a division of the family assets, a lump-sum order and property adjustment order.

McGuinness J on 23 August 1995, when giving her judgment, stated that orders made in the court would not be binding on foreign domiciled trustees of the Guernsey Trust. It would be improper to make an order directed towards the trustees of the Guernsey Trust, particularly in the absence of evidence of service.

McGuinness J stated, however, that the court has general powers under the 1989 Act to make orders altering settlements. This would include the trust fund set up by the husband. Because of the husband's role in the trust, an order was made by McGuinness J *in persona* directing the husband to take certain actions in relation to the trust including an order directing him to pay a sum to the wife to compensate her for the joint interests in the equity of the family home (which was transferred to the husband), the remainder to benefit the children's education and removing the husband's mother from the list of beneficiaries.

In each particular case involving assets or income which exist in a number of jurisdictions, a decision will have to be made on the facts. In some circumstances, it may be necessary to simply write off any possibility of acquiring a share of particular assets in a particular jurisdiction and concentrate on those available elsewhere.

7.11.1 Enforceability of foreign maintenance orders in Ireland

A situation may arise where a spouse has obtained a valid foreign divorce and a contemporaneous maintenance order. If the paying spouse then commences residing in Ireland, can the dependent spouse enforce the maintenance order obtained in the other jurisdiction in this country?

The High Court considered this question in the case of *McC v McC* [1993] 3 Fam LJ 122.

In this case, the husband and the wife married in England in 1961 and divorced in Hong Kong in 1986 on the application of the plaintiff wife. By ancillary order, maintenance was to be paid by the defendant to the plaintiff but, in 1989, he stopped doing so. The husband, an Irish citizen, then returned to Ireland and the plaintiff instituted proceedings in the circuit court claiming arrears of maintenance. The maintenance order could, under Hong Kong law, be varied retrospectively and its enforceability was raised by the defendant as a defence. This question was tried as a preliminary issue and in the circuit court it was held that the Hong Kong order was enforceable in Ireland. The defendant appealed to the High Court.

Costello J delivered the judgment of the High Court on this issue and stated that he was:

> 'of the opinion that the Irish courts have jurisdiction to enforce maintenance orders made by courts in foreign jurisdictions which are final and conclusive, that such orders can be regarded as final and conclusive when the proceedings permit the court to adjudicate on all the issues between the parties in relation to maintenance and notwithstanding that the order may be subject to variation on appeal to a higher court or by the same court if the party's circumstances change.'

In general terms, such orders made in another jurisdiction have to be final and conclusive. However, Costello J clearly indicated that the nature of any maintenance orders is that they are usually subject to variation if there are major changes in circumstances of a financial nature. Under Hong Kong law, in fact, it was possible to obtain a *retrospective* variation of a maintenance order. Costello J held that this alone was not conclusive evidence that the original order which had been made was not final and conclusive.

If it can be shown that the principle of *res judicata* applies to the order then, even though it may be subject to appeal or be varied in changed circumstances, it is a final and conclusive order which will be enforced by an Irish court.

7.11.2 Applications for periodical payment orders against spouses residing outside Ireland

Brussels Convention

Article 5(2) of the Brussels Convention of 27 September 1968 (as amended) states as follows:

> 'a person domiciled in a contracting state may, in another contracting state be sued ... in matters relating to maintenance, in the courts for the place where the maintenance creditor is domiciled or habitually resident...'

The Convention is an extension of the Hague Convention of 15 April 1958 concerning the recognition and enforcement of decisions relating to maintenance obligations in respect of children, since it ensures the recognition and enforcement of judgments granting maintenance to creditors other than children, and also of the New York Convention of 20 June 1956 on the recovery abroad of maintenance.

The purpose of the Convention was to ensure that a maintenance creditor could issue proceedings in his or her own country and not in the country where the maintenance debtor resided or was domiciled.

It was felt that the court in the place of domicile of the maintenance creditor was in the best position to know whether the creditor was in need and to determine the extent of such need.

The intention behind the Brussels Convention was to simplify the procedures for obtaining and enforcing maintenance orders in other contracting States. The Convention was introduced into the Irish legal system by means of the Jurisdiction of Courts and Enforcement of Judgments (European Communities) Act 1988.

The purpose of the Brussels Convention and the Rome Convention was to simplify procedures and ensure that the various officials in each contracting State worked in close co-operation with each other. There are very few countries remaining to which a husband may flee to avoid his financial obligations towards his wife and children.

The Maintenance Act 1994, which introduced into the Irish legal system the Rome Convention of 6 November 1990, further simplified the procedures by providing for the appointment of a central authority authorised to act on behalf of a maintenance creditor or claimant.

Definition of maintenance creditor

One of the difficulties which has arisen in relation to the Brussels Convention and its operation is the definition of 'maintenance creditor'. Article 5(2) of the

Convention states that only a 'maintenance creditor' can sue a maintenance debtor in another jurisdiction and avail of the provisions of the Brussels Convention. This is the most important article in the Convention.

This issue has been considered in some detail in the case of *F(J) v L(J)* [1996] 1 Fam LJ 17.

In this case, the applicant was an unmarried woman aged 28 years who was a mother of a child born on 3 July 1988. She alleged that the respondent was the father of the child which was disputed by the respondent who was a married man and who was employed and habitually resident in Bruges, Belgium.

The applicant sought maintenance for her child pursuant to the 1976 Act (as amended by the Status of Children Act 1987) and issued proceedings under Article 5.2 of the Brussels Convention.

It was argued in the district court that the judge had no jurisdiction to deal with this matter under the Brussels Convention as the applicant was not a 'maintenance creditor'. It was argued that he could only have become a 'maintenance creditor' if she had already obtained a maintenance order which she was attempting to enforce. It was further submitted that she could not avail of the Brussels Convention to issue proceedings against the respondent *ab initio* as no *prior* order had been made.

King DJ, on 11 February 1994, dismissed the application for want of jurisdiction. The applicant appealed to the circuit court.

The matter was eventually heard by McGuinness J who gave her judgment on 15 December 1994. In the course of the hearing in the circuit court, it was again submitted that the term 'maintenance creditor' covers only a person who has already obtained a maintenance order and that the term does not include a person such as the applicant who was merely applying for the first time for a maintenance order (a 'maintenance claimant').

McGuinness J felt that the question of interpretation of Article 5.2 of the Brussels Convention was one which 'gives rise to considerable and undesirable doubt. It is clearly a question of Community law as well as National law'.

McGuinness J therefore referred the matter to the European Court of Justice for a ruling on the interpretation of Article 5(2).

The actual question which was referred to the Court of Justice of the European Communities on 15 May 1995 by McGuinness J was as follows:

> 'Do the provisions of Article 5(2) of the Convention on Jurisdiction and Enforcement of Judgment in Civil and Commercial Matters, signed at Brussels on 27th day of September, 1968 require as a condition precedent to the institution of maintenance proceedings in the Irish courts by an applicant who is domiciled in

Ireland against a respondent who is domiciled in Belgium that the applicant has previously obtained an order for maintenance against the respondent?'

The hearing took place in Luxembourg on 21 November 1996 and the Advocate-General's opinion was given on 12 December 1996. His opinion was that no prior maintenance order was necessary and that the definition of 'maintenance creditor' included a 'maintenance claimant'.

The final order of the Court of Justice was given on 20 March 1997 and fully supported the opinion of the Advocate-General.

With the introduction of divorce in Ireland and with the increasing movement of people between various Member States of the EU, which often leads to people of different nationalities marrying, the use to which the Brussels Convention will be put in the future is of some significance. There is little doubt that it will be availed of to a far greater extent than it has been up to now and that the pursuing of maintenance debtors in other jurisdictions will become commonplace.

7.12 VARIATION OF PERIODICAL PAYMENTS ORDERS

7.12.1 Regular increases in maintenance

There is no provision in the 1976 Act, the FLA 1995 or the Divorce Act empowering the court, when making a periodical payments order, to order that the amount of the periodical payments can be increased on a regular basis as a matter of course.

Parties often agree as part of a deed of separation that maintenance payments should be increased on an annual basis in line with any increase in the Consumer Price Index or in line with increases in the husband's income.

7.12.2 Consumer Price Index

The Consumer Price Index is a statement issued each month, since 1 January 1997, by the Central Statistics Office showing the increase in the cost of living for the previous month. Until 1 January 1997, the statement of the Consumer Price Index increase was issued on only four occasions per year.

The increase is indicated by way of a percentage increase in the cost of living and is published on the fifteenth day of the relevant month. At the end of a 12-month period the annual increase in the cost of living can be ascertained and, if agreed, the maintenance payments adjusted appropriately.

7.12.3 Base date

In a deed of separation, reference is made to a base date which is a reference to a particular month for which the increase is to be ascertained, ie if the base date is 15 August 1996 then the first increase will take place on 15 August 1997. The percentage increase would be calculated by using 15 August 1996 as a base date and ascertaining the increase in the Consumer Price Index during the following 12 months.

It is far simpler to have an agreement that maintenance be increased annually in line with some measurement, such as the Consumer Price Index. If maintenance is to be increased annually, in accordance with, for example, any increases in the husband's net income, lengthy debates are likely to take place as to what this increased income is. Disputes may arise as to whether or not additional expenses should be taken into account or whether or not the husband is deliberately ensuring that his income has not increased while receiving additional payments in other ways such as trips abroad or share options, etc. Such disputes could, in many cases, lead to a further application to the court. This should be avoided if at all possible.

It is unfortunate that courts do not have the power to order that maintenance be increased on an annual basis in accordance with some formula or other. If there was an inbuilt annual increase provision, then repeat applications to the court are less likely.

7.12.4 Variation of certain financial orders

Section 22 of the 1996 Act deals with, inter alia, variation of the following orders: (a) a maintenance pending suit order; (b) a periodical payments order; (c) a secured periodical payments order; (d) a lump-sum order if, and insofar as it provides for, the payment of the lump-sum concerned *by instalments or* requires the payment of any such instalments to be secured.

In general terms, the court can vary or discharge or alter in any way it sees fit, any orders made as referred to above by taking into consideration: (a) any change in the circumstances of the case; and (b) any new evidence furnished.

7.12.5 Change in circumstances

Evidence in relation to a change in circumstances is usually adduced when an application for an increase or a reduction in a periodical payments order is made to court. If an application is made by a husband to reduce maintenance payments, then he would tend to rely on either reductions in income or increases in outgoings of a fairly substantial nature. Obviously, if a periodical payments order is made against a spouse and he loses his job and becomes unemployed, then there are sufficient grounds for a court to discharge the periodical payments order entirely.

If a husband is demoted or loses substantial overtime for some reason or suffers a diminution in his income from one source whilst retaining it from another, then the court may well feel it appropriate to reduce the maintenance payments proportionately.

Other examples of where a court may reduce maintenance payments are where, for example, the paying husband has another child or children. In addition, if he remarries, having obtained a divorce, then his second wife becomes dependent on him, and this would be a factor to be taken into consideration in deciding whether or not the maintenance should be reduced.

Similarly, if a wife in whose favour an order is made, was in employment at the time of making the order and subsequently loses this employment, then a court may, on application being made to it, *increase* the maintenance payments to be made to her.

Sometimes, it is difficult for a court to decide whether or not there has been a change in circumstances. If a periodical payments order is made by a court and an application is made three years later for an increase, does the mere fact that there has been an increase in the cost of living since the original order was made justify the making of an increased order? The answer would appear to be 'yes'.

The general attitude of the courts to such applications can be gauged from the comments made by the Supreme Court in the case of *K v K* [1993] 1 Fam LJ 12.

The original maintenance order in this case was made in November 1989 and, subsequently, inter alia, the appellant wife attempted to have the order for maintenance *for the children* increased on 12 June 1991. This claim was dismissed by the High Court and the wife appealed the decision to the Supreme Court who heard the matter in February 1992 (some two-and-a-half years after the original order).

Although there were a number of other matters dealt with by the court, the most relevant for the purposes of this discussion is the claim for an increase in the children's maintenance payments.

The wife submitted that she had moved to a different part of the country and changed the children's schools since the making of the original order. This meant that she had to drive them on a round trip of approximately 50 miles each day in order to get them to school and back. She also stated that the children were getting older and therefore more expensive. She claimed also that at the time of the making of the order, the husband had paid a sum of just under £2,000 a year in respect of one of the children attending as a school-boarder, which payment had now ceased. She also submitted that although the children were now attending a non-fee paying school, there were expenses for books and extras.

The husband's lawyers submitted that there had been no evidence of any change in circumstances in the documentation furnished by the wife, who appears to have represented herself. There were no details of the cost of the maintaining and caring for the children or any changes in that cost since November 1989 furnished to the court. It was further stated that the husband had at all times been willing to pay any extras or special amounts involved in the schooling of the children but that no claim had been made for them to him. In addition, it was pointed out that one of the other children would shortly be attending a boarding school for a year which would necessitate further payment of school fees by the husband.

Finlay J in delivering the judgment of the Supreme Court made a number of points which can be used as guidelines in assessing whether or not a variation of a periodical payments order will be made:

(a)   He stated that: 'of necessity, where the High Court, as in this case is asked by one or other of the parties to vary such an order for maintenance, it cannot and must not commence de novo to reach a new view upon the general question of maintenance, but must merely try and ascertain as to whether, from the last effective order, the situation has changed so as to warrant either an increase or decrease in the amount of maintenance'.

(b)   He said that he was: 'satisfied that the mere fact that between the time of the making of the order for £225 per week and the hearing of the motion to the High Court for an increase, the husband had by a change of the schooling arrangements been saved an obligation to pay school fees in regard to the eldest child ... cannot *of itself* constitute a ground for increasing the maintenance payable for the children. The mere fact that for a different form of maintenance, a higher figure was previously being paid by the husband, does not, in any way, automatically entitle the wife to be paid a greater sum in respect of maintenance based on a different form of education as far as the children are concerned' (author's emphasis).

(c)   Finlay J also stated that he was: 'satisfied that the court should take judicial notice of the fact that there has been an inflationary move in the reduction of the value of money, though not a very large one, since 1989'.

(d)   He was also satisfied: 'that the court can, and should, raise as an inference from the evidence accepted by the learned trial judge that there was as a matter of probability, from common experience, some additional expense as the children have grown older'.

As a result therefore, the Supreme Court increased the maintenance figure from £225 per week to £265 per week.

7.12.6   New evidence

If a court makes a periodical payments order or, indeed, a lump sum order based on information which subsequently is shown to be incorrect, then the order can be varied or discharged by a court on subsequent application to it by a spouse. In addition, if information comes to light revealing assets or income which had previously been hidden, then an application to court to vary a maintenance order or lump sum order based on the original incorrect information, will almost certainly be successful.

Again, the court will simply permit a complete re-hearing of the maintenance issue and will not allow attempts to 'fish' for further information by way of cross-examination. There must be clear evidence available to the court of new information which was not disclosed at the earlier hearing.

As has already been indicated, under s 22 of the Divorce Act, the courts have been given very wide powers to vary maintenance pending suit orders, periodical payment orders, and other financial orders.

In most cases, unless the variation of such an order has been restricted by the court on the making of the original order pursuant to s 14(2) of the Divorce Act, the following persons can make the relevant application:

(a)   either of the spouses concerned;
(b)   in the case of the death of either of the spouses by, any other person who has, in the opinion of the court, a sufficient interest in the matter or by a person on behalf of a dependent member of the family concerned;
(c)   in the case of the remarriage of either of the spouses by his or her spouse.

It is open therefore, for a second spouse, to bring an application against the first spouse in relation to a number of matters. This clearly has the effect of increasing the number of persons who can be sued in relation to matrimonial breakdown.

An example of such an occurrence would exist where a husband and wife are divorced and the wife has obtained custody of the children. The wife remarries and subsequently dies while the children are still dependents. The second husband could then, pursuant to s 22(2) of the Divorce Act issue proceedings to obtain an order increasing, for instance, the periodical payments orders made by the first husband towards the support of the children.

The court is also empowered to vary the terms of a new order already made in relation to the above matters or suspend any order or provision of such an order temporarily or permanently. The court can vary an order previously varied or further suspend or revive the operation of an order or provision previously suspended or revived under this section.

The Divorce Act goes so far as to give the court power to divest a person of property vested in him by earlier order. The courts will be reluctant to interfere in a major way with orders previously made, particularly in so far as property or lump sums are concerned but under this section, certainly have the powers to do so.

7.12.7   Discharge of payments for the support of dependent members of the family

Section 22(3) of the Divorce Act provides that an order for payments for support of a dependent member of the family:

'shall stand discharged if the member ceases to be a dependent member of the
family by reason of his or her attainment of the age of 18 years or 23 years as may
be appropriate and shall be discharged by the court, on application to it under
subsection (2) if it is satisfied that the member has, for any reason, ceased to be a
dependent member of the family'.

The use of the words 'shall stand discharged' would seem to suggest that
periodical payments which are ordered for the support of a 'dependent
member' of the family shall by operation of law immediately and automatically
cease when that member is no longer a dependant.

Although the section goes on to say that the payment shall be discharged by the
court on application to it, the suggestion seems to be that, even if there is a
delay in making such an application, no order for arrears of such maintenance
could be made. In fact, it would appear almost unnecessary to make an
application to court to discharge such an order as s 22(3) would provide a valid
defence to any claim brought by the receiving party.

7.13   TAXATION

If a husband and the wife separate or obtain a divorce, there are serious tax
implications from a number of points of view which need to be addressed.

7.13.1   Married couples living together

While a married couple are living together, they can opt for either single
assessment, joint assessment or separate assessment for income tax purposes.

Single assessment
On single assessment, each spouse is treated as a single person, with
entitlements to allowances, reliefs and rate bands exactly as if each were
unmarried. Unless both spouses earn similar salaries, it is not beneficial
because they cannot pass the unused allowances between them.

It is open to either spouse to elect that both spouses be treated as single persons
for the purpose of the Income Tax Acts. This election can be withdrawn at any
time by the spouse and ceases to have effect for the year in which it was
withdrawn. A deliberate act of election must be made, as otherwise a married
couple who are living together without having made any election are deemed
to have elected for joint assessment (Income Tax Act 1967, s 195(4)(a)).

Joint assessment
Joint assessment is the most common form of assessing the incomes of a
husband and wife who are married to each other, if they both agree. The
incomes of the husband and the wife are aggregated and taxed as the income of

the husband (or the wife since 6 April 1994). All allowances which are due to both the husband and wife are deducted from the total income. The husband or the wife as the case may be is entitled to double the rate available to a single person but, in a situation where the other spouse is also in employment, he or she will continue to receive his or her own PAYE and PRSI allowances together with any employment-related expenses allowance, half a tax table allowance where appropriate, and any other allocation of allowances, as may be agreed between the husband and the wife.

This form of assessment provides the most beneficial type of tax relief for married couples living together. Not only is the married allowance (which is double the single person allowance) available, but also the rate bands of tax are doubled and double the mortgage interest relief is available together with other additional benefits.

Either spouse may, by giving written notice to the Inspector of Taxes, withdraw the election for joint assessment.

Separate assessment

In such a situation, tax is charged separately on each spouse's income as if they were not married. The married persons allowance is divided in half between the husband and the wife and each is entitled to single rate bands. The PAYE and PRSI allowances, and any employment-related expenses or allowances are allocated to each spouse as appropriate. Other allowances and reliefs are divided between the spouses, depending on the circumstances attaching to each particular allowance or relief. If a portion of the particular allowance or relief is unused by one spouse then it can be allocated to the other.

It is open to either spouse to elect that both spouses be separately assessed. This election must be made within a period of six months prior to the end of July in the year of assessment. Any withdrawal of this election must also be made before the end of July in the year of assessment. This form of assessment is possible where a married couple have elected for, or are deemed to have elected for joint assessment and a special application for separate assessment is made.

If both the husband and the wife are working, then conflict will not arise if, because of an election for joint assessment, one spouse has all the allowances and receives a substantial net pay cheque, whilst the other spouse has lesser allowances and receives a net pay cheque of a substantially reduced amount.

The above types of assessment are available only to married couples who are actually living together.

7.13.2 Separated couples

A husband and wife will not be treated as living together for income tax purposes when they are:

(a)   separated or divorced under a court order;
(b)   separated by a deed of separation; or
(c)   'separated in such circumstances that the separation is likely to be
       permanent' (Income Tax Act 1967, s 192(1)).

If a married couple are *not* living together because of formal or informal
separation, then their entitlements to certain tax reliefs may be lost. If,
however, a couple are forced to live apart for lengthy periods because of
circumstances of employment or illness, then the couple will not be considered
to be 'separated'.

Single assessment

Generally speaking, it is most beneficial from a tax point of view for a husband
and wife who are living apart to be treated as single persons for tax purposes.

The provisions of the Finance Act 1983 apply to such persons and, where the
parties have opted for single assessment, the spouse making a maintenance
payment for the other spouse's benefit is allowed the payment as a deductible
tax allowance from income when assessing his tax payable for the year. The
spouse receiving the payment must pay tax on the moneys received by him or
her referable to him or her.

As has already been mentioned, the Divorce Act states that payments of
maintenance shall be made without deduction of income tax (s 31). In
practice, therefore, an applicant spouse should calculate his or her needs and
requirements together with those of any dependent children and estimate as
accurately as possible the *gross* amount of maintenance which needs to be paid
by the other spouse to provide for such outgoings after the payment of income
tax. The end result often provides something of a shock to both parties.

MAINTENANCE AGREEMENTS ENTERED INTO PRIOR TO 8 JUNE 1983
The situation is somewhat different when dealing with maintenance
agreements, entered into prior to 8 June 1983 (the date of coming into effect of
the Finance Act 1983). In such circumstances, the payer who is making the
maintenance payments must deduct income tax at the standard rate from the
payment. The person receiving the moneys is then taxable on the grossed up
amounts, but receives a credit in respect of tax deducted at source. As time
passes, such agreements become less and less prevalent but s 3 of the Finance
Act 1983 enables both parties to decide that the provision of the maintenance
agreement, which they had entered into prior to 8 June 1983, be treated as an
agreement of the type set out in the 1983 Act and therefore be dealt with in
exactly the same way as agreements entered into *after* the relevant date.

POST-JUNE 1983 POSITION
Maintenance payments must be of an annual or periodic nature in order to
come within the ambit of s 3 of the Finance Act 1983. Lump sum orders are
dealt with in a different way by the Revenue Commissioners.

Not only do direct money payments qualify as maintenance payments, but also certain indirect payments such as mortgage repayments, insurance premiums, VHI or BUPA premiums, cost of holidays, etc may qualify.

PAYMENTS FOR CHILDREN

It is important to be aware that in all cases where a maintenance agreement or a court order provides for any payment for the benefit of a *child*, no income tax is payable. The person making the payment is not entitled to any tax allowance concerning such payments and neither the child nor the custodial parent need pay any tax in respect of such payments.

A child includes a step-child, and an adopted child, or a child born outside marriage.

When a husband and wife are involved in divorce proceedings and make an application to court for a periodical payments order, it is important that the issue of income tax is considered in some detail. Not only should advice be taken in relation to the best possible method of assessment, the actual apportionment of the maintenance payments as between the spouse and the children, should be carefully considered. Since no income tax is payable on maintenance received for a child it may, in some cases, be more beneficial to the spouse to apportion the bulk of the maintenance moneys to the child. However, it is also necessary to take into account the fact that any maintenance payments for children need only be made up to a maximum of 23 years (if still undergoing a full-time course of education) after which date they cease.

A spouse who has been in receipt of relatively substantial maintenance payments may as a result of inadequate tax planning suddenly find that he or she is receiving a far lesser sum and may have to consider applying for a variation of a periodical payments order. As a result, he or she will incur legal expenses and undergo another court hearing concerning financial support and the marriage break-up which they thought may have been already dealt with once and for all.

Joint assessment

Despite the fact of separation, it is still possible for a couple to elect to be jointly assessed for income tax under s 4 of the Finance Act 1983. This option is not available to couples where a civil decree of nullity has been granted nor does it apply to couples where a divorce has been granted and one or other of the spouses has remarried.

Section 32 of the Divorce Act continues this option where a divorce has been granted in Ireland (with neither party having remarried), and where both spouses are resident in Ireland for tax purposes for that year of assessment. The provisions of s 4 of the Finance Act 1983 shall have effect in relation to the spouses for that year of assessment as if their marriage had not been dissolved.

Where a separated couple elect for joint assessment, no tax is payable by a receiving party on maintenance payments made to him or her and no tax allowance or deduction is available to the paying spouse.

Either party can withdraw from this form of assessment by notice in writing given to the Inspector of Taxes prior to the end of the tax year.

It is important to note that in cases of joint assessment, neither spouse would be entitled to the single parent allowance. This may lead, in certain cases, to a fairly substantial reduction in the net income of both spouses.

In effect, s 4 of the Finance Act 1983 provides a mechanism whereby separated or divorced persons can be assessed for income tax as if they were still a married couple. As has already been indicated, the election for such a form of assessment must be made in writing by *both* parties. The payments must be made pursuant to a 'maintenance arrangement' (which is defined as 'an order of court, rule of court, deed of separation, trust, covenant, agreement, arrangement, or any other act giving rise to a legally enforceable obligation or made or done in consideration of or in consequence of the dissolution or annulment of the marriage').

It is important to note that any lump sum payments made by virtue of a separation agreement do not come within the ambit of s 3 of the Finance Act 1983 because they are not 'periodical payments'. They are not made annually or monthly but are usually one-off payments (although on occasion may be made by way of instalments).

It is prudent for family law practitioners to obtain the services of an accountant or tax expert when considering maintenance and lump sum issues. Such an individual will advise on the most beneficial tax regime for both spouses and will be in a position to comment on, or advise on, various suggested schemes for payments of maintenance and lump sums.

7.13.3   Relevant tax allowances

There are certain allowances which are available and which may be obtained by either or both spouses in some cases of marital separation.

Single parent allowance

The single parent allowance may, in certain circumstances be available to both spouses. The allowance is available to a parent provided that the relevant child is resident with that parent for the whole or part of the year of assessment. It is common in divorce or separation cases for a child to be resident with *both* parents for the 'whole or part of the year of assessment'. Such 'residence' need have taken place for only one night during the relevant financial year. It is clear, however, that if there is no overnight access at all then this allowance cannot be claimed by the non-custodial parent (Income Tax Act 1967, s 138(A)(2)).

In addition, the following criteria must exist:

(a) the child must be under the age of 16 years at the commencement of the year of assessment;

(b) a child who is over the age of 16 years must be undergoing a course of full-time education;

(c) the child must be over the age of 16 years and become permanently incapacitated and prevented from maintaining himself or herself before the age of 21 years or, if over the age of 21 years, became so incapacitated while undergoing a full-time course of education.

It is also essential in order to qualify for the single parent allowance that the relevant child be maintained by the claimant at his or her expense for the whole or *part* of the year of assessment. Certainly, in many cases, both parents maintain a child from a financial point of view for part of the year of assessment. If the parents cohabit with another person, the allowance is no longer available.

If a qualifying child has his or her own independent income from any source, then this would be taken into consideration in assessing the amount of the single parent allowance.

Child allowance

Child allowance is provided for under s 141 of the Income Tax Act 1967. It is available only in respect of children who are permanently incapacitated as a result of mental or physical infirmity. In certain situations, the allowance can be divided between the husband and the wife on the basis of their contribution towards the maintenance of the relevant child. Again, the income of any relevant child is taken into consideration in ascertaining the amount of the allowance.

Mortgage interest relief

If a husband is making the mortgage repayments directly, then a wife cannot claim the interest relief on those repayments no matter what is agreed in a deed of separation if it is not a joint mortgage. If there is a joint mortgage in existence, however, the wife can claim 50% of the relief no matter who pays.

If a husband is providing maintenance to a wife and out of that amount she makes the mortgage repayments, then she is fully entitled to claim all the mortgage interest relief.

Where a husband and a wife are singly assessed for income tax pursuant to s 3 of the Finance Act 1983, then the relief available is limited to the single persons mortgage allowance. A spouse can claim mortgage interest relief only in the normal way on a loan obtained for the purposes of acquiring, repairing, developing or improving a family home or 'qualifying residence' or discharging another loan originally taken out for that purpose.

When a couple separate or divorce a 'qualifying residence' includes the residence of an individual and the residence of a former spouse. It is therefore possible to claim mortgage interest relief on two mortgages relating to two different properties, subject to the maximum single persons allowance. In some cases, therefore, it would be more tax efficient for a couple to separate, obtain two mortgages and claim the maximum possible tax relief in such circumstances rather than stay together and pay a higher amount of tax.

7.13.4 Voluntary payments

In some circumstances, a husband or a wife will make voluntary payments to the other spouse. For example, the husband may win the lottery or acquire a lump sum of some description which was unexpected and may, in a fit of generosity, decide to provide some of these moneys for his wife and children. Such payments are ignored for tax purposes. The only relevant limits would be those fixed for the purposes of capital acquisitions tax.

It is interesting that for many years the Revenue Commissioners have been accepting foreign divorce decrees at their face value. In other words, if an individual obtains a divorce decree from his first spouse in Las Vegas while both he and his wife are domiciled in Ireland, then such a divorce decree would not be recognised in Ireland. However, the Revenue Commissioners have a policy of not inquiring into the grounds for any divorce, nor do they enquire into the issue of whether or not such divorce is valid and would be recognised pursuant to the provisions of the Domicile and Recognition of Foreign Divorces Act 1986. They will *assume* that the divorce is valid and grant the usual allowances to the 'second' marriage, unless some third party interferes and makes the appropriate objections, fully supported by all relevant evidence.

7.14 DIVORCE AND SOCIAL WELFARE PROVISIONS

Only since 1970 have steps have been taken to provide social welfare assistance to persons involved in matrimonial breakdown. In that year, the deserted wives allowance was introduced for the first time and three years later, in 1973, the payment of deserted wives benefit commenced.

The situation remained somewhat disorganised and confusing until 1990 when the 'lone parents allowance' was introduced to assist all persons bringing up children on their own. The introduction of this allowance had the effect of streamlining the social welfare code insofar as it related to separated persons or lone parents.

Prior to the introduction of the Divorce Act, the Social Welfare (No 2) Act 1995 was passed. This Act ensures that the provisions of the Social Welfare Code will now apply equally to persons regardless of whether or not they are divorced, deserted or separated. The purpose behind the Act was to ensure that, if an individual obtains a divorce in Ireland, that individual will not be disadvantaged in terms of his or her social welfare entitlements. The Government Information Paper issued prior to the divorce referendum estimated that the total cost of extending such social welfare entitlements to divorced persons (even in some cases where they had remarried) would be in the region of £1m over the first five years. It is now felt that the cost incurred will be substantially greater than that.

7.14.1 Lone parents allowance

The lone parents allowance was originally introduced by ss 12–16 of the Social Welfare Act 1990 and commenced operating in November 1990. It is now governed by Chapter 9 of the Social Welfare (Consolidation) Act 1993.

The Social Welfare Act 1990 abolished certain allowances, ie the unmarried mothers allowance, deserted husbands allowance and widowers (non-contributory) pension payments. Those persons who were entitled to these allowances automatically became entitled to lone parents allowance.

The deserted wives allowance and prisoner's wives allowance are retained only for claimants over the age of 40 years, who have no qualifying children residing with them. Those claiming the widows (non-contributory) pension, who had a qualified child residing with them lost this allowance but were entitled to claim the lone parents allowance.

There are only two social welfare payments which still remain and are based on social insurance contributions rather than means-tested and these are: (a) the widows (contributory) pension; and (b) deserted wives benefit.

The introduction of the lone parents allowance was aimed at simplifying the system of social welfare payments, in particular where they related to providing for children.

The lone parents allowance is a means-tested payment and is payable to a lone parent of either sex who has at least one qualifying child residing with him or her.

There is no distinction made, as happens in cases in relation to other payments, on the basis of the sex of the applicant. A lone parent is defined as a widow or widower, a separated spouse, an unmarried person or a person whose spouse is a prisoner. A 'qualified child' is defined as a child who is under the age of 18 years or who is over the age of 18 years and under the age of 21 years and is still undergoing a course of full-time education.

Prior to the coming into operation of the Social Welfare Act 1990, there were certain persons for whom no provision had been made in the Social Welfare Code. These included: separated husbands, widowers and unmarried fathers, who had dependent children. Such persons had to rely on supplementary welfare which was a payment made in a rather arbitrary fashion based on need. It was a type of emergency payment and a decision as to whether or not it should be paid to an applicant appears to have been based on differing criteria in different areas.

In addition, separated wives who were disqualified from the deserted wives payment, because they were not deserted, will not qualify for the lone parents allowance, as long as they have a qualified child residing with them.

The deserted wives allowance remains available to women who are aged over 40 years of age but have no dependent children.

The deserted wives benefit still remains as a separate allowance with its own rules and regulations.

Means test
The lone parents allowance is means-tested, ie the income of the applicant from all sources is taken into consideration and allowances are made for certain outgoings prior to making a decision as to whether the applicant is entitled to the allowance or not. 'Means' are calculated in accordance with the rules contained in the third schedule to the Social Welfare (Consolidation) Act 1993.

An individual who is in receipt of the lone parents allowance is also permitted to obtain employment and receive income up to a certain level. In addition, 50% of any amounts earned over the threshold level are also ignored. Travelling expenses and child-minding expenses are permissible deductions together with the others itemised in the 1993 Act.

An application for lone parents allowance can be made by a spouse only if he or she and their child or children are not being maintained by the other spouse or are being maintained by the other spouse but at a rate which is less than the maximum rate of the lone parents allowance appropriate to the family size.

In addition, the spouses must have lived apart for a period of at least three months preceding the date of the application for this allowance. It is not necessary to show that one has been deserted in order to obtain the lone parents allowance. Indeed, as has already been stated, the deserted wives benefit still exists.

7.14.2   Deserted wives payments

Deserted wives allowance
It is important to understand the difference between the deserted wives allowance and the deserted wives benefit. The deserted wives allowance is now

payable only to women aged over 40 years who have no dependent children. There is no deserted husbands allowance.

A wife who is deserted and is under the age of 40 years, must have a dependent child in order to qualify for the lone parents allowance.

An applicant for the deserted wives allowance must satisfy a means test as previously discussed.

In order to establish that she has been deserted, a wife will have to show that:

(a) her husband of his own volition left her; and
(b) she
     (i)   is not being maintained by her husband, or
     (ii) is being maintained by her husband but at a rate per week which is less than the rate of the deserted wives allowance; and
(c) that she and her husband have lived apart from one another for a continuous period of at least three months immediately preceding the date of her claim (Social Welfare (Lone Parent Allowance and Other Analogous Payments) Regulation SI No 272 of 1990, art 12).

Deserted wives benefit

Up to 1992, this benefit was not means-tested. It was, and still is, based on the social insurance contributions made by *either* or *both* spouses. In assesing whether or not an applicant qualifies for this benefit, the husband's and wife's PRSI contributions *cannot* be added together. The rules for assessing the benefit are relatively complicated but, up to 1992, it was possible for an applicant wife to obtain the deserted wives benefit and also to continue to work on a full-time basis. Any earnings from her employment would not affect her entitlement to the benefit although the benefit was and is taxable in such circumstances.

Since 31 August 1992, limits have been placed on the amount of income which the recipient of the deserted wives benefit can earn and, in effect, there is now a means test in place for such benefit.

A woman who is making an application for deserted wives benefit is regarded as deserted in the same circumstances as an applicant for the deserted wives allowance. However, in addition, if an applicant can establish that her husband's conduct was such as to result in her having no option but to leave, she may also be entitled to the benefit. The concept of 'constructive desertion' appears to be relevant only to an applicant for the deserted wives benefit and not to an applicant for the deserted wives allowance. There is no doubt, however, that, in practice, in some cases, the Department of Social Welfare will grant the deserted wives allowance to applicants where there has been 'constructive desertion'.

Difficulties arise in relation to such payments when a husband and a wife have executed a deed of separation. The first clause of any such agreement usually states that the husband and the wife have agreed to live separate and apart from each other. If this is the case then the husband could not be said to have deserted the wife.

However, in practice, the Department of Social Welfare will look at the situation which existed at the time of the actual separation itself. If the husband has deserted at that stage and subsequently signs a deed of separation, then the Department of Social Welfare may still treat the applicant spouse as a deserted wife. Again, however, quite a wide discretion is given to the deciding officer as to whether or not an applicant is entitled to such a payment.

7.14.3   Liability to maintain relatives

Prior to 1990, an applicant spouse (usually the wife) was required to make 'reasonable efforts' to obtain maintenance from the other spouse (usually the husband). This requirement was interpreted strictly by the Department of Social Welfare and led to cases where applications for maintenance were made despite the fact that, clearly, the husband could not make any payments. In some cases, where the husband was in receipt of social welfare payments himself, a wife still had to go through the motions of bringing a court application in order to prove that she was making every effort to obtain maintenance from her spouse.

There was no definition of 'reasonable efforts' and clearly if a husband left the country and resided abroad, such 'efforts' would be extremely complex, expensive and difficult. However, the Department of Social Welfare expected an applicant to pursue his or her spouse through the courts in this or in any other jurisdiction where possible.

If, for instance, a wife had no idea of her husband's whereabouts, she was bound to make enquiries at his former workplace or amongst his friends, acquaintances or relatives. If he had gone to England, it was necessary for her to contact the relevant Departments of Social Welfare or Employment in England to see if they had record of his whereabouts. Such information is difficult to obtain. This whole process certainly added greatly to the stress suffered by separated couples.

Since the coming into operation of the Social Welfare Act 1990, the requirement of 'reasonable efforts' has been changed to one requiring the claimant to 'make and continue to make *appropriate* efforts, to the satisfaction of the Minister in the particular circumstances to obtain maintenance from the spouse'. The onus on the applicant spouse would therefore appear to have been lessened somewhat.

Both the Department of Social Welfare (and the Health Board in certain situations) are much more inclined now to award a particular allowance or payment to the applicant and then attempt to pursue the spouse or other liable person for a refund of such payments through the courts or otherwise. This lessens the pressure placed on an applicant spouse.

On the other hand, however, the Department of Social Welfare has only a *right* to institute proceedings against a recalcitrant husband or other person but is not *required* in all cases to do so.

Section 285 of the Social Welfare (Consolidated) Act 1993, provides that:

(a)   a man shall be liable to maintain
    (i)   his wife, and
    (ii)   any child of his under 18 or between 18 or 23 if in full-time education; and
(b)   a woman shall be liable to maintain
    (i)   her husband, and
    (ii)   any child of hers under 18 or between 18 and 23 if in full-time education.

This section applies for all the purposes of the deserted wives payments, the lone parents allowance and the supplementary welfare allowance.

Section 286(1) of the 1993 Act provides that a liable relative of a person in receipt of the deserted wives allowance or benefit, the lone parents allowance or the supplementary welfare allowance, shall be liable to contribute to the Department of Social Welfare (or the Health Board in the case of supplementary welfare allowance) such amount as the Department (or Health Board) 'may determine to be appropriate towards such a benefit or allowance'.

There are no guidelines in existence which set out how the Department of Social Welfare shall make a decision as to the appropriate amount which the liable relative should pay. Again, the amount can be relatively arbitrary although there are some general internal rules which are applied.

Once the determination is made, it cannot be appealed to an appeals officer as the decision is not made by a deciding officer. If the liable relative fails or refuses to pay the amount assessed then the Department of Social Welfare or the Health Board, as the case may be, may apply to the district court for an order directing the relevant person to make such contribution towards the appropriate benefit or allowance. In addition, the Department or the Health Board may obtain an attachment of earnings order in such circumstances.

Before making such an order on the application of the Department of Social Welfare or the Health Board, the court must be satisfied that:

(a)   the person before the court is liable to maintain the claimant;
(b)   the payment concerned was correctly made to the claimant;
(c)   at the time of the hearing the person liable to contribute has failed or neglected to make the contribution required;

(d) the person liable to contribute was, at that time, able to contribute;
(e) the procedural requirements had been complied with.

Requirement (d) is of considerable importance. The person, being pursued, must be in a position to pay. This should give him or her the right to argue in court that he does not have sufficient funds available, as a result of his own outgoings, to permit him to actually make the required payments.

7.14.4 Desertion

There is no reference in the legislation to desertion as a defence to such a claim.

In certain cases, a wife may have applied to court for a maintenance order against her husband and been refused on the grounds of desertion or because of 'lack of means' of her spouse. She may subsequently obtain one of the above-mentioned social welfare allowances and, despite the fact that there has already been a finding by the district court that no maintenance should be paid by the husband, the Department of Social Welfare or the Health Board (as the case may be) may still pursue him through the courts for a contribution towards the allowance. In effect, therefore, in certain cases the officials of the Department of Social Welfare make decisions and pursue payments through the courts whilst ignoring the decisions of judges, which have already been made after a detailed court hearing. The officials are, in a sense, exercising a quasi-judicial function which may well be unconstitutional.

Difficulties also arise in relation to maintenance agreements included in deeds of separation. A husband may agree to make certain maintenance payments to his wife who subsequently applies for the lone parents allowance. If she is granted the allowance, when the husband is pursued by the Department of Social Welfare for a contribution, he may cease making the maintenance payments pursuant to the deed of separation and make payments to the relevant Department instead. This may lead to difficulties for him, however, as his wife may still have a claim against him for any arrears of maintenance which arise on foot of the deed of separation by way of contract debt regardless of the fact that she is receiving social welfare payments.

It is common, therefore, to include in a deed of separation a clause stating that maintenance payments for a spouse will cease if he or she makes application to the Department of Social Welfare for some sort of allowance or benefit which could result in the other spouse having to make, not only maintenance payments, but also contributions towards the allowance itself.

7.14.5 Cohabitation

It is important to note that cohabitation is a bar to qualification for the lone parents allowance, deserted wives allowance, deserted wives benefit, survivors pension and widows (non-contributory) pension. An applicant cannot obtain such a payment if he or she is 'cohabiting as man and wife' (Social Welfare (Consolidation) Act 1993) with another person. The Department of Social Welfare will investigate any allegation of cohabitation and if necessary demand a refund of payments made during the period when the Department holds that the applicant was cohabiting.

As a result of a number of court cases, the deciding officer must now make known to the recipient of any allowance the basis on which it was contended that she was cohabiting and the basis upon which, if cohabitation was found, she could be required to refund the benefit received. Any such individual must be given an opportunity to deal properly with the allegations made and must be made aware of the nature and extent of the case being made against him or her (*Houlihan v Minister for Social Welfare and the Attorney General*, unreported, 23 July 1986, High Court).

7.14.6   Qualified children

The lone parents allowance is payable only to an applicant who has a qualified child residing with him or her. Once that child attains his or her majority, or completes a full-time course of education up to a maximum age of 21 years, then such payments will cease.

It may, therefore, be in the interests of an applicant wife, for instance, to obtain the deserted wives benefit rather than the lone parents allowance. Such a benefit may often be substantially higher than the lone parents allowance and may well be paid for a far longer period.

It is open to a wife to apply for the deserted wives benefit after payments of the lone parents allowance have ceased, even if they have been made for a number of years. However, it will be necessary for the applicant wife to prove desertion and this may be difficult many years after the event. It would be important in such situations for the applicant wife to retain as much documentary or other evidence as she can pending a possible application in the future.

7.14.7   Effect of divorce on the social welfare provisions

As has already been mentioned, the Social Welfare (No 2) Act 1995 attempts to ensure that the Social Welfare Code will apply equally to individuals whether they are deserted, separated or divorced.

Contributory pension scheme

The contributory pension scheme applies to widows and widowers and has been extended to enable a divorced person who has not remarried to qualify for a pension on the death of their former spouse. If the former spouse has remarried prior to his or her death, then both the first and the second spouse may qualify for the widows or widowers pension on the basis of their own insurance record or that of the deceased.

Occupational injuries benefit scheme

The benefits available to a spouse, under the occupational injuries benefit scheme when his or her spouse has died as a result of an occupational accident or disease, are now extended to the former spouse of a divorced person who has not remarried as well as to the *existing* spouse of the deceased person if he or she has remarried.

Deserted wives benefit or allowance

A woman in receipt of the deserted wives benefit or allowance who obtains a divorce decree will continue to be regarded as deserted for the purposes of these allowances unless she remarries. A divorced parent caring for children will be recognised as a lone parent and may qualify for a means-tested lone parents allowance.

Prisoner's wives allowance

A woman receiving the prisoner's wives allowance who becomes divorced will continue to qualify for this allowance provided the usual conditions are satisfied.

Chapter 8

SUCCESSION

8.1 SUCCESSION ACT 1965

8.1.1 Right of spouse to inherit

The Succession Act 1965 came into force on 1 January 1967 and was considered revolutionary at the time. Prior to that, a person was free to dispose of their assets by will in whatever manner they chose even if it was to the detriment of the dependent spouse and children. This freedom to ignore the needs of a spouse and children was circumscribed by the Part IX of that Act.

If a person now dies intestate (ie without leaving a valid will), leaving a spouse only, then the spouse is entitled to the entire estate of the deceased. If a person dies intestate leaving a spouse and a child or children, the spouse is entitled to two-thirds of the estate and the children to one-third. 'Child or children' means any child of the deceased, marital or non-marital (Status of Children Act 1987).

If a person dies testate (ie leaving a valid will), leaving a spouse only, then the spouse has a right to one half of the deceased's estate. If a person dies testate leaving a spouse and a child or children, the spouse has a right to one-third of the estate and the children to two-thirds. This share of the spouse is known as the legal right share. The right of a spouse to a legal right share has priority over devises and bequests and shares on intestacy. If a testator makes no provision by will for their spouse or makes provision which is inadequate, the spouse is entitled to elect to take either the devise or bequest under the will or to take their legal right share (1965 Act, ss 111 and 115). If a testator makes provision for a spouse which may seem fair and appropriate such as giving a spouse a life interest in their estate or naming the spouse among a class of beneficiaries for a discretionary trust, the spouse is still entitled to elect to take their legal right share as an absolute interest. The personal representative of the deceased spouse has a statutory obligation to notify the spouse of their entitlement to claim their legal right.

8.1.2 Election and appropriation

Election

The meaning of the right to elect was examined in the case of *In the matter of the Estate of Thomas Cummins deceased* (unreported, July 1996). Kelly J held that s 111 of the 1965 Act conferred a right on the surviving spouse to share in the estate of their deceased spouse and this right is recognised and protected by law. Section 115 gives a spouse the right to elect to take either the share of the estate of the deceased spouse to which they are entitled by law, or their entitlement under the will of the deceased. The surviving spouse is free to decide whether or not to exercise this right. In the case in question, the husband made no provision for his wife in his will. She survived him by only 12 hours and did not exercise her right of election. It was held that the right to share in the estate was a purely personal right and died with her. Had the wife survived, she could have decided to exercise or not to exercise her right to claim her legal right to one half share of her late husband's estate (as there were no children). Section 111 did not give rise to an automatic transfer of the legal right share to the estate of the surviving spouse. However, once a spouse has exercised his or her right, it enures for the benefit of his or her estate (*Hamilton v Armstrong* (1984) 4 ILRM 306).

Appropriation

The surviving spouse has the right to require the personal representative of the deceased spouse to appropriate the family home in or towards satisfaction of any share of the surviving spouse. The words 'dwelling and household chattels' are defined as a dwelling in which at the time of death of the deceased spouse the surviving spouse was ordinarily resident. The right of the surviving spouse, therefore, to require the dwelling to be appropriated does not apply in the context of separation or divorce if the surviving spouse is not ordinarily resident in the dwelling at the time of the deceased spouse's death. The right must be exercised by the surviving spouse within six months of a receipt of a notification by the personal representative or one year from the date of the extraction of the grant of representation whichever is the later (1965 Act, s 56).

8.1.3   Unworthiness to succeed

There are certain circumstances in which a spouse is disqualified from taking any benefit from the estate of the deceased spouse on account of their misbehaviour towards the other. The grounds of exclusion are:

(a)   a spouse who is found guilty of the murder, attempted murder or manslaughter of the other;

(b)   a spouse against whom the deceased obtained a decree of divorce *a mensa et thoro*. Such decrees are no longer available since October 1989 when the Judicial Separation and Family Law Reform Act 1989 came into operation;

(c)   a spouse who has failed to comply with a decree of restitution of conjugal rights. Since the Family Law Act 1981, no action can now rest for the restitution of conjugal rights;

(d)   a spouse who is guilty of desertion which has continued up to the death of the other for two years or more. Desertion for this purpose includes conduct which justified the deceased spouse in separating and living apart from the other;

(e)   a spouse who has been found guilty of an offence against the other punishable by imprisonment for a maximum period of at least two years or by a more severe penalty.

The effect of disqualification is that the spouse is precluded from taking any legal right share or share on intestacy and the estate is distributed as if the surviving spouse had died before the deceased spouse.

8.1.4   Renunciation

A spouse may renounce his or her legal right share either before the marriage in a pre-marriage contract or after the marriage by a renunciation of Succession Act rights often, but not necessarily, contained in a deed of separation. The renunciation must be in writing (1965 Act, s 113).

Although s 113 of the 1965 Act specifically refers to renunciation of legal right share, spouses can surrender and renounce their right to take a share of estate of the deceased spouse on intestacy.

The surviving spouse is the person first entitled to extract a grant of administration to an estate where the deceased has died intestate. In the context of separation, it is usually inappropriate for an estranged spouse to be the administrator and therefore a renunciation of entitlement to take out a grant is usually agreed.

In order to achieve a renunciation, a deed of separation will often contain the following clause:

> 'The husband and the wife hereby mutually surrender and renounce all rights either of them may have under the Succession Act 1965 to any share or legal right in the estate of the other on the other's death either testate or intestate, and hereby renounce and waive their respective rights to the extraction of a Grant of Probate or Administration in the estate of the other and undertake not to interfere in any way with the extraction of a Grant of Probate or Administration in the estate of the other provided that none of the foregoing shall impede either the husband or the wife from taking any legal action on behalf of the children to protect or defend the children's interests in the estate of either the husband or the wife or from taking any action on behalf of the children under the provisions of the Succession Act 1965' (Dublin Solicitors Bar Association 1996 precedent).

8.2   SUCCESSION AND SEPARATION

The fact that spouses are living separately and apart from each other does not of itself affect their entitlements under the 1965 Act. When granting a decree of judicial separation the court can extinguish the share that a spouse would otherwise be entitled to in the estate of the other spouse as a legal right or on intestacy under the 1965 Act. The court should only do so if it is satisfied that adequate and reasonable financial provision exists or can be made by ancillary financial relief orders for the spouse whose rights are in question. The court may also make such an order both where a spouse has applied for and has been refused any form of ancillary financial relief order, and where a spouse has not made such an application but, if he or she did, the relief would be refused.

In the case of *F(B) v F(V)* [1994] 1 Fam LJ 15, Lynch J confirmed an order extinguishing the right of a dependent wife to a share both as to legal right share and on intestacy to the estate of her husband on death. The wife had by virtue of ancillary relief orders been provided with a two-bedroomed apartment free of mortgage and the husband had agreed to assign to her the benefit of a lump sum payable by his employers on his retirement or death in service. The court ordered the husband not to prejudice the wife's entitlement nor to diminish the amount of the lump sum payment. In these circumstances, the court was satisfied that 'adequate and reasonable provision' had been made for the wife and confirmed the circuit court's order extinguishing her Succession Act rights.

In the context of separation, the courts have made extinguishing orders in circumstances where the family home has been registered in the joint names of the spouses and therefore would have passed to the dependent spouse by way of survivorship. In such cases, in order to make the extinguishing order, the court has required that other property has been transferred to the dependent spouse and/or a lump sum payment has been made and/or the dependent spouse is named as a beneficiary on a life insurance policy and the other spouse has undertaken to continue paying the premiums.

Since 1 August 1996, the court has power to make financial compensation orders similar to those which can be made in the context of divorce (see Chapter 9).

8.3   SUCCESSION AND DIVORCE

Once a divorce decree is granted, the parties are no longer married to each other and therefore the right to inherit contained in the 1965 Act is not available to a former spouse.

8.3.1   Provision out of the estate

To temper the harshness of this consequence, the court can make an order providing for a divorced spouse out of the estate of the deceased spouse if it considers it appropriate (Divorce Act, s 18(1)). No provision will be made for a spouse who has remarried (Divorce Act, s 18(2)).

8.3.2   Criteria for granting relief

Before making an order the court must be satisfied that it was not possible to make proper provision for the applicant spouse during the lifetime of the deceased spouse by way of maintenance, property adjustment, financial compensation or pension adjustment or other miscellaneous ancillary orders. The conduct of the applicant spouse must not be the reason why ancillary relief orders were not made in the first instance. In particular, the court must also have regard to the rights of any other persons having an interest in the matter and any representations made on their behalf, for example, surviving spouse or dependent member of the family or other dependent relative.

The court must have regard to all the circumstances of the case including:

(a) any lump sum order or property adjustment order made in favour of the applicant spouse; and
(b) any devise or bequest which the deceased spouse has made in favour of the applicant spouse (Divorce Act, s 18(3)).

While the court is charged with examining all the relevant circumstances, it must specifically examine whether provision of a capital nature had been given by cash lump sum or property transfer at the time of the divorce or by will at the time of death. In addition, all the criteria set out in s 20 of the Divorce Act must be considered by the court.

EXAMPLE

> The court, on granting Mr S a divorce, made a property adjustment order transferring the family home from the sole name of Mr S into the joint names of Mr S and Mrs S as joint tenants. Mrs S was given a right to reside in the home for life. Neither Mrs S nor Mr S had any children. Mr S, who was a self-employed carpenter, was also ordered to pay maintenance to his wife. No other orders were made because their circumstances at the time of the divorce were very modest and there were no other assets or money available for distribution. Mr S died. Mrs S will no longer receive maintenance. Mr S inherited a house from his unmarried aunt with whom he resided after his divorce. Mr S died testate leaving his house to a niece to whom he was very close and the remainder of his estate to his sister in England and the three children of a predeceased brother.

Applying the particular criteria of this section to this example, the court would probably take into account the following:

(a) the provision made for Mrs S at the time of the granting the divorce was modest because the assets available for distribution at that time were limited;
(b) the relief granted or not granted at the time of the divorce was not in any way due to the conduct of Mrs S;
(c) as the survivor of the joint tenancy created in the family home Mrs S is now the sole owner;
(d) no lump sum, financial compensation or pension adjustment order was made at the time of the divorce;
(e) Mr S made no provision in his will for Mrs S and left his estate to other relatives;

(f)   Mrs S will probably be entitled to a widow's pension or other statutory benefit.

If Mrs S made a claim for provision out of the estate, the beneficiaries under the will of Mr S are entitled to make representations to the court.

8.3.3   Extent of the relief

If the court is satisfied that it is appropriate to make provision for the applicant spouse, the total value of the provision must not exceed:

(a)   the share (if any) that the applicant spouse would have been entitled to take in the estate of the deceased spouse if the marriage had not been dissolved, ie the legal right share; or

(b)   the share that the applicant would have been entitled to take in the estate of the deceased spouse if the marriage had not been dissolved and if he or she died wholly or partly intestate.

The total value of the provision cannot exceed what the applicant spouse would have been entitled to either by legal right share or intestacy if they had remained married.

The provision made must take into account the value of any lump sum payment and/or property adjustment order already made in favour of the applicant. The value appears to be the value at the date of the order (Divorce Act, s 18(4)), ie the date of the order making the lump sum payment or property adjustment order. This is not altogether clear from the subsection itself. However, the fact that the value of provision in satisfaction of a legal right share for a spouse is reckoned as at the date of making the provision (1965 Act, s 116(2)) and the value of any advancement made to a child is reckoned as at the date of advancement (1965 Act, s 63(2)), it is assumed that the value of any lump sum or property adjustment order is reckoned on the date on which the order was made.

Using the example above, if the value of the house owned by Mrs S was at the time of the divorce worth £40,000 and the value of Mr S's estate on death is £60,000, the maximum that Mrs S is entitled to, pursuant to s 18(4) of the Divorce Act, is the share she would have been entitled to had the marriage not been dissolved: in other words, one-half share – her legal right share as Mr S had no children. Half of the value of the estate is £30,000; therefore, if the court was disposed to making an order in her favour, it would be limited to making provision up to a value of £10,000 only because this amount, together with the value of a half interest (£20,000) in the property transferred to Mrs S on divorce, amounts to £30,000.

If Mr S had made a bequest to Mrs S of £10,000, then she would not be successful in obtaining any relief from the court because the total value of property adjusted in her favour and the bequest made by Mr S amounts to one-half the value of his estate.

If, however, Mr S left a very substantial estate of, say, £200,000, the court might consider favourably an application and might make provision out of the estate of Mr S. The persons entitled under Mr S's will are entitled to make representations to the court and the court must have regard to them. In this instance, the court might be told that the property inherited by Mr S from his aunt was in the family for many years and Mr S very particularly wanted to leave it to his niece who had been very caring for him during his lifetime. The court will also take into account all the criteria listed in s 20 of the Divorce Act and in particular, the age of Mrs S, the duration of the marriage, the length of time they lived together and the income or benefit that Mrs S is entitled to under statute. Although it is not specifically stated, the court could have regard to the period of time which has elapsed since the granting of the divorce.

8.3.4 Impact on the administration of the estate

If provision is made for a former spouse, how does this impact on the administration of the estate?

Section 112 of the 1965 Act states that the legal right share of a spouse has priority over devises, bequests and shares on intestacy. Section 46(6) of the 1965 Act provides that 'a claim to a share as a legal right or on intestacy in the estate of a deceased person is a claim against the assets of the estate to a sum equal to the value of that share'. This means that the claim is treated as if it was a pecuniary legacy. All references to the estate are to the net estate, that is the assets remaining after payment of all expenses, debts and liabilities properly payable thereout.

This problem was examined by Henchy J, in *H v O* [1978] IR 204, who stated:

'But nowhere in the Act is there any specific statement as to how the personal representatives are to discharge the surviving spouse's legal right to one-third or one-half of the estate as the case may be. Section 112 gives the legal right priority over devises, bequests and shares on intestacy. In the general context of the Act of 1965, it must be assumed that the legislative intention was that the legal right (where elected for) is to be discharged in the same manner as if the one-half or one-third of the estate had been expressly given in the will in priority over all devises and bequests subject to the restrictions imposed by s 50 the personal representatives may sell the whole or any part of the estate for the purpose of distributing the estate amongst the persons entitled.'

An order of the court under s 18 of the Divorce Act cannot be said to be a settlement of the legal right share. It may be that if the court makes an order to make provision out of the estate, it should give to the personal representatives such directions as are necessary as to how exactly the provision is to be made.

8.3.5 Time-limits for applying

The applicant spouse must make the application to the court for relief within a period of six months from the date of the grant of probate or administration

(Divorce Act, s 18(1)). The applicant spouse is under a statutory obligation to notify the surviving spouse of the deceased and the court may also direct that any other person be notified as may be appropriate (Divorce Act, s 18(5)).

If, however, a personal representative has given notice to the former spouse of the death of the deceased spouse, that former spouse must within one month from the date of receipt of the notice notify the personal representative that:

(a) they intend to apply for relief under s 18, if that is their intention;
(b) that they have applied pursuant to s 18 and the application is pending; or
(c) that an order under s 18 has been made in their favour (Divorce Act, s 18(7)).

If the former spouse fails to notify the personal representative within the period of one month, as required, the personal representative is free to distribute the estate or any part of the estate among those entitled. This does not preclude or prejudice the right of the former spouse to follow any assets distributed into the hands of any person who may have received them. Neither does it preclude the applicant spouse from making the application within the period of six months from the date of the grant although the estate or part of it may already be distributed. The parties to whom the estate or part of it had been distributed would presumably be notified of the application at the direction of the court and be entitled to be heard.

The period of six months available from the date of the grant to a spouse to make an application is definite and absolute and should not be confused with the period of six months that a spouse has to elect to take their legal right, which only runs from the time notice is served.

8.3.6   Cessation

In view of the impact that s 18 will undoubtedly have on the administration of estates, an application can be made when the divorce decree is granted or during the lifetime of the spouses for an order blocking the operation of this section, so that either or both spouses shall not be entitled to apply under this section on the death of the other (Divorce Act, s 18(10)). This will allow spouses to achieve a clean break in relation to their estates on death and will facilitate the orderly administration of their estates. It effectively allows the court to bar any claims being made on death. It is appropriate for such an order to be sought at the time of the granting of the decree of divorce when the court has all the facts and financial circumstances of the spouse before it. If a financial compensation order or a pension adjustment order is made, the court may be satisfied that reasonable provision has been put in place to provide for a dependent spouse in the event of the other spouse predeceasing him or her. The court must also be satisfied that it is 'just' in the circumstances not to allow such an application to be made.

Remarriage

The court cannot make an order in favour of the other spouse if the other spouse has remarried since the granting of the decree of divorce from the deceased spouse.

When advising a divorced client in relation to making a will, it is essential to know if an order under s 18(10) of the Divorce Act has been obtained. If such an order has not already been made and/or in the event that the other spouse has not remarried, the client should be advised to consider making an application for an order excluding the operation of s 18. An assessment should be made of the likely value of the client's estate, the value of property and/or lump sum payments already received by the former spouse to establish the possible exposure to a s 18(10) claim.

8.3.7   Obligations and duties of personal representatives

The personal representative of a deceased spouse must make a reasonable attempt to ensure that notice of the death of the deceased spouse is given to a surviving divorced spouse or spouses (if more than one). The Divorce Act does not specify within what time-scale the personal representative should do so nor does it specify what is a reasonable attempt. The personal representative does not appear to have a duty to notify the former spouse of his or her entitlement to apply to the court under s 18 or to advise the spouse of the time-limits within which an application should be made. The obligation is to give notice of the death only. This places yet another burden on personal representatives and the solicitors who advise them. William O'Dea TD highlighted many of the dangers in his contribution to the debate on the Divorce Bill in Dail Eireann (Parliamentary Debates, Dail Eireann, 27.6.1996, vol 467, no 6, p 1806):

> 'This onus should not be put on the personal representative. We live in a small country and the onus should be on the person involved. What sanction will apply if it is established that the personal representative did not make a reasonable attempt to contact the spouse of somebody who has died with a view to their coming back to look for another share of the property? If there is no sanction, why place an obligation on somebody? The sanction, I presume, is a civil one in that they can be sued. How will it operate in practice? If the personal representative does not bring this to the notice of the spouse of somebody who has died, the time limit may elapse and the spouse who could have brought a case may suddenly discover that they could have done so had they been informed. What will be the sanction of the personal representative who made no effort to bring this to their notice? Can they sue the personal representative? What would the measure of damages be? Will the court have to calculate what the spouse would have got from the estate if they had been informed and had brought a case in time? Would that be the measure of damages against the personal representative?'

These were legitimate concerns. Some of them have been addressed by the introduction of subsections (7), (8) and (9) which were introduced as amendments by the Minister at the Select Committee Stage of the Bill in the Senate. The personal representative may now distribute the estate one month after the receipt of the notice by a surviving former spouse unless the spouse has notified the personal representative as set out above. If the applicant spouse does not so notify the personal representative, he is free to distribute the estate. The personal representative is protected against liability for distributing the estate if no notice of a claim is received (Divorce Act, s 18(8)). An applicant spouse may trace and follow any assets representing the assets of the deceased into the hands of any beneficiary who received them (Divorce Act, s 18(9)). These subsections are similar to the general protection given to personal representatives under s 47(2) and (3) of the 1965 Act.

In order for the personal representative to obtain this protection, he must make a 'reasonable attempt' to ensure that notice of the death is brought to the attention of a former spouse (or possibly several former spouses). The extent of this duty seems to lie somewhere between the particular statutory duty placed on a personal representative to notify a surviving spouse of their entitlement to elect under s 115 of the 1965 Act and the general statutory duty placed on personal representatives to give notice to creditors and others of their intention to distribute the estate. The Minister was questioned in the Senate about the definitions of 'reasonable attempt'. He replied 'that is a matter left to the discretion of the court. There is no particular definition given. In a disputed matter, it would be at the discretion of the court to define what would be reasonable in a particular circumstance' (Parliamentary Debates, Seanad Eireann, 24.10.1996, vol 149, no 1, p 26).

If an application or notification of intention to apply is made by a former spouse, the personal representative must not distribute any of the estate until such time as the application has been heard and an order made or refused. The personal representative may apply to the court for leave to make a distribution in advance of the hearing of any such application if, for example, the beneficiary of the estate is the surviving spouse of the deceased who may have dependent children and whose circumstances may be needy (Divorce Act, s 18(6)). The personal representative is free to distribute the estate if no application or notification of intention to apply is made within a period of one month from the date of receipt of the notice of death. However, to ensure that no claim can be made or that no complication arises if a claim is made after the estate or part of it is distributed, the personal representative should wait until six months have elapsed since the date of the issue of the grant of probate or administration before distributing the estate. Alternatively, the personal representative should attempt to give notice to the former spouse(s) at the earliest possible time and it may be prudent to advise them of their rights under s 18 rather just giving notice of the death and ask the spouse(s) to notify the personal representative of their intentions.

8.4 ENTITLEMENT OF CHILDREN

Nothing in the Divorce Act interferes with the entitlement of a child to seek provision from the estate of a parent if no provision is made for them in the will of that deceased parent, save that the application to court must now be made within six months of the grant not twelve months as heretofore (Divorce Act, s 46). Section 117 of the 1965 Act provides that if a court is satisfied that a testator has failed in his moral duty to make a proper provision for the child in accordance with his means, whether by will or otherwise, the court may order that such a provision, as the court thinks just, shall be made for the child out of the estate. The court must consider the matter from the point of view of a prudent and just parent, taking into account the position of each of the children of the testator and any other relevant circumstances. An order made under this section shall not affect the legal right of a surviving spouse (if the surviving spouse is the mother or father of the child) to any devise or bequest to the spouse or any share to which the spouse is entitled on intestacy. If, therefore, a testator leaves their entire estate to their spouse, who is either the mother or father of all their children, then the children have no claim. It is presumed that in the fullness of time the spouse will make provision for the children of the marriage. If, however, the testator leaves his entire estate to his spouse who is not the mother (or father) of all their children, then the child or children can make a claim for provision under s 117. Any provision, however, cannot interfere with the legal right share of the surviving spouse. It should be noted that for the purposes of s 117, the word 'child' is not limited to a minor child or to a dependant under the age of 23 but means any child of the testator. Many successful claims have been made by children who are middle-aged.

Numerous applications to the court have been made under this section and it may be that in the future further applications will be made if parents fail to provide adequately for all their children, whether by first or subsequent marriages.

EXAMPLE

> Mark Martin married Martina Martin and there were two children of the marriage, Matthew and Malachy aged 21 and 19 respectively. Mark and Martina divorced. Mark remarried Sally Smith and has one child of this marriage, Susan, who is aged four. By his will, Mark left his entire estate to Sally Smith. Mark died. Martina Martin has decided she will not make a claim against Mark's estate because she was adequately provided for at the time of the divorce. However, Matthew and Malachy believe that their father has not made proper provision for them especially as they have not yet completed their further education. Matthew and Malachy can make a s 117 claim against the estate of their father.

8.5   FOREIGN DIVORCES

Section 25 of the FLA 1995 allows the court to make provision for a former
spouse whose marriage to the deceased spouse was dissolved by a decree of
divorce granted outside the state. Originally, there was a lack of consistency in
the time-limits which applied. A former spouse by a foreign divorce decree
initially had a period of 12 months in which to make an application. This has
now been amended by s 49(j) of the Divorce Act to a period of six months so
that the same time-limits for making an application apply regardless of whether
the divorce was granted in Ireland or outside the State.

8.6   PROBATE TAX

Probate tax is a tax payable on the value of an estate in excess of £10,820 (1997
figure) of persons who died after 17 June 1993. The personal representative of
the deceased is primarily accountable for the payment of the tax and the
beneficiaries are secondarily liable. The tax is usually paid at the time when the
grant of probate or administration is being extracted.

Probate tax is not payable on assets passing from one spouse to the other by will
or intestacy. Section 36 of the Divorce Act continues this relief for former
spouses who obtain provision out of the estate of a deceased spouse pursuant to
an order under s 18.

8.7   CAPITAL ACQUISITIONS TAX

Capital acquisitions tax is a tax on gifts and inheritances received by a person.
The tax is payable by the beneficiary. There are exempt threshold amounts
based on the relationship, divided into three classes, between the disponer and
donee or successor beneficiary.

Class thresholds from the second Schedule to the Capital Acquisitions Act 1976
as indexed to 1997 are set out below.

IR£	Relationship to disponer
185,550 (Class A)	Child, minor child of deceased child, parents in respect of absolute inheritances only
24,740 (Class B)	Lineal ancestor, lineal descendant, brother, sister, child of brother or sister
12,370 (Class C)	None of the above

The threshold amounts are increased each year in line with the consumer price index.

There is no capital acquisitions tax payable on gifts (since 1 January 1990) or inheritances (since 30 January 1985) taken by one spouse from the other nor are such gifts or inheritances aggregated for the purposes of computing the tax on gifts or inheritances from other disposers. This relief continues to apply even if the spouses are separated from each other.

Section 34 maintains this relief in the context of divorce in respect of property passing either by gift or by inheritance between spouses by order of the court (Divorce Act, s 34). If a wife receives the family home by property adjustment order from her husband, this will not constitute a gift from her husband and it will not be taxable nor shall its value be taken into account in computing any liability the wife may have on other gifts or inheritances received by her. The situation is the same if she receives provision from the husband's estate pursuant to s 18 of the Divorce Act.

Nevertheless, it must be stressed that this relief applies only if the gift or inheritance is taken by virtue or in consequence of an ancillary relief order made by the court. If, for example, a divorced man makes provision for his ex-wife in his will, the value of the devise or bequest or legacy is taxable in the hands of the ex-wife, who will only have the benefit of the lowest of the three class thresholds, Class C.

8.8 EFFECT OF A DIVORCE ON EXISTING WILLS

While the contracting of a marriage automatically revokes an existing will, the granting of a divorce does not automatically do so. It is therefore important to advise all persons who have been granted a divorce that they should review their wills and make provision for their dependants in the light of the new circumstances that prevail after the divorce.

Care should also be taken in drafting wills. A will by a husband in favour of his wife, who is not specifically named, will provide for the woman who is his wife at the time of his death. Conversely, a will by a husband in favour of his wife who is specifically named will take effect in favour of that woman even though they are not legally married at the time of his death.

Marriage automatically revokes a will made prior to the marriage and not made in contemplation of that marriage and care should be taken to advise people to make a new will subsequent to their marriage. This will be particularly important for couples who have resided together for many years and have made wills in favour of each other. If such a couple marry after either one or both of them obtains a divorce, it is essential that new wills are made.

8.9   POWERS OF ATTORNEY

An enduring power of attorney in favour of a spouse will be invalidated or cease
to be in force, unless the power provides otherwise, if subsequently:

(a)   the marriage is annulled or dissolved either
      (i)   under the law of Ireland, or
      (ii)   under the law of another State and is no longer a subsisting valid
             marriage;
(b)   a decree of judicial separation has been granted;
(c)   there is a separation agreement in writing;
(d)   a protection order, interim barring order, barring order or safety order is
      made against the attorney on the application of the donor or vice versa
      (s 5(7) of the Powers of Attorney Act 1996 and s 50 of the Divorce Act).

Section 50 of the Divorce Act amends s 5(7) of the Powers of Attorney Act 1996.
The enduring power only ceases to be in force in respect of an attorney who is a
spouse and to whom s 5(7) of the Act applies. The power of attorney itself or the
appointment of a substitute or successive attorney is not invalidated.

An enduring power of attorney should provide a substitute attorney in the
event of the divorce of the appointed attorney. Alternatively, after a divorce
decree is granted, the parties should not only revise their wills but also revise
any enduring power of attorney that exists in favour of a former spouse.

Chapter 9

LIFE ASSURANCE

9.1 GENERAL

Life assurance is a contract by which one party (the insurer) agrees for a consideration (the premium) to pay money (the sum assured) to or for the benefit of the other party (the assured) upon the occurrence of a specified event. The objective of life assurance for the assured is to provide a sum to be added to his or her estate, or for the benefit of others, in the event of his or her death.

The policy holder must have an insurable interest in the life of the assured at the time when the contract is made. A person has an unlimited insurable interest in their own life. A husband and a wife have an unlimited insurance interest in the life of the other. Whether this will continue to be the case even in the context of divorce is a moot point. Most insurance companies will accept that a divorced spouse has an insurable interest in the other spouse at least to the extent that a former spouse is still financially dependent on that spouse.

9.2 TYPES OF POLICIES

9.2.1 Mortgage protection insurance

Most financial institutions, when advancing a home loan for the purchase of a property, insist that a mortgage protection policy is taken out in the amount of the loan. The amount decreases over the term of the mortgage commensurate with the amount of the outstanding loan. In the event of death, the proceeds of the policy are used to discharge the balance of the loan in full.

9.2.2 Life endowment insurance

An endowment policy from an assurance company usually provides for the payment of a principal sum at a specified date (the maturity date) or on the death of the insured, whichever is the earlier. The policy is usually for a fixed term of years (eg 20 years) and it guarantees to pay the sum assured in the event of death of the life assured within the term or on survival of the assured to the end of the term. If the policy is 'with profits' the assured will receive extra value or a bonus depending on the profitability and success of the assurance company. Bonuses are allocated from year to year and, once added, cannot be taken away. Provided the policy has not been used as collateral security for a mortgage, it can be surrendered or encashed in advance of the maturity date but this usually gives a poor return on the investment and it is better to keep the policy in place until maturity.

9.2.3   Whole of life policies

Whole of life policies provide permanent life assurance protection. The sum assured is payable only on death. In other words, the policy does not have a fixed term, or a maturity value on a specified date before death, nor does it have an investment element.

9.2.4   Joint life policies

All the different types of policies referred to above can also be taken out on joint lives. The policy usually matures on the death of the first party to die and the policy then lapses. Many consider that it is probably better to have separate policies for a husband and wife rather than a joint life policy.

9.2.5   Term policies

A term policy is a life assurance taken out for a particular period of years. For example, a husband could take out a policy of assurance on the life of his wife for a term of years to cover the period of dependency of the children. Term assurance is also used in partnership assurance and keyman assurance for company employees and shareholders.

9.2.6   Single premium policies linked

Single premium policies tend to be used as a form of investment. The funds are also easy to administer. Such policies are attractive because there is no risk element in relation to the premiums not being paid (being single premium policies) and also because the proceeds of these policies are not subject to capital gains tax or income tax.

9.2.7   Savings/educational policies

Savings/educational policies are a form of endowment assurance as the policy guarantees to pay the sum assured at a specified time, for example, so that the policy holder can pay educational expenses or on the death of the assured if before that specified time.

9.2.8   Section 60 policies

Section 60 of the Finance Act 1985 introduced relief on the proceeds of certain life assurance policies used to pay inheritance tax. The relief given is that the proceeds of the s 60 policies are exempt from tax in certain circumstances, to the extent that they are used to pay inheritance tax. Section 130 of the Finance Act 1990 extended s 60 relief to deal with simultaneous death of spouses. Policies can be single life or joint life policies. With the introduction of divorce, it is preferable to have single life policies. Joint life policies invariably provide for payment on the death of the survivor.

9.2.9 Critical illness policies

This type of policy provides cover in the event that the insured contracts and survives certain illnesses. Some policies stand alone but many others are integrated into a life assurance policy whereby the sum assured is payable on death or a part of it is paid early to the assured in the event of critical illness.

9.3 BENEFICIARIES OF THE POLICY

The benefit of a life assurance policy generally belongs to the person who takes out the policy. Thus, if Mr L took out a policy on his own life, on his death the proceeds of the policy will be paid to his estate to be distributed in accordance with his will or under the rules of intestacy. If, however, Mr L took out a policy of assurance on his own life and named his spouse, Lucy, as beneficiary, then Lucy would acquire an immediate vested interest. Since Lucy is named as the beneficiary, she is entitled to the proceeds of the policy even if she is not the wife of Mr L on his death. In the event that Lucy pre-deceases Mr L, he holds the policy in trust for her personal representative. If, however, Mr L took out a policy of assurance for the benefit of his wife (without naming a specific person) the woman who is his wife at the time of his death is the person entitled to take the benefit of the proceeds of the policy.

9.4 CREATING TRUSTS ON POLICIES

Section 7 of the Married Women's Status Act 1957 provides that:

> 'a policy of life assurance or endowment expressed to be for the benefit of, or by its express terms purporting to confer a benefit on, the wife, husband or child of insured, shall create a trust in favour of the objects named therein and the moneys payable under the policy shall not, so long as any part of the trust remains unperformed form part of the estate of the insured or be subject to his or her debts.'

The assured may therefore either by the policy or by a separate memorandum appoint trustee(s) of the moneys payable under the policy. If no trustee(s) is appointed, the policy will vest in the assured and their legal representative in trust. A child for this purpose of this section means a marital and non-marital child or children, adopted children and children to whom the insured stands in loco parentis. The main purpose of this provision is to ensure that the proceeds of the policy are paid to the trustees for the persons named and to stop the proceeds of the policy going to the estate of the assured on death.

9.5 ASSIGNMENT OF POLICIES

Policies of assurance are often assigned to a financial institution as security for a loan. Assignment of life policies is an intergral part of endowment mortgages. In such situations, the benefit of an endowment policy is assigned to the bank or building society which will reassign the policy if the mortgage is discharged in advance of the maturity date, for example if the property is sold. The financial institution usually retains the original policy document until the loan or mortgage is paid off. The benefit of a policy can also be assigned to a spouse or other named person. In order for an assignment to be effective, notice must be given to the assurance company and the assignment must be in writing although no particular form of document is required.

9.6 SURRENDER OF POLICIES

A policy of life assurance can be surrendered to the assurance company and cancelled before the maturity date. The value of the policy encashed before its due time is always substantially less than it might otherwise be. In the context of marital breakdown, if there are financial pressures the payment of premiums is often not given priority, overlooked or deliberately ignored thereby cancelling the policy. In some cases, a policy may be surrendered to provide funds to repay some pressing debt.

There are a number of companies who purchase with-profits endowment policies, in many cases for more than the surrender value quoted by the assurance company. As the increase in value can sometimes be substantial, this possibility is worth examining. The purchasing company will require details of the surrender value as given by the assurance company together with brief details of the policy, including the commencement date and end date and the premiums payable. In many instances, the purchasing company will quote a more attractive price than the surrender value proposed by the assurance company. If the assured decides to sell the policy to the purchasing company, a full assignment of the policy is executed and the interest in policy passes absolutely to the purchasing company. The purchasing company will either retain the policy until maturity or sell it on.

9.7 LIFE ASSURANCE AND SEPARATION

The FLA 1995 which came into operation on 1 August 1996 allows the court on granting a decree of judicial separation to make financial compensation orders similar to those that can be made in the context of divorce. Prior to that date, the court had no power to order a spouse to take out life assurance for the benefit of a spouse. The court would accept an undertaking from a spouse to keep a policy of assurance in place, and on that basis the court would extinguish the Succession Act rights of the other spouse. This was usually done in the context of a settlement where orders by consent were made by the court.

9.8   LIFE ASSURANCE AND DIVORCE

9.8.1   Financial compensation orders

The Divorce Act permits the court to make provision for the future financial security of a spouse and compensation for loss of opportunity by means of life assurance policies. The consequent order is called a financial compensation order as set out in s 16. The court is now able to provide for spouses by compensating them for the loss which results directly from the divorce. On granting a decree of divorce or at any time thereafter the court can make such an order. The application can be made by either spouse or by a person on behalf of a dependent member of the family. The application must be made during the lifetime of the other spouse, where a spouse is the applicant, or during the lifetime of the spouse concerned where the application is made on behalf of a dependent member of the family.

In essence, the order requires one or both spouses to do one or more of the following:

(a)   to effect a life insurance policy for the benefit of the applicant spouse or dependent member of the family.

EXAMPLE

> Mr J who is aged 37 and has three young children is ordered to take out a policy of assurance on his life in the sum of £100,000 for the benefit of his wife Mrs J. This will ensure that on his death the sum of £100,000 is available to support and maintain Mrs J and give her financial security for the future.

The spouse against whom an order is made will have to take all necessary steps to effect the assurance policy, such as complete the proposal form, undergo a medical examination, give proof of age and whatever else is necessary. There is no particular sanction for refusing or failing to do so. It may also happen that a spouse may be refused cover or be quoted a level of premium that cannot be afforded. These difficulties are not specifically dealt with by the Divorce Act but the court could review the situation if it proved impossible to implement the order;

(b)   to assign to the applicant spouse or to another person on behalf of a
       dependent member of the family the whole or a specified part of an
       existing life assurance policy already taken out on the life of the spouse or
       on their joint lives.

EXAMPLE

> Mr J took out a whole life policy for £250,000 a few years prior to the divorce
> as he was doing a lot of travelling and wanted to provide for Mrs J and his
> two children in the event of his death. The court can order Mr J to assign the
> whole or part of this policy to Mrs J. Having regard to the value of the policy
> the court may order Mr J to assign one half share to Mrs J and the other half
> to another person for the benefit of Mr J's two children.

> Mrs J also has a life assurance policy on her life. Mr J was advised this was a
> prudent thing to do by his broker so that he would have the benefit of the
> proceeds of the policy (in the event of Mrs J's death) to help with the extra
> costs of caring for dependent children while they were still small,
> particularly as their younger child, Thomas, is mentally disabled. Mr J has
> always paid the premium. In this instance, the court could order Mrs J to
> assign the benefit of the policy to Mr J.

The power of the court to provide for a dependent member of the family
by a financial compensation order will be very important if a dependent
member suffers from a mental or physical disability to such an extent that
they are unlikely ever to be able to be financially independent. The stress
and worry of having to care for such a special child or dependent adult
can be somewhat relieved if there is some degree of financial provision
put in place for that particular person.

There may be practical difficulties about giving effect to such an order in
respect of an assignment of part of a policy as it is not generally possible to
assign part of a policy. However, the spirit of the section can be achieved if
the policy is assigned to joint names or the policy could be rewritten. For
example, if a policy is worth £250,000 and the court assigned the benefit
of £100,000 to the dependent spouse, the original policy can be rewritten,
£100,000 to provide a policy for the dependent spouse and a separate
policy for £150,000 for the assured. There are certain expenses incurred
in rewriting but they should not be significant;

(c)   to order either or both spouses to pay or continue to pay the premiums on
       any life assurance policy. This allows the court to give practical effect to
       (a) and (b) above.

In the example above, Mr J may be ordered to continue paying the
premium on both policies. If the court ordered both spouses to effect a
policy of assurance, it could order them both to pay the premiums due on
their respective policies. No specific penalty is imposed for failure to
comply with this aspect of the order. If a policy actually lapses due to
non-payment of the premiums, a very serious situation could arise for the
benefiting spouse. It is in his or her interest therefore to ensure that the

premiums are paid as they fall due. If a spouse is named as a beneficiary on a policy or if the benefit of a policy has been assigned, the assurance company should be notified accordingly. A request should be made that all notices sent to the insured are copied to the benefiting spouse or other person on behalf of a dependent member of the family. This will enable action to be taken in the event that premiums are not paid on the policy or the policy is otherwise at risk of lapsing.

The court can make a financial compensation order at the time of the granting of the divorce or at any time thereafter. The court could make an order subsequent to the divorce if an existing policy had matured or had otherwise lapsed and the court was satisfied that the financial security of the spouse and/or the dependent members of the family required the cover to be continued by another policy.

9.8.2 Criteria for granting relief

Particular criteria: s 15

In deciding whether to make such an order, the court must be satisfied that the financial security of the applicant spouse or dependent member can be provided for either wholly or partly by making of the order. The meaning of 'financial security' has not been defined. It suggests that some provision is needed for the support of the spouse or dependent member of the family at some future date, for example, death while children are still dependent or death prior to likely retirement date. If a spouse has no survivor's pension in place which could provide maintenance in the event of death, then a financial compensation order could provide substitute security. Alternatively, if the applicant spouse by reason of the divorce loses the benefit (for example under a pension scheme) this could be compensated for by such an order. The forfeiture must be as a direct result of the divorce. If the applicant spouse loses the opportunity of receiving a pension benefit because of the divorce, a financial compensation order can be made.

The court can make a financial compensation order in addition to or in substitution in whole or in part for maintenance orders, property adjustment orders, pension adjustment orders and miscellaneous ancillary relief orders. The court must have regard to whether proper provision exists already or can be made by any of the above orders. Therefore if proper provision can be made without resorting to a financial compensation order, then the court should do so. However, this does not preclude the court making the order in addition to the other orders. For example, the court could make a pension adjustment order but the benefit might be relatively modest because of the short length of reckonable service accrued to the date of the divorce. The spouse cannot benefit from pension rights accruing after the divorce and, therefore, the court could make additional provision by financial compensation order. To enable the court to make an informed judgment, all possible claims for ancillary relief will have to be presented to it. The court may be more inclined to make a financial compensation order if there is an existing policy in existence provided the continuance of the payment of the premium for that policy does not put a severe strain on the income of the spouses.

A spouse can volunteer to have a financial compensation order made against them if they wish to avoid having a pension adjustment order made or if they want to block the operation of s 18(10) of the Divorce Act as discussed in Chapter 8.

General criteria: s 20
In determining whether to make a financial compensation order, the court will have regard to all the criteria set out in s 20 but will probably have particular regard to:

(a)   Section s 20(2)(a): the income and earning capacity of the spouses. Life assurance is undoubtedly a benefit to the family but there is a cost factor and if the family finances are already stretched it may or may not be possible to afford to pay for life assurance.

(b)   Section s 20(2)(b): the financial needs obligations and responsibilities which each spouse has. If a wife has no independent income and is providing full-time care to the dependent members of the family and is likely to continue to do so, then it may be necessary that her financial situation is secured in the event that her husband predeceases her.

(c)   Section s 20(2)(e): the age of the spouses and their health. The premium for life assurance may be prohibitively expensive if the spouses are elderly or suffer mental or physical disability and the court will have to take this into account.

(d)   Section s 20(2)(k): the value to each spouse of any benefit (for example a benefit under a pension scheme) which the spouse may forfeit because of the divorce. The term benefit is not defined but loss of a pension benefit will have to be valued and the value will guide the court in determining whether and if so in what amount a policy of life assurance should be taken out.

(e)   Section s 20(2)(l): the rights of other persons including a subsequent spouse. At the time of granting the divorce a spouse may be in a stable relationship with another person and the spouse may have already effected life assurance with the intention of benefiting that person and any dependent children of the relationship. The court will have to decide whether such a policy should be assigned to the spouse on divorce or whether the interests and needs of the partner are more compelling.

(f)   Section s 20(4): in regard to providing for dependent members of the family the court should particularly look at the needs of any member who is suffering from any mental or physical disability. The court will also take into account the manner in which the children are being educated and trained and what the spouses anticipated for their children. For example, if during the marriage an educational policy was taken out for each child to ensure access to tertiary education the court may order that the policy be continued to ensure equality of education advancement for all members of the family.

9.8.3 Amount of cover and cost

If a financial compensation order is being sought to provide financial security in the event of the supporting spouse's death, an approximate value of the loss of succession rights will have to be calculated. Alternatively, an actuarial calculation should be made of the capital necessary to provide maintenance at the level payable to the dependent spouse.

Cost of life assurance

Different types of policies will be appropriate to particular cases and considerations of cost will usually be paramount. If an application is made on behalf of an applicant spouse to the court for an order under s 16 of the Divorce Act, it will be necessary to obtain a quotation from a life assurance company or broker on the likely premiums payable on an appropriate policy of assurance, having regard to the age of the spouse on whose life the policy is to be taken out. This will assist the court in assessing whether a financial compensation order is affordable in the case in question.

9.8.4 Cessation and variation

Remarriage

The court cannot make a financial compensation order if the applicant spouse has remarried (Divorce Act, s 16(2)(c)). Any order already made will cease to have effect on the remarriage of the benefiting spouse insofar as it relates to that spouse (Divorce Act, s 16(2)(b)).

Death

Any order made will cease to have effect on the death of the benefiting spouse insofar as it relates to that spouse (Divorce Act, s 16(2)(b)).

Variation: s 22

Subsequent to the making of a financial compensation order, the other spouse may apply for a variation of its terms. The court has broad power to vary, discharge or suspend any provision or revive an order or provision suspended or further vary or suspend an order already varied or suspended.

The application to vary can be made by:

(a)   either of the spouses; or
(b)   in the case of death of either spouse, by another person who has sufficient interest on behalf of a dependent member of the family; or

(c)   a subsequent spouse if either spouses to the divorce has remarried.

If the court decides to vary a financial compensation order, it can decide what happens to the accumulated value of the policy taken out in compliance with the order.

Section 16(2)(d) of the Divorce Act allows the court to decide how to dispose of:

(a)   the amount representing the accumulated value of a policy effected by order under s 16(1)(i); or
(b)   the interest or the part of the interest of an existing policy assigned by order under s 16(1)(ii).

For example, on the remarriage of the benefiting spouse, either spouse can apply to have the accumulated proceeds of a policy encashed and used for an alternative purpose to that originally intended, for example for educational advancement of a dependent member of the family, or the payment of debts or simply that the proceeds of the policy be paid out to either spouse. If an application is made in respect of an interest in the policy, the court can order the benefiting spouse to assign that interest back to the other spouse. Use of the term 'make such provision (if any) as the court considers appropriate in relation to the disposal' gives the court broad powers to deal with the consequences arising by variation of the original order.

9.8.5   Taxation of the proceeds of the policy of assurance

The payment of the proceeds of a policy of assurance, either on the death of the assured or on the date of maturity of the policy may, in certain circumstances, constitute a gift or inheritance under the Capital Acquisitions Tax Act 1976. Section 30 provides that where a gift or inheritance is taken by virtue of or in consequence of an order (such as a financial compensation order) by a divorced spouse, then it shall be exempt for the purposes of the Capital Acquisitions Tax Act and shall not be taken into account in computing such tax where other gifts or inheritances are taken by the benefiting spouse. In other words, even though the persons who receives the proceeds of the policy is not a 'spouse' at the time, the spousal relief from capital aquisitions tax applies if the policy was affected or assigned in accordance with an order of the court.

There is no relief from income tax for the premiums paid on policies of life assurance.

9.8.6   Advising the client

Life assurance policies often represent a substantial or potentially substantial asset in many cases. Now that the court can compensate for loss of future benefits, practitioners will have to quantify this loss so that it can be taken into consideration. Practitioners will have to familiarise themselves with the different types of life assurance policies available. In relation to existing policies, the following information should be obtained from the client if he or she is the assured or from the legal advisors of the assured spouse:

(a) the type of policy, endowment, whole of life, etc;
(b) the sum assured;
(c) whether any beneficiary has been named on the policy;
(d) the premiums payable and whether they are paid to date;
(e) the term of the policy, ie the maturity date;
(f) a quotation giving the surrender value or market value;
(g) a quotation giving the projected sum payable on maturity;
(h) whether the policy has been assigned.

If the client is the insured, written authority should be obtained from him or her to enable this information to be furnished directly to you by the relevant assurance company.

In relation to new policies to be effected, the following information should be given to an insurance broker to obtain a quotation of the likely premiums. This information should be given in evidence at the hearing or produced to the court by affidavit:

(a) age of the spouse on whose life the policy is to be effected;
(b) age of the benefiting spouse;
(c) ages of the dependent children;
(d) amount of cover required;
(e) whether cover is required for a term of years or is to be whole of life.

Chapter 10

PENSIONS

10.1   INTRODUCTION

Today, a pension is regarded as an integral part of the total remuneration package of an employee, and consequently people are generally much more aware of the need to make provision for their retirement. Pensions come in a variety of forms and provide various benefits for the payee in retirement or for his dependants on death.

It is essential that on family breakdown any pension is properly taken account of in any financial settlement between the spouses. This chapter provides:

(a)   a brief outline of pensions legislation and the key features of the different types of scheme;
(b)   an explanation of the pensions issues which will commonly arise on separation and divorce;
(c)   an analysis of the remedies applicable to pensions provided by the Divorce Act and, in particular, the new pension adjustment order;
(d)   an explanation of the procedure involved; and
(e)   advice as to the implications for practitioners when advising their clients.

10.2   THE PENSIONS FRAMEWORK

10.2.1   Pensions Act 1990

The Pensions Act 1990 regulates occupational pension schemes and provides for equal treatment of men and women under such schemes. It also established the Pensions Board to supervise such schemes and it sets out the duties and responsibilities of pension scheme trustees. The Pensions Act 1990 also protect the rights of pension scheme members to ensure that schemes are properly administered.

10.2.2   The Pensions Board

The Pensions Board was established by the Minister for Social Welfare under the Pensions Act 1990. Its main functions as set out in its own promotional literature are:

'–   to monitor and supervise the operation of the Pensions Act and pension developments generally and if necessary to to enforce compliance with the Pension Act through the Courts;

– to issue guidelines on the duties and responsibilities of trustees of schemes and codes of practice on specific aspects of their responsibilities;
– to encourage the provision of appropriate training for trustees of schemes, and to advise the Minister on standards for trustees;
– to advise the Minister on the operation of the Pensions Act and on pensions matters generally.

The Pensions Board also wants to promote further development of pensions in Ireland through the provisions of policy guidance and advice aimed at encouraging the wider application of adequate, secure, flexible and cost-efficient pensions to meet the challenge in the coming decades of pension provision for an ageing population.'

Pension schemes must register with the Board, and most schemes must pay an annual fee to meet the Board's administrative costs. The Board can act on behalf of pension scheme members who are concerned about their scheme; it can investigate the operation of pension schemes and it has power to prosecute for breaches of the Pensions Act 1990.

The Pensions Board includes representatives of trade unions, employers, government, the pensions industry and various professional groups involved with occupational pension schemes.

10.2.3   Types of pension schemes

The purpose of pensions is to provide benefits on retirement and/or death for members and their dependents. The State has an interest in ensuring that the population as a whole has adequate pension cover particularly as people are living longer. This means that providing a reasonable standard of living for a lengthy retirement can be expensive.

Typical types of pension cover include:

(a)   a pension on retirement for the member;
(b)   a pension for a spouse on the death of the member;
(c)   the possibility of commuting part of the retirement pension to a tax free lump sum;
(d)   in the event of the death of the member while in service a lump sum payment to the member's estate or directly to the member's dependants.

Pension schemes can be divided into:

(a)   statutory pension schemes for public employees such as civil servants, teachers, gardai, etc;
(b)   occupational pension schemes established by private sector employers for their own employees;
(c)   retirement annuity contracts (often called 'personal pension plans') with insurance companies by which the self-employed and/or persons in non-pensionable employment save to provide their own pensions;

(d)   buy-out bonds with insurance companies, into which former members of
occupational schemes can transfer their entitlement.

These schemes can be further divided into defined benefit schemes and
defined contribution schemes.

Defined benefit scheme

In a defined benefit scheme, a specific level of retirement pension is promised
(usually related to salary at, and length of service up to, retirement age) and the
employer is committed to paying whatever contributions are needed to cover
the cost of the promised benefit. Most statutory schemes and many
occupational schemes with most major banks, insurance companies and larger
industrial companies are of this type.

Defined contribution scheme

In a defined contribution scheme, no specific level of benefit is promised.
Instead, stated contributions are paid in and these are accumulated until
retirement age and used to provide a pension and other benefits. The level of
pension will depend on the amount of contributions paid in and on the
investment return earned. A few statutory schemes, some occupational
schemes and all retirement annuity contracts and buy-out bonds operate on
this basis.

Social welfare pensions

When a person is aged over 65 and has retired from full-time work and can
satisfy the PRSI (pay related social insurance) contributions, he or she is
entitled to a State retirement pension from the Department of Social Welfare.
When a person is aged over 66 and can satisfy the PRSI contributions, he or she
is entitled to an old age contributory pension. Those persons who do not
qualify for an old age contributory pension may qualify for an old age
non-contributory pension which is means-tested. When a person who is in
receipt of a retirement benefit or old age contributory pension dies his or her
spouse may be entitled to a survivor's contributory pension. The Social Welfare
(No 2) Act 1995 ensures that divorced people will not be disadvantaged in
terms of their social welfare entitlements. Most defined benefit schemes take
into account the fact that a member will also be in receipt of a State pension and
the benefits payable will reflect this.

10.3   PENSIONS AND SEPARATION

The trustees of pension schemes are bound to administer the scheme by the
terms set out in the trust deed and rules. The trustees are not entitled, even at

the specific request of the member, to alter or vary the terms and make provision for a member or a dependant of that member which is outside the scope of the scheme. This has made it difficult for family law practitioners to adequately protect their clients' interests, particularly dependent spouses. The terms of certain schemes, especially statutory schemes for public servants, provide a survivors' pension and other benefits on the death of the member for the lawful spouse, in all cases, regardless of separation. The benefits arising under such schemes are unaffected by separation. In all such cases, any benefits arising under the scheme will go to the lawful spouse and not to any second partner. Other schemes give the trustees a measure of discretion in cases of separation, and the trustees must decide whether any death benefits will go to the separated spouse or the second partner, or be divided between them. The interpretation of the rules of a pension scheme was examined by Carroll J in the case of *Crowe Engineering Limited v Lynch and Others* [1992] 2 Fam LJ. Crowe Engineering Limited was trustee of a retirement and death benefit scheme. The husband was a member of the scheme and he died in service. At the time of his death, he was separated from his wife and was living with another woman.

It was held by Carroll J that on death:

(a) the benefits from the retirement and death benefit scheme did not form part of the deceased's estate;

(b) where trustees under such a scheme are given a discretion, the court will not interfere with their discretion and the court will not direct or give guidance to the trustees as to the way in which they should exercise their discretion;

(c) the wishes of the deceased as expressed in his will were not binding on the trustees;

(d) the spouse and children had no legal right to the benefit payable under the scheme other than to be considered as one of the class of persons with the possibility of benefiting;

(e) the trustees cannot exercise their discretion in advance by undertaking to dispose of the death benefit in a certain way. The trustees in this case have given an undertaking to a building society to discharge the balance due on a mortgage from the death benefit. The court held that this was ultra vires the exercise of their powers.

The FLA 1995, which came into operation on the 1 August 1996, allows the court on granting a decree of judicial separation to make pension adjustments orders similar to those that can be made by the court in the context of divorce (discussed below). In addition, s 13 of the FLA 1995 provides that the court may, on granting a decree of judicial separation, make an order directing the trustees of a scheme not to regard the separation of the spouses as a ground for disqualifying the other spouse for receipt of a benefit under the scheme a condition for the receipt of which is that the spouses should be residing together at the time when the benefit becomes payable.

10.4   PENSIONS AND DIVORCE

The following definitions are used in s 17 of the Divorce Act and practitioners should familiarise themselves with them to ensure a clear understanding of the section.

Term	Definition
Active member:	a member who is in reckonable service
Actuarial value:	the equivalent cash value of a benefit calculated by reference to appropriate financial assumptions and age and health
Approved arrangement:	an insurance contract into which entitlements under occupational pension schemes can be transferred and which is approved by the Revenue Commissioners
Contingent benefit:	is commonly known as a death-in-service benefit
Designated benefit:	the amount of the retirement benefit which is earmarked for payment to the applicant spouse
Member spouse:	a spouse who is a member of a scheme
Normal pensionable age:	the earliest age at which a member may retire, other than under any provision for early retirement on the grounds of ill health or otherwise
Pension scheme:	the definition of 'pension scheme' in the interpretation section of the Divorce Act is sufficiently broad to cover all schemes but does not cover pensions under the Social Welfare Code
Reckonable service:	the number of years service in relevant employment during membership of a scheme
Relevant employment:	employment or periods treated as employment, ie years of service which can be purchased back
Retirement benefit:	a retirement pension payable to a member on retirement or to a widow or widower on death of the member after retirement
Trustees:	the trustees of a scheme established by trust or, if not so established, a person who administers the scheme.

10.5   PENSION ADJUSTMENT ORDERS

10.5.1   The court's powers

The new legislation permits the court to adjust the pension entitlement to one or both spouses following a decree of divorce (Divorce Act, s 17). The consequent order is called a pension adjustment order.

The courts' powers differ in respect of retirement benefits and contingent benefits.

Retirement benefits

The court may make an order providing for the payment of part of the retirement benefit which has accrued for the member spouse under the scheme at the date of the divorce to either:

(a)   the other spouse (or if predeceased, their personal representative); or
(b)   a person on behalf of a dependent member of the family.

To calculate the part of the benefit 'earmarked' for payment to the spouse the order must specify two things:

(a)   the period of reckonable service to be taken into account; and
(b)   the percentage of the retirement benefit accrued to be paid to the spouse or other person.

The court will not take into account any part of the retirement benefit which accrues after the granting of the divorce decree even if the application for a pension order is made subsequent to the granting of the divorce decree. Therefore, although the court may make an order at the time of granting the decree of divorce or at any time thereafter during the lifetime of the member spouse, the court can only take into account the benefit that has accrued to the date of the divorce.

EXAMPLE 1

ORDER AFFECTING RETIREMENT BENEFIT IN A DEFINED BENEFIT SCHEME

Mr A becomes a member of the XYZ Ltd pension scheme on 1 March 1983. On 1 September 1988 he marries Mrs A, and on 1 September 1997 they are divorced.

The scheme is a defined benefit scheme under which Mr A will become entitled to a retirement pension of one-sixtieth of his final salary for every year of scheme membership, and a death-in-retirement survivor's pension of half that amount. At the time of the divorce, Mr A has been a member for fourteen years and six months, so his accrued benefit is a retirement pension of fourteen and a half sixtieths of his final salary, and a survivor's pension of seven and a quarter sixtieths.

In making a pension adjustment order, the court decides that the period of reckonable service to be taken into account is the period of the marriage, which is 1 September 1988 to 1 September 1997, or nine years. (Note that the period need not be the period of the marriage. The court might, in a suitable case, think it appropriate to specify a period beginning before the date of the marriage, if the spouses cohabited before marrying, or ending before the date of the divorce, if the spouses have been separated and living independently for some years. However, the period must end no later than the date of the divorce.)

In this case, the pension accruing during the designated period is 9/60 of Mr A's final salary. The court may also decide that 50% of this benefit is to be 'earmarked' in favour of Mrs A. Consequently, the designated benefit is a pension of four and a half sixtieths of Mr A's final salary, and two and a quarter sixtieths of the survivor's death-in-retirement pension. When Mr A retires, a benefit of four and a half sixtieths of his final salary will be paid to Mrs A. If, after retirement, Mr A dies before Mrs A, she will also receive a survivor's pension of two and a quarter sixtieths of Mr A's final salary.

It should be noted that, at the time of the divorce, it is not known what Mr A's final salary will be. Consequently, the exact annual amount of the earmarked pension will be not known until it comes into payment. The spouses may find this unsatisfactory but, given the design of the scheme, it is inevitable. It should be noted that although the court may tend to specify a percentage of 50% in favour of an applicant spouse the court could specify a higher percentage in circumstances where it felt the member spouse will have sufficient years' active service in the future to make up any loss suffered.

EXAMPLE 2

ORDER AFFECTING RETIREMENT BENEFIT IN A DEFINED CONTRIBUTION SCHEME

Consider the same facts, but in this case Mr A belongs to a defined contribution scheme under which 10% of his salary is paid every year into a pension account and accumulated to provide retirement benefits.

Again, the court orders that 50% of the retirement benefit accruing between 1 September 1988 and 1 September 1997 be earmarked for payment to Mrs A. When benefits come to be paid, the scheme trustees will calculate how much of the balance on Mr A's account is attributable to contributions paid during that period, and consequently how much of his benefits should be paid to Mrs A. The precise amount of pension will not be known until payment begins.

Contingent benefits

A common form of contingent benefit is a death-in-service lump sum of a specified sum or sum related to salary. If a member spouse dies while in employment, a lump sum becomes payable and the court now has power to order the whole or part of it to be paid to the other spouse and/or dependent members of the family.

The court can decide to pay the whole or a percentage part only of the contingent benefit to the spouse or other person or to both of them in such proportions as may be decided by the court.

The court can make a pension adjustment order in respect of both a retirement benefit and a contingent benefit. Practitioners must remember that the

application for an order in respect of a contingent benefit can be made only at
the time of granting the decree or up to one year after the divorce is granted.
The time-limit of a year is probably necessary as the insurability and state of
health of the member spouse may change.

EXAMPLE 3

ORDER AFFECTING CONTINGENT BENEFIT

> Apart from retirement benefits, Mr A's scheme also provides a death-in-service
> benefit or contingent benefit consisting of a lump sum of twice salary plus a
> survivor's pension of one-third of salary.
>
> The court orders that 100% of the death-in-service benefit be paid to Mrs A. If Mr
> A dies in service, therefore, she will receive the whole lump sum and the whole
> death-in-service pension.

Note that there is no period of reckonable service involved. Death-in-service
benefit is not treated as accruing over time, and the question of how much
accrued during the marriage is not relevant. The court specifies only the
percentage of the total benefit to be paid to the non-member spouse. If the
court specifies less than 100%, the rest of the benefit is paid in accordance with
the rules of the scheme.

10.5.2   Criteria for making orders

Although the court may make a pension adjustment order in addition to or in
substitution for orders for maintenance, both periodical and lump sum,
property adjustment and financial compensation, the court must examine in
the first instance the possibility of making proper provision for the applicant
spouse by the above-named reliefs before considering whether a pension
adjustment order is appropriate (Divorce Act, s 17(23)(b)). In other words, the
court should give priority to adjusting non-pension assets. The administration
of a pension adjustment order will be complex, and it may not be a suitable
remedy in every case. However, although a pension adjustment order may not
be possible in every case, the value of the pension rights will be important to
ensure that non-pension assets are equitably divided.

The provisions of the criteria set out in s 20 of the Divorce Act relevant to this
issue are:

(a)   Section 20(2)(d): 'the age of the spouses and the duration of the
      marriage'. If, for example, the spouses have been married for 25 years and
      the wife is aged 52 and has very little possibility of getting into pensionable
      employment, the court will be anxious to provide for her financial
      security.
(b)   Section 20(2)(f): 'the contributions that the spouses have made to the
      family'. If during the course of the marriage the husband and wife have
      agreed that provision be made for a pension, although this placed a

certain strain on the family budget, the acceptance of this modest lifestyle to achieve future security can be taken into account by the court.

(c) Section 20(2)(g): the effect on the earning capacity of the spouses of marital responsibilities assumed by, for example a wife, who may have given up her career to support her husband at home and care for the children. Even if the wife can go back to work, her earning capacity will probably be diminished and her ability to provide for her own retirement pension limited.

(d) Section 20(2)(k): the court shall have regard to the value to each spouse of any benefit (for example, a benefit under a pension scheme) which by reason of the granting of the divorce decree a spouse will be forfeit and/or lose the opportunity or possibility of acquiring.

10.5.3 Immediate commencement

If the member spouse is already in retirement when the pension adjustment order is made, the order commences immediately.

EXAMPLE 4

ORDER MADE WHEN MEMBER SPOUSE ALREADY RETIRED

Suppose Mr A joins the scheme in 1970, marries in 1980 and retired in 1995 on a final salary of £30,000. The scheme gives him a pension of one-sixtieth of final salary for every year of membership. As he has been 25 years a member, his annual pension is twenty-five sixtieths of £30,000, or £12,500.

In 2000, Mr A divorces, and a pension adjustment order is made. The designated period runs from 1980 to 2000, and the division of the benefit accruing in that period is 50%.

Because Mr A retired in 1995, benefit stopped accruing in that year. Consequently, the benefit accrued between 1980 and 2000 is only fifteen-sixtieths of £30,000, or £7,500. 50% of this, or £3,750, is earmarked for payment to Mrs A. Payment to her begins immediately from the date the pension adjustment order is made, but the order is not retrospective. The balance of Mr A's pension, £8,750, remains payable directly to him.

10.5.4 Earmarking

A pension adjustment order results in the 'earmarking' of a proportion of the member spouse's pension in favour of the non-member spouse. When the member spouse's pension falls due, the earmarked proportion is paid to the non-member spouse, and the balance to the member.

This may not happen until many years after the divorce, and in the meantime the non-member spouse needs to take care that the trustees of the scheme are aware of his or her address, so that when the time comes they can pay the earmarked benefit. Furthermore, as shown in the examples, the non-member spouse will not know the actual amount of the earmarked benefit until payment begins.

10.5.5   Pension splitting

Some non-member spouses may find these features unsatisfactory. There is an alternative procedure known as 'pension splitting' by which the earmarked proportion of the benefits can be valued, and the value (known as a 'transfer amount' s 17(4)) can be held separately for the non-member spouse either in the member spouse's scheme or (more usually) in some other scheme or arrangement. The transfer amount is then used to provide retirement benefits for the non-member spouse.

Application of the transfer amount
The non-member spouse may ask the trustees (providing the spouse furnishes the trustees with whatever information they may reasonably require) to apply the transfer amount in any one of the following three ways:

(a)   if the trustees and the spouse agree, by providing a benefit for the spouse in the scheme of the same actuarial value as the transfer amount;
(b)   by making a payment to another occupational pension scheme (for example, a scheme of which the spouse is already a member) provided the trustees of that scheme agree to accept the transfer amount;
(c)   by making a payment to an approved insurance policy, where it will be held to provide retirement benefits for the spouse. (Note that most such policies will involve charges and expenses which will be deducted from the transfer amount before providing retirement benefits).

Calculation of the transfer amount
In order to split the pension, a current value must be put on the earmarked proportion of the member's retirement benefit. This may not be unduly difficult in a defined contribution scheme. The contributions paid during the designated period are known, and it is a straightforward matter for the trustees to calculate the accumulated value at any time of those contributions. The transfer amount will be the accumulated value of the earmarked contributions.

It is not so easy, however, to place a value on the earmarked benefit in a defined benefit scheme. The member's retirement benefit will be based on the value of the final salary and this is not known until the member retires or resigns.

If the non-member spouse requests a transfer amount, the trustees will have to make an assumption about what the member's final salary would be. They will make the most conservative assumption, which is that the member's final salary will be the same as at the date of the transfer value (which will, in fact, be the case if the member resigns or retires at that time or shortly after). Consequently, the transfer value will not reflect any increase in the member's salary which might happen after the date of the transfer value. Guidelines are to issue from the Pensions Board to assist the calculation of transfer value amounts.

EXAMPLE 5

TRANSFER IN A DEFINED BENEFIT SCHEME

Mr A marries Mrs A in 1982 at the age of 23, and joins the XYZ Ltd pension scheme in 1984. In 2009, when Mr A is 50, Mr and Mrs A are divorced. A pension adjustment order is made. The relevant period is from 1982 to 2009, and the earmarking percentage is 50%.

The XYZ Ltd scheme is a defined benefit scheme providing a pension of one-sixtieth of final salary for each year of membership. Between 1982 and 2009, Mr A spent 25 years in the scheme, so his accrued benefit is twenty-five sixtieths of final salary, payable when he reaches age 65 (which will be in 2024). Twelve and a half sixtieths are earmarked in favour of Mrs A.

Assume that in 2009, immediately after the pension adjustment order is made, Mrs A seeks a transfer payment. It will be based on Mr A's salary at that time which is, £25,000. Twelve and a half sixtieths of £25,000 is £5,208.33, and the trustees will (with the help of the actuary) calculate the present value of an annual pension of £5,208.33 commencing in the year 2024.

It should be noted, however, that, in 2009, Mr A is aged only 50. He may continue to work for XYZ Ltd for another 15 years and, during that time, he can expect to receive salary increases and perhaps promotions. By the time he reaches age 65, his salary might have increased significantly. If Mr A's salary increases at 3% a year, by the time he retires it will be almost £40,000. If, instead of taking an immediate pension split, Mrs A takes no split or waits until just before Mr A's retirement, her benefits will be based on the higher salary, and she will receive an earmarked pension equal to twelve and a half sixtieths of £40,000, or £8,333.33, commencing in the year 2024, or a transfer value equivalent to this benefit.

Consequently, a spouse who takes a transfer value from a defined benefit scheme before the final salary is known may lose out significantly.

10.5.6 Compulsory splitting

When a pension adjustment order is made the benefiting spouse should decide whether and when to seek a transfer of the pension to another scheme as outlined above (s 17(5)).

If a spouse makes no application to split the pension, the trustees of the scheme may make this decision themselves at their own discretion and at their own instigation and determination. This applies to a defined contribution scheme only.

The trustees may transfer the transfer amount:

(a)   to another occupational pension scheme if the trustees of that scheme agree to accept the payment; or

(b)   make a payment to an approved arrangement, ie a buy-out bond.

This statutory right of trustees to compulsorily split the pension away from the main scheme is limited to defined contribution schemes. This is due to the fact that the value of entitlements under a defined contribution scheme are more readily calculable. As noted in EXAMPLE 5, under a defined benefit scheme, the transfer amount would generally reflect the benefits based on the member's current salary as against the final retirement benefit which will be based on the member's salary at retirement.

The purpose in having compulsory splitting is to allow trustees to smoothly administer their pension schemes and to allocate into a separate fund the appropriate share which the spouse has been held to be entitled by order of the court. The trustees must notify the benefiting spouse, or other person and also the registrar or clerk of the court when they decide to operate s 17(6) of the Divorce Act.

10.5.7   Cessation and Variation

Remarriage

The court cannot make any form of pension adjustment order if the applicant spouse has remarried (Divorce Act, s 17(23)(a)). If an order has been made in relation to a contingent benefit, it shall cease to have effect on the remarriage of the person in whose favour it was made insofar as it relates to that person (Divorce Act, s 17(19)). If an order has been made in relation to a retirement benefit, there is no automatic cessation of the order on remarriage although the member spouse could apply to the court pursuant to s 22 of the Divorce Act for the order to be varied or discharged altogether.

Death of the member spouse

Where a court has made an order in relation to a retirement benefit and the member spouse dies before payment has commenced, the trustees must within three months of the death make a payment of the transfer amount to the person in whose favour the order was made (Divorce Act, s 17(7)).

Death of the benefiting spouse

Where a court has made an order in relation to a retirement benefit and the benefiting spouse dies before the payment has commenced, the trustees shall within three months of the death of the spouse provide a payment of the transfer amount to the personal representatives of that spouse (Divorce Act, s 17(9)).

Where a court has made an order in relation to a contingent benefit and the benefiting spouse dies, the order shall cease to have effect (Divorce Act, s 17(19)).

Where as court has made an order in relation to a retirement benefit and the benefiting spouse dies after payment has commenced, the trustees shall within three months of the death of that spouse provide a payment to the personal representatives of that spouse of an amount equal to the actuarial value of the part of the designated benefit which would have been payable (but for the death of the spouse) during the lifetime of the member spouse (Divorce Act, s 17(10)).

Death of benefiting member of the family
Where a court has made an order in relation to a retirement benefit for the benefit of a dependent member of the family and that person dies before the payment of the designated benefit, then the order shall cease to have effect in so far as it relates to that person (Divorce Act, s 17(11)).

Spouse ceases to be a member of the scheme
Where a court has made an order in relation to a retirement benefit and the member spouse ceases to be a member of the scheme (otherwise than by death) the trustees at their determination may apply the transfer amount in any one of the following ways:

(a) if the trustees and the person in whose favour the pension adjustment order has been made agree, provide a benefit in the scheme of the same actuarial value as the transfer amount;
(b) make a payment to
  (i)   another occupational pension scheme if the trustees of that scheme agree to accept the payment, or make a payment to
  (ii) an approved arrangement, for example a buy-out bond (Divorce Act, s 17(8)).

It is likely that trustees will prefer the options referred to at (b) above. Keeping track of former employees and their pension entitlement is already problematic for pension administrators. Keeping track of ex-spouses of ex-employees will be even more difficult.

Variation
While s 22 of the Divorce Act allows a court to vary any ancillary orders made, s 17(26) specifically provides that an order can be made restricting to a specified extent or excluding the right to vary a pension adjustment order. If such a restriction is made, this will allow for certainty in the future. If acting for an applicant spouse, it will be essential that an order is sought excluding the

possibility of variation of any pension adjustment order made so that the applicant has the security of knowing that the order cannot be varied.

10.5.8   Obligations and duties of trustees

General

Trustees of an occupational pension scheme have duties under general trust law as well as under the Pensions Act 1990. Under trust law, the trustees must implement the terms of the trust to the letter, ensure that contributions are paid and when received are properly invested, pay to the beneficiaries their entitlements in accordance with the rules and keep proper records and books of account. Trustees must carry out their duties diligently and in good faith and seek proper professional advice when necessary.

The Pensions Act 1990 imposed further duties on the trustees of occupational pension schemes. All schemes must now register with the Pensions Board. The trustees must ensure that the contributions are received into the scheme and if not so received ascertain why not, and when received are not only properly invested but that a proper funding standard is maintained to meet the demands of the scheme. Most schemes appoint an investment manager and the trustees must exercise care in making such an appointment. Members are entitled to information on the scheme in general and their specific entitlements in particular. This is provided by s 54 of the Pensions Act 1990. Trustees will be advised to be impartial between the member and the spouse in giving relevant information and trustees cannot vary the terms of the scheme. However, where the trust deed gives the trustees discretion to act as they think appropriate in certain circumstances, they must exercise that discretion fairly in the light of all the facts and relevant information and, if necessary, they should seek advice. In the case of *Crowe Engineering Limited v Lynch and Others* [1992] 2 Fam LJ, the court held that where trustees are given discretion the court will not interfere with their discretion, unless it was made mala fide. Neither can the court direct or give guidance to the trustees as to the way in which they should execute their discretion. The trustees have a duty and they cannot abrogate their obligation. Trustees do not generally carry out the day-to-day administration of the scheme but delegate this to pension consultants. The trustees, however, remain primarily responsible so care must be taken in making such appointments.

Specific obligations imposed by the Divorce Act

The trustees must notify the registrar or clerk of the court and the other spouse within 12 months, if they have not already applied the transfer amount in accordance with s 17(5), (6), (7), (8), or (9) of the Divorce Act and where a member against whom a pension adjustment order ceases to be an active member of a pension scheme (Divorce Act, s 17(12)).

Where the trustees of the scheme compulsorily apply a transfer amount under s 17(5), (6) and (8), they must notify the benefiting spouse, or the other person concerned and the registrar or clerk of the relevant court. The trustees must also give particulars of the scheme or undertaking and particulars of the transfer amount to the benefiting spouse or other person.

Where an order has been made pursuant to s 17(2) or (3), the benefit or transfer amount shall be payable out of the resources of the scheme (Divorce Act, s 17(14)).

Once the trustees have made a payment or applied the transfer amount pursuant to s 17(5), (6), (7), (8), (9) or (10), they are discharged from any further obligation (Divorce Act, s 17(17)).

The trustees must be notified by the person who makes an application for a pension adjustment order or in respect of a variation of an existing order. A notice to trustees in the form required by the rules must be served on the trustees of the pension scheme. They must also be advised at a later stage of the date fixed for the hearing of the case. The trustees are entitled to make representations to the court and the court shall have regard to those representations before deciding whether to make a pension adjustment order (Divorce Act, s 17(18)). The Circuit Court Rules 1997 (SI No 84 of 1997), r 17 provides that trustees may make such representations by affidavit of representation to the filed and served on all parties.

Trustees must operate within the terms and rules of the scheme as set out in the trust deed. However, the court may give the trustees such directions as it considers appropriate including directions which, if complied with by the trustees, would be outside the rules of the scheme. If the trustees follow the directions of the court, they shall not be liable to any court or tribunal for loss or damage caused by non-compliance with the rules of the scheme (Divorce Act, s 17(20)).

The trustees of the scheme will receive a copy of the pension adjustment order from the registrar or clerk of the court (Divorce Act, s 17(21)).

10.5.9 Effect of order on member spouse

Where the court makes a pension adjustment order in relation to a retirement benefit, the amount of the retirement benefit payable to the member spouse shall be reduced by the amount of the designated benefit payable to the other spouse or other person pursuant to the order (Divorce Act, s 17(15)).

EXAMPLE 6

EFFECT OF PENSION ADJUSTMENT ORDER ON RETIREMENT BENEFIT

Consider the facts of Example 5 again. Assume that Mr A stays in the scheme until retiring at age 65. His total pension will then be forty-sixtieths of his final salary of £40,000, or £26,667.

However, twelve and a half sixtieths has been earmarked for payment to Mrs A, so the pension remaining payable to Mr A is only twenty seven and a half sixtieths of his salary, or £18,333.

> Note that it makes no difference whether Mrs A has waited for her earmarked benefit to come into payment or whether she has already split the pension and taken transfer amount. Once twelve and a half sixtieths of Mr A's salary is earmarked for Mrs A, the pension remaining payable to Mr A is reduced by twelve and a half sixtieths of his salary, and whether Mrs A waits and takes the benefit or takes a transfer amount will make no difference to Mr A.

Where a court makes an order in relation to a contingent benefit, the amount of the contingent benefit payable under the rules shall be reduced by an amount equal to the contingent benefit payable pursuant to the order. In addition, where a court makes an order in relation to a retirement benefit and the member spouse dies before payments have commenced, the amount of the contingent benefit payable in respect of the member spouse shall be reduced by the amount of the payment under s 17(7) (Divorce Act, s 17(16)).

EXAMPLE 7

EFFECT OF PENSION ADJUSTMENT ORDER ON CONTINGENT BENEFIT

> Suppose Mr A's scheme provides a death-in-service benefit of four times his salary and a pension adjustment order is made directing that 50% of any contingent benefit should be paid to Mrs A.

> Mr A dies at a time when his salary is £35,000. A death benefit of £140,000 will be payable, and £70,000 of it must go to Mrs A. The remaining £70,000 will be paid in accordance with the rules of the scheme (and, if Mr A has no other dependants, the rules of the scheme may well provide for it to go to Mrs A).

> Suppose, however, that the court has also made a pension adjustment order affecting the retirement benefit. When Mr A dies, then under s 17(7), a transfer amount must be paid in respect of the earmarked portion of the retirement benefit (see 10.5.7 above). Suppose that the transfer amount is £23,000.

> This amount may be deducted from the part of the contingent benefit which remains payable under the rules. Thus, the £35,000 which is not affected by the pension adjustment order may be reduced by £23,000, leaving only £12,000 to be paid under the rules.

Taxation

Payments made to a benefiting spouse will be paid net of tax (Divorce Act, s 31). As is the case with most pension payments, the administrator of the scheme will make any deductions that are necessary for income tax at the standard rate and pay the pension net of tax to the person entitled.

10.6   ADVISING THE CLIENT

10.6.1   Ascertaining information about the scheme

In order to advise clients, it will be necessary to have all relevant information on the pension scheme. Trustees of occupational pension schemes must give information on the scheme to scheme members and their spouses not only about their personal entitlement but also information about the scheme itself, how it was established, its rules, how it is run, and its financial position. Many pension schemes publish an explanatory booklet for their members which contains basic information about the scheme and how it operates. More detailed information must be made available if specifically requested (Pensions Act 1990, s 54). This section also includes a spouse of a member as a person who is entitled to general information on the scheme and a divorced spouse will also continue to be entitled to this information notwithstanding the divorce (Divorce Act, s 17(24)).

The following is a useful checklist that can be used to gather the necessary information.

(a)   a copy of the trust deed, the rules of the scheme and a copy of the last annual report. Explanatory booklets are often available to the members and are useful but should not be relied upon in place of originating documents;
(b)   the date on which the spouse joined the scheme;
(c)   whether the spouse transferred rights from another scheme into the scheme and/or whether the spouse is making additional voluntary contributions;
(d)   a copy of the last benefit statement for the spouse;
(e)   the current transfer value if the member were to leave service;
(f)   a statement quantifying the projected benefits on retirement and in particular:
    (i)   the lump sum payable in the event of death in service;
    (ii)   the pension payable to a spouse in the event of death of the member while in service or post retirement;
    (iii) the maximum lump sum which the member can commute and the impact of this on the retirement benefit;
    (iv)   the level of pension available to the spouse in the event that the member does not commute;
    (v)   the normal retirement date on which the figures are based and the possibility of the member taking early retirement.

As already stated, each member of a pension scheme and their spouse is entitled to certain information. When this information is obtained, expert assistance will be needed to establish the nature and value of the entitlements of the member spouse in the scheme.

Once an application has been made, an applicant spouse or applicant person (Divorce Act, s 17(25)) or the court may direct the trustees of a scheme to provide information within a specified period of time on the following:

(a)   a calculation of the value and the amount of the retirement benefit or contingent benefit concerned that is payable under the scheme and has accrued at the time of the making of that order; and

(b)   a calculation of the amount of the contingent benefit concerned that is
       payable under the scheme.

10.6.2   Ascertaining the value of entitlements

When this information is obtained, expert assistance will be needed to establish
the nature and value of the entitlements of the member spouse in the scheme.

All other assets of the applicant and member spouse must be valued and a
decision made as to whether it is more appropriate to seek an adjustment of
non-pension assets. If a decision is made to pursue the application for a pension
adjustment order, expert evidence will have to be presented to the court to
support the application.

10.6.3   Advising the applicant spouse

If it is considered appropriate to apply for a pension adjustment order, the civil
bill should clearly set out the relief being sought. The court will want to know
what the applicant hopes to achieve. Is the applicant looking for a pension
adjustment order in respect of a retirement benefit only or in respect of a
retirement benefit and/or in respect of a contingent benefit?

The applicant will have to have an expert witness to give evidence and
information to the court on the critical matters of:

(a)   reckonable service;
(b)   amount and value of the retirement benefit which has accrued;
(c)   the amount of the contingent benefit.

The expert should also try to assist the court in establishing the likely value of
the designated benefit to the applicant spouse if the court specifies various
periods of reckonable service and various percentage shares. The court will
need to know the age of the spouses, the length of the reckonable service, the
length of the marriage and the length of time the spouses lived together and
the ages of any dependent member of the family.

The practitioner will have to discuss with the client and the expert on how best
to present the application. It may be that an application will be made by a
spouse for a pension adjustment order in respect of a retirement benefit with a
further application being made for a pension adjustment order in respect of a
contingent benefit in respect of the dependent children of the family.
Practitioners are reminded that an application in respect of a contingent
benefit must be made within one year of the granting of the divorce decree.

If the court grants a pension adjustment order in respect of a retirement
benefit, the practitioner must ensure that an order under s 17(26) of the
Divorce Act is made excluding the possibility of variation at any time in the
future.

If a pension adjustment order is made the client will need the assistance of the expert to decide whether it is more appropriate for the designated benefit to remain within the scheme or whether the pension should be split and transferred away from the scheme and, if so, when would be the most appropriate time for this to be done.

10.6.4 Advising the member spouse

If acting for a member spouse who does not wish a pension adjustment order to be made against him or her, at the very least the value of the benefits being lost or forfeited by the applicant spouse will have to be quantified.

If the value of the benefits being lost is insignificant then the court may decline to make such a pension adjustment order and attempt to make appropriate provision from non-pension assets.

The court will want to know the age of the spouses, the length of reckonable service in the pension scheme, the age of the dependants of the family and the length of the marriage. The member spouse may have to offer other forms of security to the applicant spouse in lieu of a pension adjustment order. For example, if a husband member spouse does not wish to have his pension entitlements fettered in any way by a pension adjustment order, he may have to offer or consent to a financial compensation order being made against him instead. If acting for a member spouse, an application to block the possibility of variation at any time in the future should be opposed to allow the court vary the order if circumstances in the future warrant, for example, the marriage of the applicant spouse.

10.7 COSTS

10.7.1 Costs to the scheme

Direct

The direct costs to a pension scheme of dealing with a court application by a spouse for a pension adjustment order, and the costs of implementing the order if made and of complying with any directions of the court, will be borne by the member spouse or the applicant spouse or both as the court may determine (Divorce Act, s 17(22)(a)). In making this determination the court shall have regard, inter alia, to the representations made by the trustees (Circuit Court Rules 1997 (SI No 84 of 1997), r 35(6)).

If a party fails to pay the costs in accordance with an order of the court, the trustees may apply to the court for an order that the amount be deducted from any benefit payable from the scheme to that person (Divorce Act, s 17(22)(b)).

PRIOR TO MAKING AN ORDER

If the trustees are served with a notice in accordance with s 17(18) of the Divorce Act by the applicant spouse that they have applied for a pension adjustment order, at the very least the trustees will have to record that fact and open a file on the case. A decision will have to be made on whether representation should be made to the court. The trustees may notify their views in advance to the member spouse and the applicant spouse.

The court can on its own initiative direct the trustees to provide calculations which will help the court make a decision. These include:

(a)   a calculation of the value and amount of the retirement benefit that has accrued to the time; and

(b)   a calculation of the amount of a contingent benefit that is payable under the scheme.

The calculations will require a careful assessment of the figures following guidelines to be published by the Pensions Board and will require a considerable level of expertise.

Pension administrators may liaise with member spouses and their legal advisors to see if a form of consent order can be agreed in advance of a court hearing and, if so, on what terms.

AFTER AN ORDER IS MADE

Trustees of pension schemes will be notified by the registrar or clerk of the court if a pension adjustment order is made. No further action may be required until a member spouse retires or receives their pension. If a pension is already payable, immediate steps must be taken to divide the pension in accordance with the order of the court.

If a spouse obtains a pension adjustment order, the benefiting spouse will have a claim on the assets of the scheme in their own right and so there will be an additional set of records to be maintained.

The trustees may, in certain circumstances, have the spouse's benefit transferred out of the scheme altogether to another scheme or to a buy-out bond (Divorce Act, s 17(6) and (8)). This will eliminate the spouse from the administrative records and should reduce costs.

Indirect

There will, undoubtedly, be indirect administrative costs to pension schemes generally. At the very least, pension administrators will have to establish a system whereby the information which is required by members and their spouses in divorce situations is readily available on request. There will have to be a system for receiving notifications from applicant spouses that pension adjustment applications are being made to the court and a procedure for deciding whether representations to the court are necessary in the particular case. In addition, where orders are made, records must be kept of the non-member spouse's entitlement and procedures established to ensure that the order is observed.

10.7.2   Costs to the parties

Direct

Any costs incurred by the trustees of the pension scheme by being notified that a pension adjustment application has been made, and in making representations to the court or in complying with a pension adjustment order made by the court or in complying with a direction of the court, will be borne by the member spouse or by the applicant spouse in such proportion as the court may determine and if the court does not so determine shall be borne by the member and the applicant spouse equally.

If a person fails to pay the amount of costs ordered by the court, the trustees can apply to the court for a further order that the amount can be deducted by the trustees from any benefit payable to that person.

There will also be other costs to the spouses both to the member spouse and to the applicant spouse.

Costs to the applicant spouse

PRIOR TO THE APPLICATION
The applicant spouse will need expert advice. The first step will be to obtain all relevant information and establish the nature and value of the pension entitlements of the member spouse. As the issue of pensions must be considered in the context of total family assets, a precise value of the pension benefits will have to be carried out by an actuary and their advice obtained on whether to seek a pension adjustment order at all or whether a distribution of other available assets is preferable in the circumstances of each case.

If the applicant spouse decides to proceed with an application for a pension adjustment order, the pension expert or actuary may have to attend court to give evidence to the court, support the application and assist the court in making the most appropriate order. The costs of this expert will form part of the costs of the action but will have to be paid for by the applicant at first instance.

AFTER THE ORDER IS MADE
If a pension adjustment order is made in favour of the applicant spouse, he or she will then need assistance to help decide whether to leave the benefit within the scheme or whether to seek to have the transfer amount transferred to another scheme or arrangement and, if so, to which one to achieve the best possible result. The cost of such advice will have to be paid for by the applicant spouse.

Costs to the member spouse

The costs to the member spouse may be less onerous than for the applicant spouse. The information on the pension scheme should be readily available to the member spouse. However, the member spouse cannot expect the pension administrator to assist and guide them in deciding how best to deal with an application for a pension adjustment order without the necessity of obtaining independent actuarial advice. The trustees will comply with their statutory obligations in relation to providing information under the Pensions Act 1990 but they will be advised to be impartial between the member and their spouse and to provide information, not advice.

Chapter 11

FOREIGN DIVORCES

11.1 INTRODUCTION

Since the passing of the Family Law (Divorce) Act 1996, the relevance of divorce decrees obtained in other jurisdictions requires detailed consideration.

It is interesting that a relatively high proportion of separated persons in Ireland have obtained foreign divorce decrees. According to the 1991 census, 8.9 per cent of all separated women in 1991 and 14.5 per cent of all separated men in 1991 were divorced abroad.

Spouses who have obtained such foreign divorce decrees are often confused as to their legal status, and practitioners are now sometimes asked to advise such persons on a number of issues such as:

(a) If a spouse has obtained a foreign divorce decree which is recognised in the Republic of Ireland, can that person also obtain a divorce decree in Ireland pursuant to the Divorce Act?
(b) If a spouse obtained a foreign divorce decree which is *not* recognised in the Republic of Ireland, may that person apply for a divorce decree in Ireland pursuant to the provisions of the Divorce Act?
(c) If a spouse is in a position to obtain a foreign divorce decree which would be recognised in Ireland and also a decree of divorce in Ireland, what criteria should be used to decide where the application should be brought?
(d) If a spouse is unsure as to whether or not his or her foreign decree of divorce is recognised in Ireland, what steps can be taken to clarify the position?

Such questions assume particular importance in relation to issues such as Succession Act rights, financial support, income tax and social welfare payments. Discussions on the recognition of foreign divorces revolve to a large degree around the question of domicile. This concept is discussed in detail later.

11.2 CONSTITUTIONAL POSITION

Article 41.3.3. of the 1937 Constitution states as follows:

'No person whose marriage has been dissolved under the civil law of any other

> State but is a subsisting valid marriage under the law for the time being in force within the jurisdiction of the Government and Parliament established by this Constitution shall be capable of contracting a valid marriage within that jurisdiction during the lifetime of the other party to the marriage so dissolved.'

This Article was not affected in any way by the provisions of the 15th Amendment of the Constitution Act 1995.

The wording of Article 41.3.3 of the Constitution enabled the Oireachtas to legislate for the recognition of such foreign divorce decrees. The relevant part of Article 41.3.3 which would suggest such an interpretation is the reference to the 'law for the time being in force within the jurisdiction of the Government and Parliament . . .'. This gives 'a National Parliament jurisdiction to decide by legislation that Decrees of dissolution made by the Courts of other States are to be recognised by our Courts' (Kenny J, *Bank of Ireland v Caffin*, 1971 IR 123). The Supreme Court in the case of *Gaffney v Gaffney*, 1975 IR 133 agreed with Kenny J's interpretation of this Article. Such legislation was enacted in July 1986 by the passing of the Domicile and Recognition of Foreign Divorces Act 1986 which came into operation on 2 October 1986.

11.3 PRE-1937 POSITION

Before 1937, if a foreign divorce decree were to be recognised and considered valid in Ireland, it was necessary for both the husband and the wife to have been domiciled in the country which granted the divorce.

The definition of 'domicile' is of fundamental importance in this area. It does not simply mean that both spouses were *resident* in a particular jurisdiction at the time of the application for the divorce, but is far more complex. This concept is discussed in some detail below.

11.4 THE DOMICILE AND RECOGNITION OF FOREIGN DIVORCES ACT 1986

The requirement that both spouses had to be domiciled in the jurisdiction which granted the decree of divorce in order to ensure that the decree was recognised by the Irish courts continued until 1986.

The situation changed fundamentally in 1986 and s 5(1) of the 1986 Act provided that:

> 'for the rule of law that a divorce is recognised if granted in a country where *both* spouses are domiciled, there is hereby substituted a rule that a divorce shall be recognised if granted in the country where *either* spouse is domiciled.'

In considering whether or not a foreign divorce decree is valid and would be recognised under Irish law, the courts are not concerned about the grounds for the granting of such decree. The Irish courts do not feel it appropriate to comment upon whether or not the grounds for the granting of a decree in another jurisdiction are reasonable or otherwise. The Irish court is concerned to ensure that the relevant foreign court had jurisdiction to grant the divorce in the first place. The courts in Ireland will hold that a foreign court had jurisdiction *only* if one of the spouses were domiciled in that jurisdiction at the time of the issuing of divorce proceedings.

11.5   PLACE OF MARRIAGE

The place were the marriage ceremony took place is largely irrelevant. It is sometimes thought by spouses that because, for example, they went on holiday to England, and married each other there, that they are entitled to obtain an English decree of divorce which would be recognised in Ireland, despite the fact they have never even resided in England. Such a view is incorrect. The place of marriage may be of some evidential relevance in claiming domicile in a particular jurisdiction, but even then it is only one of many factors to be considered.

11.6   DOMICILE OF ORIGIN

Every person acquires at birth a 'domicile of origin'. The country of birth is sometimes not the deciding factor. What is important is the domicile of the parent or parents as the case may be. A child born within a marriage takes the domicile of his or her father. A child born outside of marriage takes the mother's domicile. A child's domicile can change during his or her minority along with changes in the relevant parent's domicile. A child only has a dependent domicile until he or she attains the age of 18 years.

11.7   DOMICILE OF CHOICE

Despite the fact that an individual obtains his or her domicile at birth, it is possible to change this domicile by way of choice. In order to change a domicile of origin, a person must actually reside in another jurisdiction and have a firm *intention to reside there permanently*. For a divorce decree to be granted in such a jurisdiction and to be recognised in Ireland, one of the spouses must be domiciled in that jurisdiction 'at the time of the institution of the proceedings for Divorce' (s 5(7) of the 1986 Act).

The burden of proof is very heavy in such situations and it is often very difficult to ascertain the real 'intention' of a spouse or spouses when they are residing away from their domicile of origin. The test is an extremely subjective one.

It is possible for an individual to acquire a number of domiciles of choice during his or her lifetime. A person can intend to reside permanently in a particular country but because of a change in circumstances in the future move to another jurisdiction with the intention of remaining in *that* jurisdiction for the rest of his or her life. In some instances, the cessation of a particular domicile of choice will lead to the old domicile of origin reviving itself.

11.7.1 The case of *M(C) v M(T)*, 1988 ILRM 456

It is worthwhile considering this case in some detail in order to understand the concept of 'Domicile'.

Facts

In this case, the plaintiff wife and defendant husband were both born in England and had an English domicile of origin. They married in London in September of 1974 and had two children. The husband was a leading songwriter and record producer and worked to a large degree both in London and Los Angeles.

The couple lived in London for approximately one year after the marriage but the husband then became concerned about the very large tax payments which he was making. He took advice from specialists and was advised to take up residence outside of the UK for at least one year in order to reduce his tax bill. Ultimately, the couple moved to Ireland in order to minimise their tax liability and take advantage of the special tax concessions available to artists in Ireland at that time. The couple moved to Ireland in early 1979. They purchased and renovated a substantial property in Kinsale, Co Cork and lived as a family continuously until the marriage broke down in August 1985.

Once the couple had split up the husband moved back to England and the wife and children continued living in Ireland. The husband felt that the tax regime in England had improved substantially and that he could afford to reside there. The husband gave evidence that he intended to purchase a property in England and remain there permanently. While living in England the husband initiated divorce proceedings on 7 July 1986 and obtained a divorce decree on 3 March 1987. The wife did not file her answer within the appropriate time and was refused an extension of time to do so on application to the court. In June 1986, the wife had issued separate proceedings in Ireland for a maintenance order for herself and the two children, interim maintenance and an order granting a declaration as to the wife's legal and equitable interest in the husband's songwriting/music business. The wife also looked for a declaration that she was solely entitled to certain properties. Her case came on for hearing in the High Court on 15 February 1988.

If the English divorce decree were considered to be valid pursuant to the provisions of the 1986 Act then the wife could bring none of her applications to court in the usual way as she was no longer 'a spouse'. If, however, the divorce decree was not recognised in Ireland then the applicant wife was still a spouse and entitled to bring any claims for reliefs which were available under the Family Law legislation in existence at that time.

Although this case was decided prior to the coming into operation of the 1986 Act, the meaning of 'domicile' was discussed at some length by Barr J in his judgment.

Barr J stated that the 'Domicile of Origin of a person continues until it is proved to have been intentionally and voluntarily abandoned and supplanted by another'. He further stated that he 'was satisfied that the husband was motivated primarily by financial considerations in deciding to come to Ireland' in the first place. Such a move, according to Barr J, did not 'establish per se an intention on his part to make his permanent home in Ireland and to abandon his domicile of origin'. He pointed to the distinction between setting up home for an *indefinite* period in a particular place and setting up a *permanent* home in such a place. Barr J also felt that the main reason why the husband remained in Ireland was the financial advantages available to the family. Barr J was satisfied 'that the husband never had an intention to abandon his domicile of origin or to establish a permanent home in this jurisdiction ...'.

Although the husband had made a number of declarations in documents including his will that he was domiciled in Ireland, these were not considered of relevance by the court in reaching its judgment.

The divorce decree was therefore recognised in Ireland as the husband's domicile of origin (England) still existed and, at that time, it was felt that a wife took her husband's domicile. The wife therefore had no right to bring any applications to court pursuant to Irish Family Law legislation which granted remedies to spouses.

11.7.2 The case of *K(A) v K(J)*, Circuit Court, 1996 1 Fam LJ 22

This case contains a detailed discussion of the area of domicile which is of further help in understanding the concept.

Facts

The parties were married in 1974 and had five children, three of whom were dependent. Following physical and mental ill-treatment, the wife left the family home and went to England with the children in September 1992. While in England she petitioned for divorce and ultimately obtained a decree absolute. In that petition, she claimed to be domiciled in England in order to satisfy the jurisdictional requirements of the courts. In October 1994, she returned to Ireland and applied to the court to have the husband barred from the family home. At that time, a barring order could only be obtained against a spouse and the husband submitted that his wife had obtained a decree of divorce in England which was recognised in Ireland pursuant to the 1986 Act and that therefore she could not apply for a barring order against him.

The Circuit Court considered the preliminary issue in June 1995 and McGuinness J made an order which found as follows:

(1)   The burden of proof in establishing the acquisition of the domicile of choice is on the person seeking to establish it.
(2)   The statements by a party as to their domicile are not conclusive and must be approached with caution.
(3)   The wife had *not* abandoned her Irish domicile of origin and acquired a domicile of her choice in England.
(4)   The foreign decree of divorce does not fall within the rules for recognition laid down in the Domicile and Recognition of Foreign Divorces Act 1986 and it is therefore of no effect in the jurisdiction of the Irish courts.

Therefore, since the wife was still 'a spouse', she was entitled to apply for a barring order. (Since the passing of the Domestic Violence Act 1996, it is open to a person to apply for a barring order against a partner to whom he or she is not married.)

In her judgment, McGuinness J referred to a number of other discussions on the issue of Domicile and, in particular, to the comments of Dicey and Morris (*Conflict of Laws*, 12th edn, Sweet & Maxwell, p 128) who stated:

> 'a person who intends to spend the rest of his life in another country clearly has the necessary intention, even though he does not consider his determination to be irrevocable. It is, however, rare for the *animus manendi* to exist in this positive form; more frequently a person simply resides in a country without any intention of leaving it and such a state of mind may suffice for the acquisition of a domicile of choice. The fact that a person contemplates that he might move is not decisive; thus a person who intends to reside in a country indefinitely may be domiciled there although he envisages the possibility of returning one day to his native country. If he has in mind the possibility of such a return should a particular contingency occur, the possibility will be ignored if the contingency is vague and indefinite, for example making a fortune or suffering some ill-defined deterioration in health; but if it is a clearly foreseen and reasonably anticipated contingency, for example the termination of employment, succession to entailed property, a change in the relative levels of taxation as between two countries, or the death of one's spouse, it may prevent the acquisition of a domicile of choice. If a person intends to reside in a country for a fixed period only he lacks the *animus manendi* however long that period may be. The same is true where a person intends to reside in a country for an indefinite time but clearly intends to leave the country at some time.'

McGuinness J then went on to discuss the issue of domicile of choice. She referred to the comments of Professor William Binchy in his book *The Irish Conflicts of Law* (Butterworths, p 43) where he stated:

> 'two elements must be established in order to acquire a domicile of choice. These are *residence* and *intention*. It must be proved that the person in question resided in a certain country with the intention of remaining there permanently or indefinitely ... In many decisions the words "permanent" and "indefinite" are used interchangeably ... Every case must depend on its own special facts.'

McGuinness J referred to the comments of Lord Westbury in *Udny v Udny*, 1869 LR 1 ST and DIV 441, 458 where he stated:

> 'The law derives from the fact of a man fixing voluntarily his sole or chief residence in a particular place, with an intention of continuing to reside there for an unlimited time. This is a description of the circumstances which create or constitute domicile and not a definition of the term. There must be residence, freely chosen and not prescribed or dictated by any external necessity such as the duties of office, the demands of creditors, or the relief from illness ...'

The court then went on to consider the issue of the onus of proof. McGuinness J referred to the decision in *Winans v Attorney-General*, 1904 AC 287, where it is stated in the headnote that:

> 'the onus of proving that a domicile has been chosen in substitution for the domicile of origin lies upon those who assert that the domicile of origin has been lost. The domicile of origin continues unless the fixed and settled intention of abandoning the first domicile and acquiring another as the sole domicile is clearly shown.'

McGuinness J stressed the 'strength and tenacity of the domicile of origin as opposed to the domicile of choice'.

11.8   DEPENDENT DOMICILE OF MINOR

Section 4 of the Domicile and Recognition of Foreign Divorces Act 1986 deals with the issue of the dependent domicile of a minor. The domicile of a minor at any time when his father and mother are living apart shall be that of his mother if:

> '(a)   the minor then has his home with her and has no home with his father; *or*
> (b)   the minor has at any time had his domicile by virtue of paragraph (a) of this subsection and has not since had a home with his father' (s 4(1)(b)).

> 'The domicile of a minor if his mother is dead shall be that which she last had before she died if at her death the minor had his domicile by virtue of subsection 1 of this section and has not since had a home with his father' (s 4(2)).

11.9   DIFFERENT JURISDICTIONS

In a number of countries such as, for example, the United States, there may be two or more divorce systems applying in different States or territorial units. The provisions of the 1986 Act shall 'have effect as if each territorial unit were a separate country' (s 5(2)).

The Act went on to specifically refer to divorces granted in England and Wales, Scotland, Northern Ireland, the Isle of Man and the Channel Islands and stated that a divorce granted in any of those jurisdictions shall be recognised if either spouse is domiciled in any one of those jurisdictions (s 5(3)). An applicant spouse may therefore, for instance, be domiciled in the Isle of Man and obtain a divorce decree in Scotland which will be recognised in Ireland.

Section 5(4) of the 1986 Act then deals with the situation where both spouses are domiciled outside of the State and obtain a decree of divorce in a country where *neither* of them are domiciled. In such instances, the divorce will be recognised in Ireland: 'if it is recognised in the country or countries where the spouses are domiciled'.

11.10   TIME OF GRANTING DECREE

Section 5 of the 1986 Act: 'shall apply to a Divorce granted *after* the commencement of this Act' (s 5(5)).

Where proceedings were commenced before the passing of the Act but the decree was granted thereafter, then the Act will still apply.

It was understood in 1986 that this section indicated that for a divorce decree granted in a foreign jurisdiction prior to the coming into operation of the 1986 Act to be recognised in Ireland, *both* spouses had to be domiciled in the relevant jurisdiction at the date of the institution of the proceedings for divorce.

However, as a result of the judgment in the Supreme Court, *W v W* [1993] 3 Fam LJ 106, the situation is somewhat different. In this case the relevant divorce decree was obtained in England on 25 October 1972. The case largely revolved around the issue of 'dependent domicile' which will be discussed later.

In *W v W* the court held, inter alia, that the rule of dependent domicile did not survive the enactment of the Constitution (see below). The court then considered what effect the removal of that rule had on the common law rules with regard to the recognition of foreign divorces which applied prior to 2 October 1986 (the date of the coming into operation of the Domicile and Recognition of Foreign Divorces Act 1986).

Egan J summarised the view of the majority of the judges in this case by stating:

'in my view the appropriate basis of recognition in these circumstances for divorces obtained prior to the 1st of October 1986, which would be consistent both with the Constitution and with the general principles of international law, would be a recognition of divorce, if granted by the courts, of a country in which *either* of the parties to a marriage was domiciled at the time of the proceedings for divorce.'

Blayney J referred to various English judgments and held that the original common law rule was a judge-made rule and that therefore judges could change it if they so wished.

11.11   DEPENDENT DOMICILE OF WIFE

Prior to the coming into operation of the 1986 Act (2 October 1986), it was assumed that from a legal point of view a married woman automatically took her husband's domicile once she married him. If the husband's domicile changed then so did the wife's.

Before 1986, when the husband was domiciled abroad since the wife always took her husband's domicile, any possible requirement that *both* spouses needed to be domiciled in the jurisdiction where a divorce decree was granted was satisfied.

Egan J in the case of *W v W* (above) in discussing the concept of dependent domicile stated that there was: 'even an element of absurdity in the rule as its application could mean that a married woman could be held to be domiciled in a country where she had never set foot and never intended to visit' (p 115).

Section 1(1) of the 1986 Act purported to abolish the concept of 'dependent domicile'. This section stated:

'from the commencement of this Act the domicile of a married woman shall be an independent domicile and shall be determined by reference to the same factors as in the case of any other person capable of having an independent domicile, and, accordingly, the rule of law whereby upon marriage a woman acquires the domicile of her husband and is during the subsistence of the marriage incapable of having any other domicile is hereby abolished.'

Section 1(2) goes on to: state that:

'this section applies to the parties to every marriage irrespective of where and under what law the marriage takes place and irrespective of the domicile of the parties at the time of the marriage.'

Reference is made in s1(1) to: 'the *rule of law* whereby upon marriage a woman acquires the domicile of her husband'. It would now appear that, as a result of a number of court decisions, such a 'rule of law' has in fact not existed in this jurisdiction since the 1937 Constitution came into effect.

The issue was first mentioned by Walsh J, in the case of *Gaffney v Gaffney*, 1975 IR 133, where he stated at p 152 that: 'in a case where the wife has never physically left her domicile of origin while her deserting husband may have established a domicile in another jurisdiction' the concept of the wife automatically taking her husband's domicile may be challenged on the basis that it is unconstitutional.

This argument was strengthened by the comments of Barr J in the case of *M(C) v M(T)* (above), when he stated that it was his view that the concept of dependent domicile no longer existed and indicated that he: 'would have no hesitation whatever in holding that the old rule was a relic of matrimonial female bondage which was swept away by the principles of equality before the law and equal rights in marriage as between men and women which are enshrined in the Constitution – see, in particular, Article 40(1 and 3) and Article 41'.

The position in relation to the concept of dependent Domicile was clarified once and for all by the Supreme Court in *W v W* (1993) 3 Fam LJ 106. In this case, the wife had applied for a decree of judicial separation and ancillary orders pursuant to the 1989 Act and an issue arose as to the recognition of an English divorce decree obtained in 1972 and the subsequent validity of the marriage of the plaintiff and the defendant having regard to the common law rule of dependent domicile of a married woman. O'Hanlon J stated a case for the determination of the Supreme Court who held, inter alia (Egan and Blayney JJ; Finlay CJ and O'Flaherty J; Hederman J dissenting), that:

(1)   The dependent domicile rule, that the domicile of a married woman is the same as that of her husband is contrary to Article 40.1 of the Constitution and did not survive its enactment.

(2)   The recognition of foreign divorces is identified as part of our legal system by Article 41.3 of the Constitution and is regulated by it. In the absence of statutory regulation prior to 2 October 1986 the appropriate basis for recognition of foreign divorces obtained prior to that date would be to recognise the divorce whereby it was granted by a court in a country where *either* party to a marriage was domiciled at the date of the proceedings.

It is therefore now clear that the concept of 'dependent domicile' has not existed since 1937, although, mistakenly, it was assumed that it did. It is also important to note in this case that the Supreme Court, in effect, retrospectively validated certain foreign divorce decrees by stating that such divorce decrees would be recognised in this jurisdiction if one of the spouses was domiciled in the jurisdiction which granted the decree at the date of the institution of the proceedings. Prior to this judgment, it was felt that *both* spouses needed to be so domiciled.

The position now is that the only divorces where there is still a requirement that *both* spouses be domiciled in the relevant jurisdiction are those which were granted prior to 1937. It is unlikely that there will be many applications to court in the future concerning the validity of decrees granted so many years ago.

11.12 INVALID FOREIGN DIVORCES

It would appear that where a divorce decree has been granted in another jurisdiction and it is *not* recognised in Ireland as a result of the fact that neither of the spouses were domiciled in the jurisdiction which granted the decree at the time of the institution of the proceedings, then either spouse may apply for a divorce decree pursuant to the provisions of the Divorce Act. The fact that one of the spouses may have colluded in the obtaining of an invalid divorce decree cannot of itself prevent the court holding that such a decree is irrelevant and granting a divorce decree pursuant to the Divorce Act. A person cannot be estopped from claiming a decree of divorce is invalid merely because he or she had applied for an invalid decree in the first place (see *Gaffney v Gaffney* (above)).

However, the fact that one or both of the spouses may have been involved in executing documents which contained untruths could well be a factor which the court may take into account when making decisions relating to various ancillary matters such as maintenance, lump sum orders or property adjustment orders. The principle that an applicant 'must come to equity with clean hands' is of some relevance in this area. Such an issue has not yet arisen in the Irish courts but may very well be relevant in the future.

11.13 RELIEF ORDERS PURSUANT TO PART III OF FLA 1995

If a party to a marriage obtains a foreign divorce decree which is recognised in the jurisdiction of the Irish courts then it would appear that neither of the spouses can bring an application for a divorce decree under the Divorce Act. It is only possible for a spouse to obtain *one* valid and recognised decree of divorce and it is not open to a spouse to obtain a divorce decree in a number of jurisdictions.

However, the provisions of the FLA 1995 allow such an individual to make an application to the Irish courts for the necessary relief orders where a marriage has been dissolved, or a spouse is legally separated outside of the State.

Section 23 of the FLA 1995 deals with the various relief orders available which, with certain exceptions (largely relating to interim relief and preliminary orders), are similar to the ancillary orders available to an applicant for a decree of judicial separation pursuant to the provisions of both the 1989 Act and the 1995 Act.

One of the difficulties which arose for parties who had obtained a foreign divorce decree which was recognised in Ireland, was that neither of the ex-spouses could apply to the Irish courts for relief as such reliefs were, in general terms, only available to spouses.

For instance, an Italian couple may have married and divorced in Italy with the ex-wife subsequently moving to reside in Ireland. She may have built up substantial business or property interests and, prior to the passing of the FLA 1995, her ex-husband would have been unable to apply to the Irish court for a periodical payments order, a lump sum order or a property adjustment order. Because of the provisions contained in s 23 of the FLA 1995 such reliefs are now available.

It is important to note, however, that the court will not make a relief order in favour of an applicant who has remarried (FLA 1995, s 23(3)(2)(d)).

Before an application can be made to court for a relief order, the applicant must obtain the permission of the court to make the application in the first place. Such an application for permission may be made ex parte and 'the court shall not grant such leave (to bring the application) unless it considers that there is a substantial ground for so doing' and if one of the conditions referred to in s 27 is complied with (s 23(3)(a)).

The conditions referred to in s 27 is as follows:

(a)   either of the spouses concerned was domiciled in the State on the date of the application ... or was so domiciled on the date on which the divorce or the judicial separation concerned took effect in the country or jurisdiction in which it was obtained; or

(b)   either of the spouses was ordinarily resident in the State throughout the period of one year ending on either of the dates aforesaid; or

(c)   on the date of the institution of the proceedings aforesaid either or both of the spouses had a beneficial interest in land situated in the State.

It is only when the court is satisfied that it is appropriate in all the circumstances to make a relief order that it will do so (s 26). This section further sets out the matters to which the court shall have regard in deciding whether or not to make a relief order.

Such matters include the 'connection' of the spouses with the Irish State, the State which granted the decree of divorce or any other State; any orders of a financial nature already made on the granting of the decree of divorce; the extent to which the order has been complied with or is likely to be complied with; the entitlement of the applicant or a dependent member of a family to apply for financial relief in another jurisdiction; the availability in the State of any property in respect of which a relief order can be made; the extent to which the relief order is likely to be enforceable and the length of time which has elapsed since the date of the divorce or legal separation concerned (s 26(a) to (i)).

11.14   DECLARATIONS AS TO MARITAL STATUS

Partly because of the fact that the definition of domicile revolves around such a subjective test (ie an intention to reside permanently) and partly because there are an increasing number of couples living together who have been divorced and have gone through further ceremonies of marriage, there will often be great uncertainty as to whether or not a foreign divorce decree is recognised in Ireland. Where there is any doubt, the Registrar of Marriage is reluctant to marry a couple in such circumstances but will require a court declaration as to the marital status of one or both parties to the proposed marriage.

Such declarations as to marital status are provided for in Part IV of the FLA 1995.

Section 29 specifies the declarations in relation to a marriage which can be made by the court; these are as follows:

(a)   that the marriage was at its inception a valid marriage;
(b)   that the marriage subsisted on a date specified in the application;
(c)   that the marriage did not subsist on a date so specified, not being the date of the inception of the marriage;
(d)   that the validity of a divorce, annulment or legal separation obtained under the civil law of any other country or jurisdiction in respect of the marriage is entitled to recognition in the State;
(e)   that the validity of a divorce, annulment or legal separation so obtained in respect of the marriage is not entitled to recognition in the State.

It is important to note that such an application may be made by 'either of the spouses concerned' or 'by any other person who ... has a sufficient interest in the matter ...'. The latter type of applicant may include a personal representative of a deceased spouse or a guardian of a dependent member of the family.

It is also arguable that, in certain circumstances, the Revenue Commissioners could bring such an application as they may well be considered to be a 'person who has a sufficient interest in the matter', when raising income tax assessments against persons who base the validity of their marriage on the recognition of an earlier foreign divorce decree.

11.15   PROCEDURE

Pursuant to the Circuit Court Rules (SI No 84 of 1997), the application for a declaration of marital status shall be by way of the Family Law Civil Bill. The

Civil Bill shall set out the nature of the applicant's reason for seeking the declaration and give full details of the marriage and divorce (where appropriate) in respect of which the declaration is sought. Where possible, a certified copy of the marriage certificate should be attached to the Civil Bill.

The Family Law Civil Bill should also set out how the jurisdiction requirements of s 29(2) of the FLA 1995 are satisfied. These requirements are that either of the spouses should be domiciled in the State on the date of the application or had been ordinarily resident in the State throughout the period of one year ending on that date or have died before that date, and either:

(a)   was at the time of death domiciled in the State; or
(b)   had been ordinarily resident in the State throughout the period of one year ending on that date.

The summons should also provide particulars of any previous or pending proceedings in relation to any marriage concerned or to the matrimonial status of a party to any such marriage, the relief being sought and any other relevant facts. Subsequently, a defence must be filed and a notice of trial served. The courts will endeavour to give such applications priority.

One spouse cannot apply for such a declaration without notifying the other spouse concerned or the personal representative of such a spouse. The other spouse, or personal representative as the case may be, must be joined in the proceedings (s 29(3)). If the court feels it necessary, it can order that the Attorney-General should be added as a party to any such proceedings (s 29(4)). Once an application is made for a declaration under this section and one of the parties alleges that the marriage concerned is or was void or voidable and should be annulled, 'the court may treat the application ... as an application for a decree of nullity of marriage and may forthwith proceed to determine the matter accordingly and may postpone the determination of the application under subsection 1' (s 29(7)).

When making such declarations, the court will endeavour to ensure that its order does not conflict with 'a previous final judgment or decree of a court of competent jurisdiction of a country or jurisdiction other than the State ... unless the judgment or decree was obtained by fraud or collusion' (s 30(3)). This provision is an attempt to ensure that allegations will not be made against the Irish courts that they are interfering in orders made by courts in other jurisdictions without good reason.

11.16   NOTIFICATION TO REGISTRAR

'Notification of a declaration under section 29 (other than a declaration relating to a legal separation) shall be given by the Registrar of the Court to An

Tard Chlaraitheoir' (s 30(4)). The Tard Chlaraitheoir is the Chief Registrar of Births, Deaths and Marriages who will receive a notification of the Declaration and make any necessary amendment or alteration to the relevant marriage certificate or certificates.

11.17 COSTS

The only reference to the costs of making such an application is contained in s 30(2) and only then insofar as the costs of the Attorney-General are concerned. The court is empowered to make any order it sees fit for the payment of all or part of the Attorney-General's costs in the proceedings under this section by any of the other parties to the proceedings.

11.18 WHERE AND WHEN SHOULD DIVORCE APPLICATIONS BE MADE?

Difficulties arise for practitioners in situations where it is possible for a spouse to obtain a foreign divorce decree which would be recognised in Ireland and also a divorce decree in Ireland pursuant to the provisions of the Divorce Act. In making a decision as to where divorce proceedings should be issued, the question of location of any family assets is of the utmost importance. If, for instance, most of the family assets are in Ireland it makes sense to apply for a divorce decree in this jurisdiction. The opposite would be the case if most of the assets were held in a foreign jurisdiction. The ultimate decision would depend on the facts of each particular case.

Practitioners will have to take great care in advising their clients in such circumstances. Consideration will have to be given to the risks involved in instituting divorce proceedings in Ireland and to the benefits which are likely to accrue to an individual. The institution of divorce proceedings may of itself, as has already been discussed, lead to the respondent spouse deciding to reopen issues which had already been dealt with by way of deed of separation. The necessity to file and serve a detailed affidavit of means at the same time as issuing the Family Law Civil Bill may suggest to a respondent spouse that he or she should pursue a share of particular assets or income of which he or she was not aware until proceedings were issued.

Because the test of domicile, in relation to the recognition of foreign divorce decrees, is such a subjective one, it is often extremely difficult for practitioners to be certain as to the validity of a foreign divorce. Where an individual has a foreign divorce decree, a decision will have to be made as to whether a spouse should make an application for a declaration as to marital status pursuant to Part IV of the FLA 1995 or ignore the foreign divorce and simply apply for a decree of divorce pursuant to the Divorce Act. If a practitioner is advising a client who has amassed substantial assets since the granting of the foreign divorce, then it would be wise to advise the client to apply for a declaration as to the status of the divorce decree. If, however, the relevant spouse is in financial difficulties and is aware that the other party is wealthy, he or she may well be advised to institute proceedings for a divorce decree under the Divorce Act and apply for various ancillary orders of a financial nature.

In some cases, a spouse may be well advised to refrain from making any application at all under the Divorce Act until it has been operating for a number of years, and spouses may be more certain of the eventual outcome of such an application.

Chapter 12

DISCOVERY, FINANCIAL DISCLOSURE, AND ANTI-AVOIDANCE

12.1 FINANCIAL DISCLOSURE

In order to advise clients about the financial relief orders which are likely to be made on divorce, practitioners must be as familiar as possible with the assets and liabilities and income of their client and the other spouse.

Secton 38(6) of the Divorce Act mirrors s 38(7) of the FLA 1995 and specifically provides that in proceedings for any ancillary relief orders each spouse must give such particulars of his or her property and income as may reasonably be required for the purposes of the proceedings to:

(a) the other spouse;
(b) any dependent member of the family who is an applicant;
(c) a person acting on behalf of any dependent member of the family;
(d) and the dependent member of the family must give similar particulars to the spouses.

The important words in this section are 'as may reasonably be required'. What may be reasonable will differ from case to case. In practice, the amount of documentation varies from minimal information contained on a few pages of paper to mountains of documentation, much of which may be irrelevant and unnecessary.

The Divorce Act, by using the words 'as may reasonably be required,' tries to ensure that practitioners do not get carried away in their quest for information. There has from time to time been judicial criticism in England (eg in *Evans v Evans* [1990] 1 FLR 319; *P v P* [1989] 2 FLR 241) as to the amount of legal costs and other professional fees incurred in divorce proceedings in an attempt to ascertain the true value of the assets of the spouses. In some cases, the fees and costs have almost exceeded the value of the assets at issue between the parties. Practitioners, therefore, must attempt to do the utmost for their client to ascertain the true financial position of the other spouse, but advise the client on costs and expenses so that they can make an informed decision on what level of enquiry is necessary.

It would undoutedly have been useful to have a specific provision which clearly states that spouses must make financial disclosure. Instead, the wording of the provision is weak. Are not all particulars relevant, especially financial particulars, not only 'such particulars as may reasonably be required'?

Section 38(7) of the Divorce Act allows the court to give directions to a person to comply with s 38(6) in the event that a spouse or applicant fails or refuses to do so. If used broadly, this power could prove a valuable procedure by allowing the court to manage and direct the parties' attention to the information and disclosure which is critical. The earlier that all the financial information is available to the parties and their advisors, the better the chance of reaching agreement. The new Circuit Court Rules (SI No 84 of 1997) facilitate the furnishing of such information by directing that a detailed affidavit of means be filed and served at the same time as the issuing and serving of the Family Law Civil Bill.

12.2   USUAL DOCUMENTS REQUIRED

The extent of the particulars required will vary from case to case. The particulars must be supported by vouching documentation.

In a situation where, for example, the husband is in salaried employment, the following documents will be required as a minimum:

(a)   P60 for one, two or three years;
(b)   sequence of pay slips to show up-to-date income and any deductions at source;
(c)   bank or credit card statements for one, two or three years;
(d)   any deposit account with banks, building society, post office or credit union;
(e)   statement on the mortgage of the family home;
(f)   Statement of pension details;
(g)   details of life insurance policies.

In a situation, where for example, the husband is self-employed and/or has various businesses and/or investment properties the following documents will be required:

(a)   accounts of each of the business or companies for two to five years;
(b)   up-to-date valuation of investment properties;
(c)   details of all expenses, bonuses, dividends paid by the business or company;
(d)   income tax returns and documents referred to for two to five years;
(e)   bank or credit statements for two to five years;
(f)   any deposit account with banks, building society, post office or credit union both in and outside the State;
(g)   statement on the mortgage of the family home;
(h)   statement of pension details;
(i)   details of life insurance policies.

12.3   AFFIDAVIT OF MEANS

The Rules of the Circuit Court, SI No 159 of 1991 and SI No 84 of 1997, in relation to judicial separation and divorce proceedings where financial relief is sought require both spouses to file an affidavit of means setting out the following information at the time of application if applying for ancillary relief. Either party may request the other party to vouch for all or any of the items referred to in an affidavit of means within 14 days of the request. If a party fails to file an affidavit of means or give vouching documentation when requested, the court may make an order for discovery and/or such other order as may be necessary. The affidavit of means shall be in the form prescribed by the rules and shall set out in schedules the following information.

First Schedule—Assets:
- (a) all assets, whether held in the party's sole name or jointly with another or in the sole name of another and held on trust for the spouse;
- (b) the manner in which the assets are held;
- (c) whether they are subject to a mortgage or other charge or lien;
- (d) the names of any bank, building society or other financial institution in which any of the aforementioned assets are deposited or held;
- (e) details of any life assurance policy which exists.

Second Schedule—Income:
- (a) all income currently received and receivable from whatever source and the source of such income;
- (b) details of all deductions from such income, whether by way of PAYE, PRSI, social welfare or otherwise; and
- (c) such further and other details as are appropriate.

Third Schedule—Debts and liabilities: all debts and liabilities and the person(s) to whom such debts and/or liabilities are due.

Fourth Schedule—Personal expenditure: a list of the spouse's expenditure on such personal items as food, rent and/or mortgage, transport, medical, clothing, holiday, entertainment and such other items as are appropriate in the circumstances.

Fifth Schedule—Pensions: details of all pension information known to the deponent and relevant to the proceedings, the nature of the pension scheme, the benefits payable thereunder, normal pensionable age and period of reckonable service. Where the information has been obtained from the trustees of the pension scheme concerned under the Pensions Act 1990 such information should be exhibited and where such information has not been obtained, the deponent should depose to the reason(s) why such information has not been obtained.

In the case of *L(J) v L(J)* [1996] 1 Fam LJ at p 36, McGuinness J commented as follows:

'The affidavit of means, if properly set out in accordance with the rules, provides the court with a clear and comprehensive framework of financial information. At a later stage, additional financial detail can be provided through the process of discovery and the financial information contained, both in the affidavits of means and in the discovery can be tried and tested through oral evidence and cross-examination thus giving the court as clear and complete a picture as possible of the family finances. If, however, the financial framework of the affidavits is missing, the process of examination and cross-examination based on the discovery material can be both confusing and unproductive, as indeed was the position in this case.'

An affidavit of means must be sworn at the same time as issuing a Family Law Civil Bill for a divorce decree and must be served along with the Civil Bill and affidavit of welfare on the respondent spouse.

12.4 DISCOVERY

12.4.1 General

Discovery is a pre-hearing process whereby the parties to the case obtain a list of the relevant documents from the other side and are given copies of the documents so listed. The list is contained in an affidavit sworn on oath and known as an affidavit of discovery. The purpose of discovery is to ensure that all relevant information and documents, whether beneficial or detrimental to the parties' case are produced in advance of the hearing. This helps identify the critical issues of the case and in many cases assists resolution of some or all of the issues, because the parties and their legal advisors have a full and complete picture of the financial circumstances of their own client and of the other spouse.

12.4.2 Voluntary discovery

It is preferable that parties to proceedings agree to make voluntary discovery. Order 31, r 12(4) of the Rules of the Superior Court provides that a party to the case may request the other side to make voluntary discovery of all relevant documents and suggest a reasonable period of time to swear the approrpriate affidavits. If an agreement for voluntary discovery is made, it has the same effect as if it had been directed by order of the court. If a party refuses to agree to make discovery, or does not agree to make it on the terms sought, or fails to file the affidavit of disovery within the period specified, then an application for an order for discovery can be made to the court.

12.4.3 Application to the court

Order 31, r 21 of the Rules of the Superior Court provides that the application shall be made to the Master of the High Court; Order 29 of the Rules of the Circuit Court provides that the application is to be made to the circuit court. The application is made by notice of motion which does not need to be grounded on an affidavit. Many orders are made by consent, but where there is a dispute the court has discretion in deciding whether or not to make an order. The court may limit the date from which the documents need to be produced.

For example, a wife may seek discovery of all financial documents covering a period of five years while the husband may consent to discovery for a period of two years only. The court can decide on this issue and on the relevance of certain documents or categories of documents.

The court will decide on the issue of relevance of documents on the basis of:

(a)   their necessity for fairly disposing of the case; and
(b)   so as to save costs.

Having regard to the provision in s 37(6) of the Divorce Act that the parties must give 'such particulars' of his or her property and income as may 'reasonably be required for the purposes of proceedings', this may limit the scope of the documentation to be discovered.

The order of discovery will specify who is to swear the affidavit. In a divorce application, this will usually be each of the spouses. The order will also specify the period of time in which the affidavit is to be sworn. Usually a period of four, six or eight weeks is allowed depending on the scope of the order and the nature and extent of the assets.

12.4.4   Affidavit of discovery

The affidavit of discovery for High Court proceedings should be in the form of Form 10 contained in Appendix C of the Rules of the Superior Court and the affidavit of discovery for circuit court proceedings should be in the form attached to the schedule to the rules or such variations of that form as the circumstances of the case may necessitate.

Once the affidavits of discovery have been filed and exchanged, both parties and their legal advisors are entitled to inspect the discovery documents of the other. If the documents are not voluminous, the facility of copying all the relevant documents and furnishing them to the other side is usually adopted. Practitioners should take care in preparing affidavits of discovery and ensure that all relevant documents are listed and, for ease of reference, categories of documents should be grouped together. The term document used in the context of discovery not only means documents in the conventional sense but also photographs, tape-recordings and computer disks.

The affidavit must list not only the documents that are in the physical possession of the party swearing the affidavit but also those documents within the party's power to procure.

12.4.5   Application for further and better discovery

If a spouse is dissatisfied with the affidavit of discovery made by the other spouse, he or she may seek an order for further and better discovery. Such an order will not be made merely on the belief that documents have been omitted. There must be some reason for believing that the affidavit is incomplete. The process cannot simply be used as a 'fishing expedition'. There must be clear reasons why the further documentation is sought.

If the affidavit of discovery is correct at the date on which it is sworn, there is no continuing obligation on the party to make further discovery of documents which come into existence after the date of the swearing of the affidavit. If, however, a party traces or locates a document which should have been discovered if it had been in their possession at the date of swearing the affidavit, then they should file a supplemental affidavit listing that document.

12.4.6   Third party discovery

Sometimes it is necessary to obtain orders for third party discovery. A spouse may seek an order for discovery against a third party who is not a party to the proceedings if there are documents in that party's possession, custody or power of procurement and they are relevant to the issues arising between the spouses. Order 29 of the Rules of the Superior Court provides that the court may make an order for discovery against a party who is not a party to the action. The documents must be relevant to the issue. The onus is on the party applying for the third party discovery to show the relevance of the documents and the court had discretion whether to grant the order. Application for third party discovery is by notice of motion which must be served on the other party and the third party. The affidavit grounding the application must include an undertaking by the party seeking the order to indemnify the third party in respect of all costs reasonably incurred by the third party in answering the motion and complying with any order made. Such costs will form part of that party's costs if an order for costs is ultimately made against the other spouse at the hearing of the action. For example, if a wife makes an application for third party discovery against the company in which her husband is a shareholder and the company complies with the order of discovery so made, the wife must discharge the company's reasonable legal costs in meeting the case and complying with the order. However, the costs so paid by the wife will form part of the costs that she may claim against the husband if costs are awarded in her favour at the hearing of the case.

An application for third party discovery is common when a husband is not only employed by a company but is also a shareholder. He may be working with partners who are also shareholders of the company and who may be reluctant to reveal information. In such circumstances, it may be necessary to obtain a court order to force the production of certain documents. Before embarking on such a process, however, an applicant should be aware that there could be substantial additional legal costs involved. In some cases, the production of all relevant documentation could involve substantial photocopying and collating.

The costs involved, even in relation to the time expended by staff of the company in complying with the order, can be considerable. It is important to be as precise as possible about the documents being sought when making such an application.

12.4.7 Discovery of privileged documents

As will be seen from the form of affidavit of discovery, a party making discovery may object to the production of some of the documents listed in the affidavit on the basis of legal professional privilege. This extends to any letter or communication to or from a legal advisor.

This issue was examined by McGuinness J in the case of *L(T) v L(V)* [1995] 1 Fam LJ 7. Both husband and wife had filed affidavits of discovery. However, the applicant wife submitted that there were a number of items missing from the husband's discovery including, in particular, a blue book or diary which it was alleged contained financial information concerning his private medical practice. The pocket diaries were produced to the court. Most of the material in the diaries consisted of notes made at the suggestion of the respondent's solicitor with a view to instructing the solicitor and as such were covered by legal professional privilege. However, counsel for the wife submitted that the notes in the diary were not specifically documents of instruction to a solicitor and counsel and were thus not covered by professional legal privilege. In the alternative, it was argued that the documents contained matters relevant to the welfare of the children and that legal professional privilege should not be applied to them.

McGuiness J, with the consent of both parties, read the diaries. She concluded that the notes in the diaries fell into two categories. The first category consisted of some sparse notes made from time to time of what appeared to be fees received from private patients and the second category consisted of day-to-day notes concerning the parties and their children. The judge concluded that many solicitors and counsel who regularly practice in the field of family law often advise their clients to keep careful notes of current developments and happenings as they affect both the parties and the children. These notes are made for the specific purpose of instructing solicitors and counsel and assists the preparation for the hearing of the action. Having comprehensively reviewed many English and Irish authorities, particularly where discovery was ordered on the grounds of welfare of the children, McGuinness J concluded that the material contained in the diary was not of such a nature that the interests of the children required it to disclosed by way of discovery. Therefore she refused discovery in relation to the respondent's diary for the year 1994. In relation to the diary for 1993, since it contained references to fees received from private patients, the judge identified the pages on which this relevant information was contained and ordered that these pages be discovered.

12.4.8   Documents relevant to the welfare of children

Difficulties can sometimes arise where the interests of children are concerned. It is quite clear that all parties concerned in a matrimonial case have a duty to furnish and produce all documentation touching on the interests or welfare of the children. For example, a practitioner may be acting on behalf of a mother who is seeking an order for custody of her children in the course of divorce proceedings. The husband may be opposing this application strenuously and seeking custody himself. If, directly or indirectly, a report from a psychiatrist comes to light which states that the wife has dangerous psychotic tendencies which only manifest themselves on occasion, then that practitioner, despite the clients wishes, has a duty to reveal this report to the court. This example is rather extreme, but difficulties such as this do arise from time to time. Everyone must give priority to the interests of the children.

This issue was also discussed in the case of *L(T) v L(V)* [1995] 1 Fam LJ referred to above. The 1994 diary consisted of day-to-day notes concerning the parties and their children. These notes commenced after the issuing of the wife's proceedings in February 1994. It was accepted that these notes were made on the instructions of the respondent's solicitors and were prepared for the purpose of litigation. Thus, they would in the normal way be covered by legal professional privilege. However, McGuinness J then considered in some detail the question of whether or not documents, containing matters relevant to the welfare of children, should be disclosed to the court in breach of the normal legal professional privilege rule. The judge referred to the case of *S M and M M v G M and Others* [1985] 5 ILRM 186. The then President of the High Court, Finlay P, in that case, which involved the refusal of the Adoption Board and the Adoption Society to furnish certain documents to the applicants on the basis that they were privileged, stated:

> 'I have no doubt that the best interests of the child in regard to the determination of those proceedings when considered in the context of discovery, depends upon the discovery of such documents being made as would enable all the parties to those proceedings to present their case to the full. In detail, this means that the plaintiffs as prospective adoptive parents should be in a position to adduce the maximum amount of evidence establishing their suitability as custodians of the child and to defend themselves against any challenges or criticisms of that suitability and that the mother should have a like advantage and opportunity.'

Where the interests of a child were at issue, those interests were superior to the statutory privilege claimed by the Board. McGuinness J went on to consider a number of English decisions which clearly showed that legal professional privilege could be overridden in cases where the interests of the child required this. A number of these judgments referred to the furnishing of reports which had been obtained and which one or other of the parties wished to withhold as they were not particularly helpful to their case.

McGuinness J concluded that: 'in each case the desirability of a disclosure must, on the facts of the case, be weighted against the desirability of maintaining the privilege and the decision taken in light of the interests of the child concerned'. She accepted that the power to override the normal privilege in such cases should be exercised only rarely and only when the court is satisfied that it is necessary.

12.4.9 Inadmissible documents

Section 9 of the Divorce Act states that:

> 'an oral or written communication between either of the spouses concerned and a third party for the purposes of seeking assistance to effect a reconciliation or to reach agreement between them on some or all of the terms of a separation or a divorce (whether or not made in the presence or with the knowledge of the other spouse), and any record of such communication made or caused to be made by either of the spouses concerned or such a third party, shall not be admissible as evidence in any court.'

This section encourages both the husband and the wife to engage in marriage counselling, mediation, or discussions with their solicitor without fear that any third parties will be forced to disclose information or documents relating to their discussions. Any relevant documents may not be subpoenaed by any person.

12.5 RESPONSIBILITY OF THE PRACTITIONER

12.5.1 Obtaining the financial information

No practitioner can advise a client on the fairness or appropriateness of concluding a settlement without obtaining full financial disclosure. Neither can they properly present their client's application for ancillary relief to the court without such disclosure being made to them in advance of the hearing.

In many cases, the filing of the affidavit of means with the documents to vouch the information contained therein will be sufficient, but there will be many cases where further enquiry is essential. Some clients misinterpret the function of the practitioner who is seeking financial disclosure. They do not see the necessity of the process and only see it as a delaying tactic.

Some dependent spouses seem to be satisfied to reach agreement with the other spouse without financial disclosure and in some cases resent the warnings urged on them by their advisors. Caution should be exercised by practitioners in advising clients on the fairness of settlement terms agreed in cases where little or no disclosure had been made because of the client's unwillingness to so instruct, and, for their own protection, should express their concern in writing to the client.

However, a balance must be struck between making no enquiry at all and not knowing when sufficient information has been obtained.

In England, the courts have become alarmed at the high costs being incurred, especially by comparison to the value of the assets at issue. In the case of *Evans v Evans* [1990] 1 FLR 319, Booth J gave the following guidelines to practitioners, a summary of which are set out as follows:

(a)   affidavit evidence should be confined to relevant facts and should not be prolix or diffused;

(b)   enquiries should be made in one comprehensive questionnaire;

(c)   if possible, valuations should be carried out by jointly instructed valuers, failing that, valuers for both spouses should try to agree a valuation;

(d)   while a broad assessment of the value of a shareholding in a private company may be necessary, the expense of a precise valuation should be avoided when it is clear that the company will not be sold;

(e)   all professional witnesses should be careful not to be partisan;

(f)   care should be taken in deciding what evidence (other than professional evidence) should be adduced and emotive issues, which are not material should be avoided;

(g)   solicitors on both sides should try to agree what bundles of documents should be presented to the court;

(h)   a chronology of material facts should be agreed;

(i)   in substantial assets cases a pre-trial review should take place to explore the possibility of settlement or narrow the issues;

(j)   solicitors and counsel should advise their clients on the issue of costs;

(k)   the desirability of reaching settlement should always be borne in mind.

Most family practitioners already conduct their cases on this basis. However, there is a constant tension between pursuing matters energetically in the interests of the client and thereby involving them in legal costs, and making minimal enquiry and facing the possibility of an action for negligence. Practitioners also have an obligation to the court to make all relevant financial information available to it; otherwise the court cannot properly exercise its discretion.

12.5.2   Presentation of financial information

It is important for practitioners to present the information on the financial circumstances of their clients and the other party to the proceedings to the court in as clear, systematic and understandable a way as is possible.

In the case of *L(J) v L(J)* [1996] 1 Fam LJ at p 36, McGuinness J criticised the presentation of the financial disclosure to the court. She stated:

> 'Although the financial issues are of prime importance in this case the financial evidence before the court was of a most confusing and unsatisfactory nature. An order and cross-order for discovery were made, ... affidavits of discovery were sworn and documents exchanged. During the trial a great deal of time was spent in detailed cross-examination of both parties arising out of the discovery of

documents. Finally the entire documents were handed into court … However what was entirely lacking was a clear and systematic picture of the present financial position of each party's assets and liabilities resources and needs.'

The judge stressed that it should not be the business of the trial judge at the hearing to sift through large quantities of discovery documents to try to ascertain basic information which should have been set out in the affidavit of means.

12.5.3 Analysis of financial information

Having obtained financial information through the process of discovery the practitioner must analyse information and documents very carefully. In cases where the assets comprise more than the family home and bank or building society accounts, it may be necessary to instruct an accountant experienced in this area. The accountant can assist the following ways:

(a) examining the financial documents and presenting a report to the solicitor of the assets and income of the spouse in question;

(b) preparing a schedule of whatever further documents he or she may require to carry out a comprehensive investigation and a list of queries arising out of the documents already furnished;

(c) identifying assets which could be transferred from one spouse to the other without undue complication;

(d) giving overall taxation advice, and specifically on the tax implications of the orders likely to be made by the court or agreed by the parties;

(e) giving evidence to the court in support of the client's case and assisting the court in matters which are complex.

Other experts may also be required to analyse the information furnished. In the context of pension adjustment orders, the expertise of a pension consultant or actuary will be necessary and in the context of financial compensation orders the advice of an insurance broker should be obtained to ascertain if the existing policies are sufficient to provide security for the spouse and dependant or whether increased cover is necessary.

12.5.4 Independent enquiries

Apart from ensuring that full and proper discovery is made by the spouses to an action, practitioners should also carry out certain investigations themselves. A substantial amount of relevant information concerning the financial and property affairs of the spouses can be obtained by independent enquiry.

Searches can be carried out in the Land Registry and Registry of Deeds to ascertain who are the registered owners of any property and whether there are any judgments registered against the property.

Up-to-date valuations of all property should be obtained prior to any court hearings. If a value can be agreed with the other side, this is preferable, but, failing that an independent valuation should be carried out, not only of the family home, but of all other property and assets.

If spouses are jointly assessed for income tax, then both of them are entitled to obtain copies of all income tax returns together with copies of all supporting documentation which have been filed with the Revenue Commissioners. A spouse therefore may obtain copies of the income tax returns of the other spouse directly from the Revenue Commissioners. This may go some way towards clarifying the income position of the other spouse. The Revenue Commissioners have an obligation to treat both spouses equally insofar as the furnishing of information or documents is concerned.

12.5.5   Banker's Books Evidence Acts 1879 and 1959

It is open to either spouse to apply to the court for an order under the Banker's Book Evidence Acts 1879 and 1959. The making of such an order enables the applicant spouse or his or her legal representatives to actually go into a named bank or building society and examine the accounts which may be held by them in respect of the other spouse.

12.6   ANTI-AVOIDANCE PROVISIONS

12.6.1   Reviewable dispositions

Section 137 of the Divorce Act gives power to the court in relation to transactions intended to prevent or reduce relief. The provision is similar to that contained in s 29 of the Judicial Separation and Family Law Reform Act 1989 (now replaced by s 36 of the FLA 1995) although the format of the section is somewhat different.

References to 'defeating a claim for financial relief' are references to:

(a)   preventing relief being granted to the person concerned whether for the benefit of that person or a dependent member of the family;
(b)   limiting the relief granted; or
(c)   frustrating or impeding the enforcement of an order granting relief (Divorce Act, s 37(1)).

A reviewable disposition is defined as a disposition made by a spouse to any other person, but does not include a disposition made for valuable consideration (other than marriage) to a person who acts in good faith and without notice of intention to defeat a claim for relief.

Relief means any of the financial or material benefits which can be ordered by the court by way of maintenance, lump sum order, property adjustment order or residence in the family home, pension adjustment or financial compensation order or, indeed, any form of ancillary relief.

To ensure that a disposal is not being made with the purpose or effect of defeating a claim for financial relief, all statutory declarations given on the sale or mortgage of property and any other agreements made in respect of property (for example, sale of shares in a private company) include the declaration or warranty that the transaction is not intended to defeat a claim by a spouse.

After the institution of proceedings for divorce but, prior to the application being heard, if the court is satisfied that:

(a)   the other spouse or any other person proposes to make any disposition of or to transfer out of the jurisdiction or otherwise deal with any property, the court can make an order restraining that other spouse or other person from so doing or otherwise protecting the claim;

(b)   the other spouse or other person has made a reviewable disposition, the court can make an order setting aside that disposition, if to do so would allow the court grant relief or different relief than would otherwise be granted. In cases where relief has already been granted by the court, and a spouse had made a reviewable disposition, the court may make an order setting aside that disposition.

The powers of the court are also extended so that the court may make such directions as it considers necessary for the implementation of its orders, including a provision requiring the making of any payment or the disposal of any property (Divorce Act, s 37(3)).

The class of persons against whom an order can be made include not only the other spouse but any other person. If a person is taken to mean not only a natural person but an artificial person, then it could include a company. In the Interpretation Act 1937, the word 'person' is construed as importing a body corporate as well as an individual. This is an important extension of the relief. In many cases, a husband may own the vast majority of shares in a private company which in turn may own valuable assets. It would appear open to the court to make a restraining order against the company if it was transferring assets out of the jurisdiction or otherwise dealing with property. It could also make such an order if a property were held by a person in trust or as a nominee for a spouse.

The same rules as in the FLA 1995 apply in relation to intention. If the disposition has taken place less than three years before the date of the application, it will be presumed (unless the contrary is shown) that the other spouse or other person has disposed of the property with the intention of defeating the applicant's claim in relief. The court, however, must be satisfied that the disposition would have the consequence or did in fact have the consequence of defeating the applicant's claim for relief (Divorce Act, s 37(4)).

12.6.2   Advising the client

Practitioners are from time to time asked by clients how they can manage their affairs to minimise their exposure to ancillary relief orders being made against them. It is not uncommon for a spouse to seek advice on how they might 'rearrange' their financial affairs. Clients should be warned of the risk of an application for interlocutory restraining orders being made against them and the negative impact such an order could have on the final outcome of the case. Whilst there does not appear to be any reported judgments on the circumstances in which orders have been made under s 29 of the 1989 Act, in practice if a spouse has a real and genuine concern, which can be established, that the other spouse may be dealing in property at a time when the terms of separation or divorce are being negotiated or an application for judicial separation or divorce is anticipated or has been commenced and is waiting to come on for hearing, then the court will make restraining orders, even ex parte. If an application is made, the reality is that the burden of showing a compelling reason why the restraining order should not be made or if already made should not be continued is shifted to the spouse against whom the application is made.

It is prudent for practitioners when advising their clients of the necessity for making full and financial disclosure to advise them of the provisions of s 37 of the Divorce Act and the harmful consequences that could flow if a court was satisfied that they were deliberately dealing with their property or transferring it out of the jurisdiction with the intention of defeating a claim for relief.

In the case of *O'L v O'L* [1996] 2 Fam LJ at p 66, McGuinness J in an application by the wife for ancillary relief orders, was 'very much concerned about the vagueness of her (the wife's) financial evidence.' In the intervening period between the hearing of the case and final judgment being given, certain matters came to light which showed that the applicant wife had clearly failed to make proper discovery of all her financial assets and, in particular, of moneys lodged to a credit union account and other investment moneys. McGuinness J concluded her judgment as follows:

> 'with regard to cost I had intended to direct that the husband should pay a contribution towards the wife's costs. However given the discovery of the additional financial evidence after the date of trial and the subsequent general unreliability of the wife's financial evidence, I have decided to make no order as to the costs.'

Chapter 13

COURT RULES

13.1 JURISDICTION OF THE COURTS

The circuit court concurrently with the High Court has jurisdiction to hear and determine applications for divorce. At the time of publication, the High Court had not revised its rules to deal with divorce applications so it is presumed that the special summons procedure used for judicial separation will continue to apply. The circuit court is known as the Circuit Family Court and the majority of applications will be at this level. An applicant must make the application to the court of the circuit in which the applicant or the respondent resides or carries on any business, profession or occupation. An applicant cannot pick the circuit he or she feels is most convenient. Either the applicant or the respondent must live or work there. The Circuit Family Court has not generally in the past, in the context of judicial separation, heard applications where the rateable valuation of any land or property, the subject matter of the proceedings, exceeds £200. Section 38(2) of the Divorce Act allows the circuit court to hear such applications unless application is made by any person having an interest in the proceedings to have the case transferred to the High Court. Section 38(4) of the Divorce Act allows the circuit court to determine whether the rateable valuation would or would not exceed £200 in cases where the land has not been given a rateable valuation.

Section 39 gives jurisdiction to the court to grant a decree of divorce if, but only if, either:

(a) either of the spouses concerned was domiciled in the State at the date of the institution of the proceedings;
OR
(b) either of the spouses was ordinarily resident in the State throughout the period of one year ending on that date, ie the date of the institution of the proceedings.

It is only necessary for one spouse to satisfy the domicile or ordinary residence requirement and this does not have to be the applicant spouse. Thus the fact that a person may be ordinarily resident in Ireland for one year will allow their spouse to apply for a divorce in Ireland, if he or she wishes to do so.

13.2 FAMILY LAW CIVIL BILL

The Circuit Court Rules 1997 (SI No 84 of 1997), contain the rules for making applications to the Circuit Family Court for divorce. In addition, these rules relate to applications for judicial separation, decrees of nullity, declarations as to marital status, relief after foreign divorces and property determination applications. The rules came into operation on 27 February 1997. Applications are to be made by Family Law Civil Bill. Every Family Law Civil Bill must set out in numbered paragraphs the relief being sought and the grounds relied upon to support the application. The Civil Bill must contain the following information:

(i)   the date and place of marriage of the parties;

(ii)   the length of time the parties have lived apart, including the date upon which the parties commenced living apart and the addresses of both of the parties during that time where known;

(iii)   details of any previous matrimonial relief sought and/or obtained and details of any previous separation agreement entered into between the parties (where appropriate, a certified copy of any relevant court order and/or deed of separation/separation agreement should be annexed to the Civil Bill;

(iv)   the names and ages and dates of birth of any dependent children of the marriage;

(v)   details of the family home(s) and/or other residences of the parties including, if relevant, details of any former family home/residence to include details of the manner of occupation/ownership thereof;

(vi)   where reference is made in the Civil Bill to any immovable property, whether it is registered or unregistered land and a description of the land/premises so referred to;

(vii)   the basis of jurisdiction under the 1996 Act;

(viii) the occupation(s) of each party;

(ix)   the grounds relied upon for the relief sought;

(x)   each section of the 1996 Act under which relief is sought.

When the Family Law Civil Bill has been prepared and signed by the applicant or the solicitor for the applicant, the original is filed at the appropriate circuit court office and the County Registrar enters it and usually allocates the case a number. At the time of the issuing of the Civil Bill, the solicitor for the applicant must file the appropriate certificate under s 6 of the Divorce Act. In addition, at the time of the issuing of the Civil Bill, the applicant must file an affidavit of means if any financial relief is sought and an affidavit of welfare if there are dependent children.

13.3   AFFIDAVIT OF MEANS

If the Family Law Civil Bill for divorce contains an application for financial relief, the applicant and respondent must file affidavits of means. The affidavit of means must contain details of the parties' income, assets, debts, expenditure and other liabilities wherever situated and from whatever source and, to the best of the deponent's knowledge, information and belief, the income, assets, debts, expenditure and other liabilities wherever situate and from whatever source of any dependent member of the family. If a pension adjustment order is sought, the affidavit should insofar as possible state the nature of the pension scheme, the benefits payable thereunder, the normal pensionable age and the period of reckonable service of the member spouse. Although r 19 of the Circuit Court Rules deals only with the issue of pensions in the context of s 12 of the FLA 1995, it is presumed that similar information should be given when seeking a pension adjustment order in the context of divorce.

Is it necessary in every case for the parties to file affidavits of means? The rules state that it is only necessary to do so where financial relief is sought. Financial relief is not defined in the rules by reference to any particular section or sub-section of the Divorce Act. Is it appropriate to assume that any ancillary relief order sought pursuant to Part III of the Divorce Act is a financial relief order? If so, do spouses who have been separated for a very long time and who have no financial connection with each other and who have no children or no dependent children need to obtain nil orders, for example in respect of maintenance, or an order blocking the operation of s 18 allowing for provision to be made from the estate of the deceased spouse? The answers to these questions would appear to be yes. Do spouses who have signed a deed of separation some years previously need to have the terms of the deed in relation to custody, maintenance and property made orders of the court or is it sufficient to continue to rely on the contractual obligations of the spouses in the deed? It is submitted that it is preferable to have the arrangements made part and parcel of the divorce decree.

Undoubtably there will be cases where a dependent spouse will be encouraged to claim additional financial relief other than that which is provided in a deed of separation, if the affidavit of means filed by the other spouse discloses greater income and assets than the dependent spouse understood to be the position.

Practitioners will need guidance from the court on these practical issues. However, it should be understood that a financial package which a spouse found acceptable in the context of separation may not necessarily be acceptable in the context of divorce and it is appropriate for practitioners, particularly if they are representing a dependent spouse, to obtain full disclosure from the other spouse by affidavit of means.

13.4 AFFIDAVIT OF WELFARE

At the time of the issue of the Family Law Civil Bill for divorce, an applicant must file an affidavit of welfare if there are any dependent children. The affidavit of welfare must give details of the children born to the applicant and the respondent or adopted by them and details of other children of the family or to which either of the parties stand in loco parentis. Details must be furnished as to the address at which the children reside, the number of rooms, whether the house is rented or owned and, if so, the extent of the mortgage and what is proposed for the children's living arrangements in the context of divorce. The affidavit must also give details of the education and training of each of the children and if any of them have any special educational needs. The affidavit must give details of child care and what arrangements are made to look after the children on a day-to-day basis and give details of the work commitments of both parents. The affidavit must set out the arrangements for the maintenance and support of the children, the manner in which support is made and the extent of it. Details should also be given on what contact the children have with the other parent, the extent of the access and visiting arrangements and whether there are overnight stays and holidays. Details should also be given on the children's health and whether they suffer from any illness or disability and it should also give details of the health of the applicant and the respondent. If any of the children have been under the care of the Health Board or under the supervision of a social worker or probation officer, details must also be given.

The purpose of the affidavit of welfare is to ensure that both parties focus on the needs of the children and how best they can be met in the context of divorce. The affidavit also gives to the court the particular information it requires to ensure that the needs of the children are met.

13.5   SERVICE OF DOCUMENTS

Rule 8 provides that all Family Law Civil Bills must be served by registered post on the respondent at his or her last known address or alternatively may be served personally on the respondent by any person over the age of 18 years. At the time of service of the Family Law Civil Bill, the appropriate s 6 certificate should also be served in addition to the affidavit of means and the affidavit of welfare. If the respondent spouse lives outside Ireland, the usual application must be made for leave to issue and serve the Civil Bill out of the jurisdiction. If there is any difficulty with service in accordance with the rules, the County Registrar can make an order giving directions as to service of the Civil Bill. This power is contained in the Court and Court Officers Act 1995, Second Schedule.

13.6   APPEARANCE, DEFENCE AND COUNTERCLAIM

If a respondent, having been served with a Family Law Civil Bill and the other documents as required intends to contest the application or in any way participate in the proceedings, he or she shall enter an appearance. Such an appearance is generally entered by a solicitor acting on behalf of the respondent but it may be filed by the respondent personally. A respondent to an application to divorce may file a defence to the application if he or she disputes any claims being made by the applicant. In addition, the respondent may file a counterclaim. The counterclaim should set out in numbered paragraphs the matters which are required to be inserted in a Family Law Civil Bill as discussed at **13.2**. In addition, it must outline the grounds on which the respondent seeks a decree of divorce and specify whether the respondent intends to apply for any ancillary relief and, if so, what relief. In addition, the respondent must file an affidavit of means as discussed at **13.3**. The respondent must also file an affidavit of welfare if there are dependent children. If the respondent agrees with the facts as averred to in the affidavit of welfare filed on behalf of the applicant, the respondent may file a shortened version of the affidavit confirming his/her agreement. In circumstances where the respondent disagrees with the affidavit of welfare filed by the applicant, a separate affidavit of welfare including all the matters referred to at **13.4** should be sworn by the respondent.

13.7   NOTICE OF TRIAL

When a respondent has filed a defence and, if appropriate, a counterclaim, the applicant may file a notice of trial or a notice to fix a date for trial as appropriate. In circuits other than Dublin, at least 10 days' notice of trial must be given to the respondent and all other necessary parties, for example the trustees of a pension scheme and it shall be for the sittings of the court next ensuing after the expiration of that 10-day period. In relation to the Dublin circuit, a notice to fix a date for trial shall give 10 days' notice to the respondent and all other necessary parties, and the County Registrar shall fix a date for the hearing of the case including trustees of a pension scheme. In the event that an applicant fails to serve a notice for trial or a notice to fix a date for trial, the respondent may do so. If there are two or more actions between the parties, the court may order that the actions be tried together and make such further orders in relation to costs as may be appropriate.

13.8   MOTION FOR JUDGMENT

If a respondent does not enter an appearance or file a defence then the applicant may apply to the court for judgment in default of appearance/ defence. Fourteen clear days' notice must be given to the respondent of the notice of motion. The court may on hearing the case give judgment in the applicant's case and may make such orders as are appropriate. When a respondent is served with a notice of motion for judgment in default of appearance/defence, the respondent may lodge a defence not later than 7 days after the service of the notice of motion and if he or she does so, the motion for judgment will be struck out and the respondent shall be responsible for the applicant's costs.

13.9　JUDGMENT BY CONSENT

In a case where both the husband and the wife are agreed in respect of all the reliefs being sought by the applicant and a defence in accordance with the rules has been filed and served by the respondent which reflects this agreement, either the applicant or the respondent may apply to the court for judgment by way of notice of motion. This procedure may be viewed as divorce by consent. Undoubtedly, if a couple have lived apart for the requisite period, and if there is no reasonable prospect of reconciliation, and if they are agreed on the financial provision, they may proceed by this route. However, it is expected that judges, mindful of their obligation to uphold the provisions of the Constitution, will make careful and diligent enquiry of the parties and their circumstances to ensure that all requirements have been strictly observed, before granting the divorce decree.

13.10　THE HEARING

Section 38(5) of the Divorce Act provides that the existing arrangements for the conduct and hearing of proceedings for judicial separation in the Circuit Family Court shall apply to proceedings for divorce. Section 32 of the 1989 Act directs that the Circuit Family Court shall sit to hear and determine proceedings at a different place or at different times or on different days from those on which the ordinary sittings of the circuit court are held. Section 33 of the 1989 Act provides that proceedings in the Circuit Family Court and family law proceedings before the High Court shall be as informal as is practicable and consistent with the administration of justice. Neither the judges nor the barristers and solicitors shall wear wigs or gowns in the Circuit Family Court or in family law proceedings before the High Court. All proceedings for divorce shall be heard otherwise than in public and the costs of any proceedings shall be at the discretion of the court. Rule 35 of the Circuit Court Rules 1997 provides that the costs between parties may be measured by the judge and, if not so measured, shall be taxed, in default of agreement by the parties, by the County Registrar according to such scale of costs as may be prescribed. If a party is aggrieved by such taxation, he or she may appeal to the court and have the costs reviewed by it.

APPENDICES

Appendix 1

FAMILY LAW (DIVORCE) ACT 1996

(1996 No 33)

ARRANGEMENT OF SECTIONS

PART I

PRELIMINARY AND GENERAL

PART II

THE OBTAINING OF A DECREE OF DIVORCE

PART III

PRELIMINARY AND ANCILLARY ORDERS IN OR AFTER PROCEEDINGS FOR DIVORCE

PART IV

INCOME TAX, CAPITAL ACQUISITIONS TAX, CAPITAL GAINS TAX, PROBATE TAX AND STAMP DUTY

PART V

MISCELLANEOUS

ACTS REFERRED TO

Capital Gains Tax Acts	
Censorship of Publications Act 1929	1929, No 21
Criminal Damage Act 1991	1991, No 31
Criminal Evidence Act 1992	1992, No 12
Defence Act 1954	1954, No 18
Domestic Violence Act 1996	1996, No 1
Enforcement of Court Orders Act 1940	1940, No 23
Family Home Protection Act 1976	1976, No 27
Family Law Act 1995	1995, No 26
Family Law (Maintenance of Spouses and Children) Act 1976	1976, No 11
Finance (1909–10) Act 1910	1920, c 8
Finance Act 1972	1972, No 19
Finacne Act 1983	1983, No 15
Finance Act 1993	1993, No 13
Finance Act 1994	1994, No 13
Guardianship of Infants Act 1964	1964, No 7
Income Tax Act 1967	1967, No 6
Income Tax Acts	
Insurance Act 1989	1989, No 3
Judicial Separation and Family Law Reform Act 1989	1989, No 6
Maintenance Act 1994	1994, No 28
Partition Act 1868	1868, c 40
Partition Act 1876	1876, c 17
Pensions Act 1990	1990, No 25
Pensions (Amendment) Act 1996	1996, No 18
Powers of Attorney Act 1996	1996, No 12
Registration of Title Act 1964	1964, No 16
Social Welfare Acts	
Status of Children Act 1987	1987, No 26
Succession Act 1965	1965, No 27

An act to make provision for the exercise by the courts of the jurisdiction conferred by the Constitution to grant decrees of divorce, to enable the courts to make certain preliminary and ancillary orders in or after proceedings for divorce, to provide, as respects transfers of property of divorced spouses, for their exemption from, or for the abatement of, certain taxes (including stamp duty) and to provide for related matters.

[27 November 1996]

PART I

PRELIMINARY AND GENERAL

1 Short title and commencement

(1) This Act may be cited as the Family Law (Divorce) Act 1996.

(2) This Act shall come into operation on the day that is 3 months after the date of its passing.

2 Interpretation

(1) In this Act, save where the context otherwise requires—
'the Act of 1964' means the Guardianship of Infants Act 1964;
'the Act of 1965' means the Succession Act 1965;
'the Act of 1976' means the Family Law (Maintenance of Spouses and Children) Act 1976;
'the Act of 1989' means the Judicial Separation and Family law Reform Act 1989;
'the Act of 1995' means the Family Law Act 1995;
'the Act of 1996' means the Domestic Violence Act 1996;
'conveyance' includes a mortgage, lease, assent, transfer, disclaimer, release and any other disposition of property otherwise than by a will or a *donatio mortis causa* and also includes an enforceable agreement (whether conditional or unconditional) to make any such disposition;
'the court' shall be construed in accordance with section 38;
'decree of divorce' means a decree under section 5;
'decree of judicial separation' means a decree under section 3 of the Act of 1989;
'decree of nullity' means a decree granted by a court declaring a marriage to be null and void;
'dependent member of the family', in relation to a spouse, or the spouses, concerned, means any child—
  (a) of both spouses or adopted by both spouses under the Adoption Acts 1952 to 1991, or in relation to whom both spouses are in *loco parentis*, or
  (b) of either spouse or adopted by either spouse under those Acts, or in relation to whom either spouse is in *loco parentis*, where the other spouse, being aware that he or she is not the parent of the child, has treated the child as a member of the family,
who is under the age of 18 years or if the child has attained that age—
  (i) is or will be or, if an order were made under this Act providing for periodical payments for the benefit of the child or for the provision of a lump sum for the child, would be receiving full-time education or instruction at any university, college, school or other educational establishment and is under the age of 23 years, or
  (ii) has a mental or physical disability to such extent that it is not reasonably possible for the child to maintain himself or herself fully;
'family home' has the meaning assigned to it by section 2 of the Family Home Protection Act 1976, with the modification that the references to a spouse in that section shall be construed as references to a spouse within the meaning of this Act;
'financial compensation order' has the meaning assigned to it by section 16;
'Land Registry' and 'Registry of Deeds' have the meanings assigned to them by the Registration of Title Act 1964;
'lump sum order' means an order under section 13(1)(c);
'maintenance pending suit order' means an order under section 12;
'member', in relation to a pension scheme, means any person who, having been admitted to membership of the scheme under its rules, remains entitled to any benefit under the scheme;
'pension adjustment order' means an order under section 17;
'pension scheme' means—
  (a) an occupational pension scheme (within the meaning of the Pensions Act 1990), or

(b)   (i)   an annuity contract approved by the Revenue Commissioners under section 235 of the Income Tax Act 1967, or a contract so approved under section 235A of that Act,

(ii) a trust scheme, or part of a trust scheme, so approved under subsection (4) of the said section 235 or subsection (5) of the said section 235A, or

(iii) a policy or contract of assurance approved by the Revenue Commissioners under Chapter II of Part I of the Finance Act 1972, or

(c)   any other scheme or arrangement (including a personal pension plan and a scheme or arrangement established by or pursuant to statute or instrument made under statute other than under the Social Welfare Acts) that provides or is intended to provide either or both of the following, that is to say:

(i)   benefits for a person who is a member of the scheme or arrangement ('the member') upon retirement at normal pensionable age or upon earlier or later retirement or upon leaving, or upon the ceasing of, the relevant employment,

(ii) benefits for the widow, widower or dependants of the member, or for any other persons, on the death of the member;

'periodical payments order' and 'secured periodical payments order' have the meanings assigned to them by section 13;

'property adjustment order' has the meaning assigned to it by section 14;

'trustees', in relation to a scheme that is established under a trust, means the trustees of the scheme and, in relation to a pension scheme not so established, means the persons who administer the scheme.

(2) In this Act, where the context so requires—

(a)   a reference to a marriage includes a reference to a marriage that has been dissolved under this Act,

(b)   a reference to a remarriage includes a reference to a marriage that takes place after a marriage that has been dissolved under this Act,

(c)   a reference to a spouse includes a reference to a person who is a party to a marriage that has been dissolved under this Act,

(d)   a reference to a family includes a reference to a family as respects which the marriage of the spouses concerned has been dissolved under this Act,

(e)   a reference to an application to a court by a person on behalf of a dependent member of the family includes a reference to such an application by such a member and a reference to a payment, the securing of a payment, or the assignment of an interest, to a person for the benefit of a dependent member of the family includes a reference to a payment, the securing of a payment, or the assignment of an interest, to such a member,

and cognate words shall be construed accordingly.

(3) In this Act—

(a)   a reference to any enactment shall, unless the context otherwise requires, be construed as a reference to that enactment as amended or extended by or under any subsequent enactment including this Act,

(b)   a reference to a Part or section is a reference to a Part or section of this Act unless it is indicated that reference to some other enactment is intended,

(c)   a reference to a subsection, paragraph, subparagraph or clause is a reference to the subsection, paragraph, subparagraph or clause of the provision in which the reference occurs unless it is indicated that reference to some other provision is intended.

3 Repeal

Section 14(2) of the Censorship of Publications Act 1929, is hereby repealed.

4 Expenses

The expenses incurred by the Minister for Equality and Law Reform, the Minister for Health or the Minister for Justice in the administration of this Act shall, to such extent as may be sanctioned by the Minister for Finance, be paid out of moneys provided by the Oireachtas.

PART II

THE OBTAINING OF A DECREE OF DIVORCE

5 Grant of decree of divorce and custody etc, of children

(1) Subject to the provisions of this Act, where, on application to it in that behalf by either of the spouses concerned, the court is satisfied that—

  (a) at the date of the institution of the proceedings, the spouses have lived apart from one another for a period of, or periods amounting to, at least four years during the previous five years,

  (b) there is no reasonable prospect of a reconciliation between the spouses, and

  (c) such provision as the court considers proper having regard to the circumstances exists or will be made for the spouses and any dependent members of the family,

the court may, in exercise of the jurisdiction conferred by Article 41.3.2° of the Constitution, grant a decree of divorce in respect of the marriage concerned.

(2) Upon the grant of a decree of divorce, the court may, where appropriate, give such directions under section 11 of the Act of 1964 as it considers proper regarding the welfare (within the meaning of that Act), custody of, or right of access to, any dependent member of the family concerned who is an infant (within the meaning of that Act) as if an application has been made to it in that behalf under that section.

6 Safeguards to ensure applicant's awareness of alternatives to divorce proceedings and to assist attempts at reconciliation

(1) In this section 'the applicant' means a person who has applied, is applying or proposes to apply to the court for the grant of a decree of divorce.

(2) If a solicitor is acting for the applicant, the solicitor shall, prior to the institution of the proceedings concerned under section 5—

  (a) discuss with the applicant the possibility of a reconciliation and give to him or her the names and addresses of persons qualified to help to effect a reconciliation between spouses who have become estranged,

  (b) discuss with the applicant the possibility of engaging in mediation to help to effect a separation (if the spouses are not separated) or a divorce on a basis agreed between the applicant and the other spouse and give to the applicant the names and addresses of persons qualified to provide a mediation service for spouses who have become estranged, and

   (c) discuss with the applicant the possibility (where appropriate) of effecting a separation by means of a deed or agreement in writing executed or made by the applicant and the other spouse and providing for their separation.

(3) Such a solicitor shall also ensure that the applicant is aware of judicial separation as an alternative to divorce where a decree of judicial separation in relation to the applicant and the other spouse is not in force.

(4) If a solicitor is acting for the applicant—

   (a) the originating document by which the proceedings under section 5 are instituted shall be accompanied by a certificate signed by the solicitor indicating, if it be the case, that he or she has complied with subsection (2) and, if appropriate, subsection (3) in relation to the matter and, if the document is not so accompanied, the court may adjourn the proceedings for such period as it considers reasonable to enable the solicitor to engage in the discussions specified in subsection (2), and, if appropriate, to make the applicant aware of judicial separation,

   (b) if the solicitor has complied with paragraph (a), any copy of the originating document aforesaid served on any person or left in an office of the court shall be accompanied by a copy of the certificate aforesaid.

(5) A certificate under subsection (4) (a) shall be in a form prescribed by rules of court or a form to the like effect.

(6) The Minister may make regulations to allow for the establishment of a Register of Professional Organisations whose members are qualified to assist the parties involved in effecting a reconciliation, such register to show the names of members of those organisations and procedures to be put in place for the organisations involved to regularly update the membership lists.

7   Safeguards to ensure respondent's awareness of alternatives to divorce proceedings and to assist at reconciliation

(1) In this section 'the respondent' means a person who is the respondent in proceedings in the court under section 5.

(2) If a solicitor is acting for the respondent, the solicitor shall, as soon as may be after receiving instructions from the respondent in relation to the proceedings concerned under section 5—

   (a) discuss with the respondent the possibility of a reconciliation and give to him or her the names and addresses of persons qualified to effect a reconciliation between spouses who have become estranged,

   (b) discuss with the respondent the possibility of engaging in mediation to help to effect a separation (if the spouses are not separated) or a divorce on a basis agreed between the respondent and the other spouse and give to the respondent the names and addresses of persons qualified to provide a mediation service for spouses who have become estranged, and

(c) discuss with the respondent the possibility (where appropriate) of effecting a separation by means of a deed or agreement in writing executed or made by the applicant and the other spouse and providing for their separation.

(3) Such a solicitor shall also ensure that the respondent is aware of judicial separation as an alternative to divorce where a decree of judicial separation is not in force in relation to the respondent and the other spouse.

(4) If a solicitor is acting for the respondent—
  (a) the memorandum or other document delivered to the appropriate officer of the court for the purpose of the entry of an appearance by the respondent in proceedings under section 5 shall be accompanied by a certificate signed by the solicitor indicating, if it be the case, that the solicitor has complied with subsection (2) and, if appropriate, subsection (3) in relation to the matter and, if the document is not so accompanied, the court may adjourn the proceedings for such period as it considers reasonable to enable the solicitor to engage in the discussions specified in subsection (2) and, if appropriate, to make the applicant aware of judicial separation,
  (b) if paragraph (a) is complied with, any copy of the document aforesaid given or sent to the other party to the proceedings or his or her solicitor shall be accompanied by a copy of the relevant certificate aforesaid.

(5) A certificate under subsection (4)(a) shall be in a form prescribed by rules of court or a form to the like effect.

8 Adjournment of proceedings to assist reconciliation or agreements on the terms of the divorce

(1) Where an application is made to the court for the grant of a decree of divorce, the court shall give consideration to the possibility of a reconciliation between the spouses concerned and, accordingly, may adjourn the proceedings at any time for the purpose of enabling attempts to be made by the spouses, if they both so wish, to effect such a reconciliation with or without the assistance of a third party.

(2) Where, in proceedings under section 5, it appears to the court that a reconciliation between the spouses cannot be effected, it may adjourn or further adjourn the proceedings for the purpose of enabling attempts to be made by the spouses, if they both so wish, to reach agreement, with or without the assistance of a third party, on some or all of the terms of the proposed divorce.

(3) If proceedings are adjourned pursuant to subsection (1) or (2), either or both of the spouses may at any time request that the hearing of the proceedings be resumed as soon as may be and, if such a request is made, the court shall, subject to any other power of the court to adjourn proceedings, resume the hearing.

(4) The powers conferred by this section are additional to any other power of the court to adjourn proceedings.

(5) Where the court adjourns proceedings under this section, it may, at its discretion, advise the spouses concerned to seek the assistance of a third party in relation to the effecting of a reconciliation between the spouses or the reaching of agreement between them on some or all of the terms of the proposed divorce.

9 Non-admissibility as evidence of certain communications relating to reconciliation, separation or divorce

An oral or written communication between either of the spouses concerned and a third party for the purpose of seeking assistance to effect a reconciliation or to reach agreement between them on some or all of the terms of a separation or a divorce (whether or not made in the presence or with the knowledge of the other spouse), and any record of such a communication, made or caused to be made by either of the spouses concerned or such a third party, shall not be admissible as evidence in any court.

10 Effect of decree of divorce

(1) Where the court grants a decree of divorce, the marriage, the subject of the decree, is thereby dissolved and a party to that marriage may marry again.

(2) For the avoidance of doubt, it is hereby declared that the grant of a decree of divorce shall not affect the right of the father and mother of an infant, under section 6 of the Act of 1964, to be guardians of the infant jointly.

PART III

PRELIMINARY AND ANCILLARY ORDERS IN OR AFTER PROCEEDINGS FOR DIVORCE

11 Preliminary orders in proceedings for divorce

Where an application is made to the court for the grant of a decree of divorce, the court, before deciding whether to grant or refuse to grant the decree, may, in the same proceedings and without the institution of proceedings under the Act concerned, if it appears to the court to be proper to do so, make one or more of the following orders—
  (a) a safety order, a barring order, an interim barring order or a protection order under the Act of 1996,
  (b) an order under section 11 of the Act of 1964;
  (c) an order under section 5 or 9 of the Family Home Protection Act 1976.

12 Maintenance pending suit orders

(1) Where an application is made to the court for the grant of a decree of divorce, the court may make an order for maintenance pending suit, that is to say, an order requiring either of the spouses concerned to make to the other spouse such periodical payments or lump sum payments for his or her support and, where appropriate, to make to such person as may be specified in the order such periodical payments for the benefit of such (if any) dependent member of the family and, as respects periodical payments, for such period beginning not earlier than the date of the application and ending not later than the date of its determination, as the court considers proper and specifies in the order.

(2) The court may provide that payments under an order under this section shall be subject to such terms and conditions as it considers appropriate and specifies in the order.

13   Periodical payments and lump sum orders

(1) On granting a decree of divorce or at any time thereafter, the court, on application
to it in that behalf by either of the spouses concerned or by a person on behalf of a
dependent member of the family, may, during the lifetime of the other spouse, or, as the
case may be, the spouse concerned, make one or more of the following orders, that is to
say—
    (a)   a periodical payments order, that is to say—
        (i)   an order that either of the spouses shall make to the other spouse such
            periodical payments of such amount, during such period and at such times
            as may be specified in the order, or
       (ii)   an order that either of the spouses shall make to such person as may be so
           specified for the benefit of such (if any) dependent member of the family
           such periodical payments of such amount, during such period and at such
           times as may be so specified,
    (b)   a secured periodical payments order, that is to say—
        (i)   an order that either of the spouses shall secure, to the satisfaction of the
            court, to the other spouse such periodical payments of such amounts,
            during such period and at such times as may be so specified, or
       (ii)   an order that either of the spouses shall secure, to the satisfaction of the
           court, to such persons as may be so specified for the benefit of such (if any)
           dependent member of the family such periodical payments of such
           amounts, during such period and at such times as may be so specified,
    (c)   (i)   an order that either of the spouses shall make to the other spouse a lump
           sum payment or lump sum payments of such amount or amounts and at
           such time or times as may be so specified, or
       (ii)   an order that either of the spouses shall make to such person as may be so
           specified for the benefit of such (if any) dependent member of the family a
           lump sum payment or lump sum payments of such amount or amounts and
           at such time or times as may be so specified.

(2) The court may—
    (a)   order a spouse to pay a lump sum to the other spouse to meet any liabilities or
        expenses reasonably incurred by that other spouse before the making of an
        application by that other spouse for an order under subsection (1) in
        maintaining himself or herself or any dependent member of the family, or
    (b)   order a spouse to pay a lump sum to such person as may be specified to meet any
        liabilities or expenses reasonably incurred by or for the benefit of a dependent
        member of the family before the making of an application on behalf of the
        member for an order under subsection (1).

(3) An order under this section for the payment of a lump sum may provide for the
payment of the lump sum by instalments of such amounts as may be specified in the
order and may require the payment of the instalments to be secured to the satisfaction of
the court.

(4) The period specified in an order under paragraph (a) or (b) of subsection (1) shall
begin not earlier than the date of the application for the order and shall end not later
than the death of the spouse, or any dependent member of the family, in whose favour
the order is made or the other spouse concerned.

(5) (a) Upon the remarriage of the spouse in whose favour an order is made under paragraph (a) or (b) of subsection (1), the order shall, to the extent that it applies to that spouse, cease to have effect, except as respects payments due under it on the date of the remarriage.

   (b) If, after the grant of a decree of divorce, either of the spouses concerned remarries, the court shall not, by reference to that decree, make an order under subsection (1) in favour of that spouse.

(6) (a) Where a court makes an order under subsection (1)(a), it shall in the same proceedings, subject to paragraph (b), make an attachment of earnings order (within the meaning of the Act of 1976) to secure payments under the first mentioned order if it is satisfied that the person against whom the order is made is a person to whom earnings (within the meaning aforesaid) fall to be paid.

   (b) Before deciding whether to make or refuse to make an attachment of earnings order by virtue of paragraph (a), the court shall give the spouse concerned an opportunity to make the representations specified in paragraph (c) in relation to the matter and shall have regard to any such representations made by that spouse.

   (c) The representations referred to in paragraph (b) are representations relating to the questions—
      (i) whether the spouse concerned is a person to whom such earnings as aforesaid fall to be paid, and
      (ii) whether he or she would make the payments to which the relevant order under subsection (1)(a) relates.

   (d) References in this subsection to an order under subsection (1)(a) include references to such an order as varied or affirmed on appeal from the court concerned or varied under section 22.

14   Property adjustment orders

(1) On granting a decree of divorce or at any time thereafter, the court, on application to it in that behalf by either of the spouses concerned or by a person on behalf of a dependent member of the family, may, during the lifetime of the other spouse or, as the case may be, the spouse concerned, make a property adjustment order, that is to say, an order providing for one or more of the following matters:

   (a) the transfer by either of the spouses to the other spouse, to any dependent member of the family or to any other specified person for the benefit of such a member of specified property, being property to which the first-mentioned spouse is entitled either in possession or reversion,

   (b) the settlement to the satisfaction of the court of specified property, being property to which either of the spouses is so entitled as aforesaid, for the benefit of the other spouse and of any dependent member of the family or of any or all of those persons,

   (c) the variation for the benefit of either of the spouses and of any dependent member of the family or of any or all of those persons of any ante-nuptial or post-nuptial settlement (including such a settlement made by will or codicil) made on the spouses,

   (d) the extinguishment or reduction of the interest of either of the spouses under any such settlement.

(2) An order under paragraph (b), (c) or (d) may restrict to a specified extent or exclude the application of section 22 in relation to the order.

(3) If, after the grant of a decree of divorce, either of the spouses concerned remarries, the court shall not, by reference to that decree, make a property adjustment order in favour of that spouse.

(4) Where a property adjustment order is made in relation to land, a copy of the order certified to be a true copy by the registrar or clerk of the court concerned shall, as appropriate, be lodged by him or her in the Land Registry for registration pursuant to section 69(1)(h) of the Registration of Title Act 1964, in a register maintained under that Act or be registered in the Registry of Deeds.

(5) Where—
  (a) a person is directed by an order under this section to execute a deed or other instrument in relation to land, and
  (b) the person refuses or neglects to comply with the direction or, for any other reason, the court considers it necessary to do so,
the court may order another person to execute the deed or instrument in the name of the first-mentioned person; and a deed or other instrument executed by a person in the name of another person pursuant to an order under this subsection shall be as valid as if it had been executed by that other person.

(6) Any costs incurred in complying with a property adjustment order shall be borne, as the court may determine, by either of the spouses concerned, or by both of them in such proportions as the court may determine, and shall be so borne in such manner as the court may determine.

(7) This section shall not apply in relation to a family home in which, following the grant of a decree of divorce, either of the spouses concerned, having remarried, ordinarily resides with his or her spouse.

15 Miscellaneous ancillary orders

(1) On granting a decree of divorce or at any time thereafter, the court, on application to it in that behalf by either of the spouses concerned or by a person on behalf of a dependent member of the family, may, during the lifetime of the other spouse or, as the case may be, the spouse concerned, make one or more of the following orders:
  (a) an order—
    (i) providing for the conferral on one spouse either for life or for such other period (whether definite or contingent) as the court may specify of the right to occupy the family home to the exclusion of the other spouse, or
    (ii) directing the sale of the family home subject to such conditions (if any) as the court considers proper and providing for the disposal of the proceeds of the sale between the spouses and any other person having an interest therein,
  (b) an order under section 36 of the Act of 1995,
  (c) an order under section 5, 7 or 9 of the Family Home Protection Act 1976,
  (d) an order under section 2, 3, 4 or 5 of the Act of 1996,
  (e) an order for the partition of property or under the Partition Act 1868, and the Partition Act 1876,

(f)   an order under section 11 of the Act of 1964,

and, for the purposes of this section, in paragraphs (b), (c) and (d), a reference to a spouse in a statute referred to in paragraph (b), (c) or (d) shall be construed as including a reference to a person who is a party to a marriage that has been dissolved under this Act.

(2) The court, in exercising its jurisdiction under subsection (1) (a), shall have regard to the welfare of the spouses and any dependent member of the family and, in particular, shall take into consideration—

(a)   that, where a decree of divorce is granted, it is not possible for the spouses concerned to reside together, and

(b)   that proper and secure accommodation should, where practicable, be provided for a spouse who is wholly or mainly dependent on the other spouse and for any dependent member of the family.

(3) Subsection (1) (a) shall not apply in relation to a family home in which, following the grant of a decree of divorce, either of the spouses concerned, having remarried, ordinarily resides with his or her spouse.

16   Financial compensation orders

(1) Subject to the provisions of this section, on granting a decree of divorce or at any time thereafter, the court, on application to it in that behalf by either of the spouses concerned or by a person on behalf of a dependent member of the family, may, during the lifetime of the other spouse or, as the case may be, the spouse concerned, if it considers—

(a)   that the financial security of the spouse making the application ('the applicant') or the dependent member of the family ('the member') can be provided for either wholly or in part by so doing, or

(b)   that the forfeiture, by reason of the decree of divorce, by the applicant or the member, as the case may be, of the opportunity or possibility of acquiring a benefit (for example, a benefit under a pension scheme) can be compensated for wholly or in part by so doing,

make a financial compensation order, that is to say, an order requiring the other spouse to do one or more of the following:

(i)   to effect such a policy of life insurance for the benefit of the applicant or the member as may be specified in the order,

(ii) to assign the whole or a specified part of the interest of the other spouse in a policy of life insurance effected by that other spouse or both of the spouses to the applicant or to such person as may be specified in the order for the benefit of the member,

(iii) to make or to continue to make to the person by whom a policy of life insurance is or was issued the payments which that other spouse or both of the spouses is or are required to make under the terms of the policy.

(2) (a) The court may make a financial compensation order in addition to or in substitution in whole or in part for orders under section 13, 14, 15 or 17 and in deciding whether or not to make such an order it shall have regard to whether proper provision having regard to the circumstances exists or can be made for the spouse concerned or the dependent member of the family concerned by orders under those sections.

(b) An order under this section shall cease to have effect on the re-marriage or death of the applicant in so far as it relates to the applicant.

(c) The court shall not make an order under this section in favour of a spouse who has remarried.

(d) An order under section 22 in relation to an order under paragraph (i) or (ii) of subsection (1) may make such provision (if any) as the court considers appropriate in relation to the disposal of—

  (i) an amount representing any accumulated value of the insurance policy effected pursuant to the order under the said paragraph (i), or

  (ii) the interest or the part of the interest to which the order under the said paragraph (ii) relates.

17 Pension adjustment orders

(1) In this section, save where the context otherwise requires—

'the Act of 1990' means the Pensions Act 1990;

'active member' in relation to a scheme, means a member of the scheme who is in reckonable service;

'actuarial value' means the equivalent cash value of a benefit (including, where appropriate, provision for any revaluation of such benefit) under a scheme calculated by reference to appropriate financial assumptions and making due allowance for the probability of survival to normal pensionable age and thereafter in accordance with normal life expectancy on the assumption that the member concerned of the scheme, at the effective date of calculation, is in a normal state of health having regard to his or her age;

'approved arrangement', in relation to the trustees of a scheme, means an arrangement whereby the trustees, on behalf of the person for whom the arrangement is made, effect policies or contracts of insurance that are approved of by the Revenue Commissioners with, and make the appropriate payments under the policies or contracts to, one or more undertakings;

'contingent benefit' means a benefit payment under a scheme, other than a payment under subsection (7) to or for one or more of the following, that is to say, the widow or the widower and any dependents of the member spouse concerned and the personal representative of the member spouse, if the member spouse dies while in relevant employment and before attaining any normal pensionable age provided for under the rules of the scheme;

'defined contribution scheme' means a scheme which, under its rules, provides retirement benefit, the rate or amount of which is in total directly determined by the amount of the contributions paid by or in respect of the member of the scheme concerned and includes a scheme the contributions under which are used, directly or indirectly, to provide—

(a) contingent benefit, and

(b) retirement benefit the rate or amount of which is in total directly determined by the part of the contributions aforesaid that is used for the provision of the retirement benefit;

'designated benefit', in relation to a pension adjustment order, means an amount determined by the trustees of the scheme concerned, in accordance with relevant guidelines, and by reference to the period and the percentage of the retirement benefit specified in the order concerned under subsection (2);

'member spouse', in relation to a scheme, means a spouse who is a member of the scheme;

'normal pensionable age' means the earliest age at which a member of a scheme is entitled to receive benefits under the rules of the scheme on retirement from relevant employment, disregarding any such rules providing for early retirement on grounds of ill health or otherwise;

'occupational pension scheme' has the meaning assigned to it by section 2(1) of the Act of 1990;

'reckonable service' means service in relevant employment during membership of any scheme;

'relevant guidelines' means any relevant guidelines for the time being in force under paragraph (c) or (cc) of section 10(1) of the Act of 1990;

'relevant employment', in relation to a scheme, means any employment (or any period treated as employment) or any period of self-employment to which a scheme applies;

'retirement benefit', in relation to a scheme, means all benefits (other than contingent benefits) payable under the scheme;

'rules', in relation to a scheme, means the provisions of the scheme, by whatever name called;

'scheme' means a pension scheme;

'transfer amount' shall be construed in accordance with subsection (4);

'undertaking' has the meaning assigned to it by the Insurance Act 1989.

(2) Subject to the provisions of this section, where a decree of divorce ('the decree') has been granted, the court, if it so thinks fit, may, in relation to retirement benefit under a scheme of which one of the spouses concerned is a member, on application to it in that behalf at the time of the making of the order for the decree or at any time thereafter during the lifetime of the member spouse by either of the spouses or by a person on behalf of a dependent member of the family, make an order providing for the payment, in accordance with the provisions of this section, to either of the following, as the court may determine, that is to say—

    (a) the other spouse and, in the case of the death of that spouse, his or her personal representative, and

    (b) such person as may be specified in the order for the benefit of a person who is, and for so long only as he or she remains, a dependent member of the family,

of a benefit consisting, either, as the court may determine, of the whole, or such part as the court considers appropriate, of that part of the retirement benefit that is payable (or which, but for the making of the order for the decree, would have been payable) under the scheme and has accrued at the time of the making of the order for the decree and, for the purpose of determining the benefit, the order shall specify—

    (i) the period of reckonable service of the member spouse prior to the granting of the decree to be taken into account, and

    (ii) the percentage of the retirement benefit accrued during that period to be paid to the person referred to in paragraph (a) or (b), as the case may be.

(3) Subject to the provisions of this section, where a decree of divorce ('the decree') has been granted, the court, if it so thinks fit, may, in relation to a contingent benefit under a scheme of which one of the spouses concerned is a member, on application to it in that behalf not more than one year after the making of the order for the decree by either of the spouses or by a person on behalf of a dependent member of the family concerned,

make an order providing for the payment, upon the death of the member spouse, to either of the following, or to both of them in such proportions as the court may determine, that is to say—

(a) the other spouse, and
(b) such person as may be specified in the order for the benefit of a dependent member of the family,

of, either, as the court may determine, the whole, or such part (expressed as a percentage) as the court considers appropriate, of that part of any contingent benefit that is payable (or which, but for the making of the order for the decree, would have been payable) under the scheme.

(4) Where the court makes an order under subsection (2) in favour of a spouse and payment of the designated benefit concerned has not commenced, the spouse in whose favour the order is made shall be entitled to the application in accordance with subsection (5) of an amount of money from the scheme concerned (in this section referred to as a 'transfer amount') equal to the value of the designated benefit, such amount being determined by the trustees of the scheme in accordance with relevant guidelines.

(5) Subject to subsection (17), where the court makes an order under subsection (2) in favour of a spouse and payment of the designated benefit concerned has not commenced, the trustees of the scheme concerned shall, for the purpose of giving effect to the order—

(a) on application to them in that behalf at the time of the making of the order or at any time thereafter by the spouse in whose favour the order was made ('the spouse'), and
(b) on the furnishing to them by the spouse of such information as they may reasonably require,

apply in accordance with relevant guidelines the transfer amount calculated in accordance with those guidelines either—

(i) if the trustees and the spouse so agree, in providing a benefit for or in respect of the spouse under the scheme aforesaid that is of the same actuarial value as the transfer amount concerned, or
(ii) in making a payment either to—
(I) such other occupational pension scheme, being a scheme the trustees of which agree to accept the payment, or
(II) in the discharge of any payment falling to be made by the trustees under any such other approved arrangement,
as may be determined by the spouse.

(6) Subject to subsection (17), where the court makes an order under subsection (2) in relation to a defined contribution scheme and an application has not been brought under subsection (5), the trustees of the scheme may, for the purpose of giving effect to the order, if they so think fit, apply in accordance with relevant guidelines the transfer amount calculated in accordance with those guidelines, in making a payment to—

(a) such other occupational pension scheme, being a scheme the trustees of which agree to accept the payment, or
(b) in the discharge of any payment falling to be made by the trustees under such other approved arrangement,

as may be determined by the trustees.

(7) Subject to subsection (17), where—

(a) the court makes an order under subsection (2), and

(b) the member spouse concerned dies before payment of the designated benefit concerned has commenced,

the trustees shall, for the purpose of giving effect to the order, within 3 months of the death of the member spouse, provide for the payment to the person in whose favour the order was made of an amount that is equal to the transfer amount calculated in accordance with relevant guidelines.

(8) Subject to subsection (17), where—

(a) the court makes an order under subsection (2), and

(b) the member spouse concerned ceases to be a member of the scheme otherwise than on death,

the trustees may, for the purpose of giving effect to the order, if they so think fit, apply, in accordance with relevant guidelines, the transfer amount calculated in accordance with those guidelines either, as the trustees may determine—

(i) if the trustees and the person in whose favour the order is made ('the person') so agree, in providing a benefit for or in respect of the person under the scheme aforesaid that is of the same actuarial value as the transfer amount concerned, or

(ii) in making a payment, either to—

(I) such other occupational pension scheme, being a scheme the trustees of which agree to accept the payment, or

(II) in the discharge of any payment falling to be made under such other approved arrangement,

as may be determined by the trustees.

(9) Subject to subsection (17), where—

(a) the court makes an order under subsection (2) in favour of a spouse ('the spouse'),

(b) the spouse dies before the payment of the designated benefit has commenced,

the trustees shall, within 3 months of the death of the spouse, provide for the payment to the personal representative of the spouse of an amount equal to the transfer amount calculated in accordance with relevant guidelines.

(10) Subject to subsection (17), where—

(a) the court makes an order under subsection (2) in favour of a spouse ('the spouse'), and

(b) the spouse dies after payment of the designated benefit has commenced,

the trustees shall, within 3 months of the death of the spouse, provide for the payment to the personal representative of the spouse of an amount equal to the actuarial value, calculated in accordance with relevant guidelines, of the part of the designated benefit which, but for the death of the spouse, would have been payable to the spouse during the lifetime of the member spouse.

(11) Where—

(a) the court makes an order under subsection (2) for the benefit of a dependent member of the family ('the person'), and

(b) the person dies before payment of the designated benefit has commenced,

the order shall cease to have effect in so far as it relates to that person.

(12) Where—

(a) the court makes an order under subsection (2) or (3) in relation to an occupational pension scheme, and

(b) the trustees of the scheme concerned have not applied the transfer amount concerned in accordance with subsection (5), (6), (7), (8) or (9), and

(c) after the making of the order, the member spouse ceases to be an active member of the scheme,

the trustees shall, within 12 months of the cessation, notify the registrar or clerk of the court concerned and the other spouse of the cessation.

(13) Where the trustees of a scheme apply a transfer amount under subsection (6) or (8), they shall notify the spouse (not being the spouse who is the member spouse) or other person concerned and the registrar or clerk of the court concerned of the application and shall give to that spouse or other person concerned particulars of the scheme or undertaking concerned and of the transfer amount.

(14) Where the court makes an order under subsection (2) or (3) for the payment of a designated benefit or a contingent benefit, as the case may be, the benefit shall be payable or the transfer amount concerned applied out of the resources of the scheme concerned and, unless otherwise provided for in the order or relevant guidelines, shall be payable in accordance with the rules of the scheme or, as the case may be, applied in accordance with relevant guidelines.

(15) Where the court makes an order under subsection (2), the amount of the retirement benefit payable, in accordance with the rules of the scheme concerned to, or to or in respect of, the member spouse shall be reduced by the amount of the designated benefit payable pursuant to the order.

(16) (a) Where the court makes an order under subsection (3), the amount of the contingent benefit payable, in accordance with the rules of the scheme concerned in respect of the member spouse shall be reduced by an amount equal to the contingent benefit payable pursuant to the order.

(b) Where the court makes an order under subsection (2) and the member spouse concerned dies before payment of the designated benefit concerned has commenced, the amount of the contingent benefit payable in respect of the member spouse in accordance with the rules of the scheme concerned shall be reduced by the amount of the payment made under subsection (7).

(17) Where, pursuant to an order under subsection (2), the trustees of a scheme make a payment or apply a transfer amount under subsection (5), (6), (7), (8), (9) or (10), they shall be discharged from any obligation to make any further payment or apply any transfer amount under any other of those subsections in respect of the benefit payable pursuant to the order.

(18) A person who makes an application under subsection (2) or (3) or an application for an order under section 22(2) in relation to an order under subsection (2) shall give notice thereof to the trustees of the scheme concerned and, in deciding whether to make the order concerned and in determining the provisions of the order, the court shall have regard to any representations made by any person to whom notice of the application has been given under this section or section 40.

(19) An order under subsection (3) shall cease to have effect on the death or remarriage of the person in whose favour it was made in so far as it relates to that person.

(20) The court may, in a pension adjustment order or by order made under this subsection after the making of a pension ajustment order, give to the trustees of the scheme concerned such directions as it considers appropriate for the purposes of the pension adjustment order including directions compliance with which occasions non-compliance with the rules of the scheme concerned or the Act of 1990; and a trustee of a scheme shall not be liable in any court or other tribunal for any loss or damage caused by his or her non-compliance with the rules of the scheme or with the Act of 1990 if the non-compliance was occasioned by his or her compliance with a direction of the court under this subsection.

(21) The registrar or clerk of the court concerned shall cause a copy of a pension adjustment order to be served on the trustees of the scheme concerned.

(22) (a) Any costs incurred by the trustees of a scheme under subsection (18) or in complying with a pension adjustment order or a direction under subsection (20) or (25) shall be borne, as the court may determine, by the member spouse or by the other person concerned or by both of them in such proportion as the court may determine and, in the absence of such determination, those costs shall be borne by them equally.

    (b) Where a person fails to pay an amount in accordance with paragraph (a) to the trustees of the scheme concerned, the court may, on application to it in that behalf by the trustees, order that the amount be deducted from the amount of any benefit payable to the person under the scheme or pursuant to an order under subsection (2) or (3) and be paid to the trustees.

(23) (a) The court shall not make a pension adjustment order in favour of a spouse who has remarried.

    (b) The court may make a pension adjustment order in addition to or in substitution in whole or in part for an order or orders under section 13, 14, 15 or 16 and, in deciding whether or not to make a pension adjustment order, the court shall have regard to the question whether proper provision, having regard to the circumstances, exists or can be made for the spouse concerned or the dependent member of the family concerned by an order or orders under any of those sections.

(24) Section 54 of the Act of 1990 and any regulations under that section shall apply with any necessary modifications to a scheme if proceedings for the grant of a decree of divorce to which a member spouse is a party have been instituted and shall continue to apply notwithstanding the grant of a decree of divorce in the proceedings.

(25) For the purposes of this Act, the court may, of its own motion, and shall, if so requested by either of the spouses concerned or any other person concerned, direct the trustees of the scheme concerned to provide the spouses or that other person and the court, within a specified period of time—

    (a) with a calculation of the value and the amount, determined in accordance with relevant guidelines, of the retirement benefit, or contingent benefit, concerned that is payable (or which, but for the making of the order for the decree of divorce concerned, would have been payable) under the scheme and has accrued at the time of the making of that order, and

    (b) with a calculation of the amount of the contingent benefit concerned that is payable (or which, but for the making of the order for the decree of divorce concerned, would have been payable) under the scheme.

(26) An order under this section may restrict to a specified extent or exclude the application of section 22 in relation to the order.

18   Orders for provision for spouse out of estate of other spouse

(1) Subject to the provisions of this section, where one of the spouses in respect of whom a decree of divorce has been granted dies, the court, on application to it in that behalf by the other spouse ('the applicant') not more than 6 months after representation is first granted under the Act of 1965 in respect of the estate of the deceased spouse, may by order make such provision for the applicant out of the estate of the deceased spouse as it considers appropriate having regard to the rights of any other person having an interest in the matter and specifies in the order if it is satisfied that proper provision in the circumstances was not made for the applicant during the lifetime of the deceased spouse under section 13, 14, 15, 16 or 17 for any reason (other than conduct referred to in subsection (2)(i) of section 20 of the applicant).

(2) The court shall not make an order under this section in favour of a spouse who has remarried since the granting of the decree of divorce concerned.

(3) In considering whether to make an order under this section the court shall have regard to all the circumstances of the case including—
    (a) any order under paragraph (c) of section 13(1) or a property adjustment order in favour of the applicant, and
    (b) any devise or bequest made by the deceased spouse to the applicant.

(4) The provision made for the applicant concerned by an order under this section together with any provision made for the applicant by an order referred to in subsection (3)(a) (the value of which for the purposes of this subsection shall be its value on the date of the order) shall not exceed in total the share (if any) of the applicant in the estate of the deceased spouse to which the applicant was entitled or (if the deceased spouse died intestate as to the whole or part of his or her estate) would have been entitled under the Act of 1965 if the marriage had not been dissolved.

(5) Notice of an application under this section shall be given by the applicant to the spouse (if any) of the deceased spouse concerned and to such (if any) other persons as the court may direct and, in deciding whether to make the order concerned and in determining the provisions of the order, the court shall have regard to any representations made by the spouse of the deceased spouse and any other such persons as aforesaid.

(6) The personal representative of a deceased spouse in respect of whom a decree of divorce has been granted shall make a reasonable attempt to ensure that notice of his or her death is brought to the attention of the other spouse concerned and, where an application is made under this section, the personal representative of the deceased spouse shall not, without the leave of the court, distribute any of the estate of that spouse until the court makes or refuses to make an order under this section.

(7) Where the personal representative of a deceased spouse in respect of whom a decree of divorce has been granted gives notice of his or her death to the other spouse concerned ('the spouse') and—
    (a) the spouse intends to apply to the court for an order under this section,

(b) the spouse has applied for such an order and the application is pending, or

(c) an order has been made under this section in favour of the spouse,

the spouse shall, not later than one month after the receipt of the notice, notify the personal representative of such intention, application or order, as the case may be, and, if he or she does not do so, the personal representative shall be at liberty to distribute the assets of the deceased spouse, or any part thereof, amongst the parties entitled thereto.

(8) The personal representative shall not be liable to the spouse for the assets or any part thereof so distributed unless, at the time of such distribution, he or she had notice of the intention, application or order aforesaid.

(9) Nothing in subsection (7) or (8) shall prejudice the right of the spouse to follow any such assets into the hands of any person who may have received them.

(10) On granting a decree of divorce or at any time thereafter, the court, on application to it in that behalf by either of the spouses concerned, may, during the lifetime of the other spouse or, as the case may be, the spouse concerned, if it considers it just to do so, make an order that either or both spouses shall not, on the death of either of them, be entitled to apply for an order under this section.

19 Orders for sale of property

(1) Where the court makes a secured periodical payments order, a lump sum order or a property adjustment order, thereupon, or at any time thereafter, it may make an order directing the sale of such property as may be specified in the order, being property in which, or in the proceeds of sale of which, either or both of the spouses concerned has or have a beneficial interest, either in possession or reversion.

(2) The jurisdiction conferred on the court by subsection (1) shall not be so exercised as to affect a right to occupy the family home of the spouse concerned that is enjoyed by virtue of an order under this Part.

(3) (a) An order under subsection (1) may contain such consequential or supplementary provisions as the court considers appropriate.

(b) Without prejudice to the generality of paragraph (a), an order under subsection (1) may contain—

(i) a provision specifying the manner of sale and some or all of the conditions applying to the sale of the property to which the order relates,

(ii) a provision requiring any such property to be offered for sale to a person, or a class of persons, specified in the order,

(iii) a provision directing that the order, or a specified part of it, shall not take effect until the occurrence of a specified event or the expiration of a specified period,

(iv) a provision requiring the making of a payment or payments (whether periodical payments or lump sum payments) to a specified person or persons out of the proceeds of the sale of the property to which the order relates, and

(v) a provision specifying the manner in which the proceeds of the sale of the property concerned shall be disposed of between the following persons or such of them as the court considers appropriate, that is to say, the spouses concerned and any other person having an interest therein.

(4) A provision in an order under subsection (1) providing for the making of periodical payments to one of the spouses concerned out of the proceeds of the sale of property shall, on the death or remarriage of that spouse, cease to have effect except as respects payments due on the date of the death or remarriage.

(5) Where a spouse has a beneficial interest in any property, or in the proceeds of the sale of any property, and a person (not being the other spouse) also has a beneficial interest in that property or those proceeds, then, in considering whether to make an order under this section or section 14 or 15(1)(a) in relation to that property or those proceeds, the court shall give to that person an opportunity to make representations with respect to the making of the order and the contents thereof, and any representations made by such a person shall be deemed to be included among the matters to which the court is required to have regard under section 20 in any relevant proceedings under a provision referred to in that section after the making of those representations.

(6) This section shall not apply in relation to a family home in which, following the grant of a decree of divorce, either of the spouses concerned, having remarried, ordinarily resides with his or her spouse.

20 Provisions relating to certain orders under sections 12 to 18 and 22

(1) In deciding whether to make an order under section 12, 13, 14, 15(1)(a), 16, 17, 18 or 22 and in determining the provisions of such an order, the court shall ensure that such provision as the court considers proper having regard to the circumstances exists or will be made for the spouses and any dependent member of the family concerned.

(2) Without prejudice to the generality of subsection (1), in deciding whether to make such an order as aforesaid and in determining the provisions of such an order, the court shall, in particular, have regard to the following matters:
   (a) the income, earning capacity, property and other financial resources which each of the spouses concerned has or is likely to have in the foreseeable future,
   (b) the financial needs, obligations and responsibilities which each of the spouses has or is likely to have in the foreseeable future (whether in the case of the remarriage of the spouse or otherwise),
   (c) the standard of living enjoyed by the family concerned before the proceedings were instituted or before the spouses commenced to live apart from one another, as the case may be,
   (d) the age of each of the spouses, the duration of their marriage and the length of time during which the spouses lived with one another,
   (e) any physical or mental disability of either of the spouses,
   (f) the contributions which each of the spouses has made or is likely in the foreseeable future to make to the welfare of the family, including any contribution made by each of them to the income, earning capacity, property and financial resources of the other spouse and any contribution made by either of them by looking after the home or caring for the family,
   (g) the effect on the earning capacity of each of the spouses of the marital responsibilities assumed by each during the period when they lived with one another and, in particular, the degree to which the future earning capacity of a spouse is impaired by reason of that spouse having relinquished or foregone the opportunity of remunerative activity in order to look after the home or care for the family,

(h) any income or benefits to which either of the spouses is entitled by or under statute,

(i) the conduct of each of the spouses, if that conduct is such that in the opinion of the court it would in all the circumstances of the case be unjust to disregard it,

(j) the accommodation needs of either of the spouses,

(k) the value to each of the spouses of any benefit (for example, a benefit under a pension scheme) which by reason of the decree of divorce concerned, that spouse will forfeit the opportunity or possibility of acquiring,

(l) the rights of any person other than the spouses but including a person to whom either spouse is remarried.

(3) In deciding whether to make an order under a provision referred to in subsection (1) and in determining the provisions of such an order, the court shall have regard to the terms of any separation agreement which has been entered into by the spouses and is still in force.

(4) Without prejudice to the generality of subsection (1), in deciding whether to make an order referred to in that subsection in favour of a dependent member of the family concerned and in determining the provisions of such an order, the court shall, in particular, have regard to the following matters:

(a) the financial needs of the member,

(b) the income, earning capacity (if any), property and other financial resources of the member,

(c) any physical or mental disability of the member,

(d) any income or benefits to which the member is entitled by or under statute,

(e) the manner in which the member was being and in which the spouses concerned anticipated that the member would be educated or trained,

(f) the matters specified in paragraphs (a), (b) and (c) of subsection (2) and in subsection (3),

(g) the accommodation needs of the member.

(5) The court shall not make an order under a provision referred to in subsection (1) unless it would be in the interests of justice to do so.

21 Retrospective periodical payments orders

(1) Where, having regard to all the circumstances of the case, the court considers it appropriate to do so, it may, in a periodical payments order, direct that—

(a) the period in respect of which payments under the order shall be made shall begin on such date before the date of the order, not being earlier than the time of the institution of the proceedings concerned for the grant of a decree of divorce, as may be specified in the order,

(b) any payments under the order in respect of a period before the date of the order be paid in one sum and before a specified date, and

(c) there be deducted from any payments referred to in paragraph (b) made to the spouse concerned an amount equal to the amount of such (if any) payments made to that spouse by the other spouse as the court may determine, being payments made during the period between the making of the order for the grant of the decree aforesaid and the institution of the proceedings aforesaid.

(2) The jurisdiction conferred on the court by subsection (1)(b) is without prejudice to the generality of section 13(1)(c).

22 Variation, etc, of certain orders under this Part

(1) This section applies to the following orders:
  (a) a maintenance pending suit order,
  (b) a periodical payments order,
  (c) a secured periodical payments order,
  (d) a lump sum order if and in so far as it provides for the payment of the lump sum concerned by instalments or requires the payment of any such instalments to be secured,
  (e) an order under paragraph (b), (c) or (d) of section 14(1) in so far as such application is not restricted or excluded pursuant to section 14(2),
  (f) an order under subparagraph (i) or (ii) of section 15(1)(a),
  (g) a financial compensation order,
  (h) an order under section 17(2) insofar as such application is not restricted or excluded pursuant to section 17(26),
  (i) an order under this section.

(2) Subject to the provisions of this section and section 20 and to any restriction or exclusion pursuant to section 14(2) or 17(26) and without prejudice to section 16(2)(d), the court may, on application to it in that behalf—
  (a) by either of the spouses concerned,
  (b) in the case of the death of either of the spouses, by any other person who has, in the opinion of the court, a sufficient interest in the matter or by a person on behalf of a dependent member of the family concerned, or
  (c) in the case of the remarriage of either of the spouses, by his or her spouse,
if it considers it proper to do so having regard to any change in the circumstances of the case and to any new evidence, by order vary or discharge an order to which this section applies, suspend any provision of such an order or any provision of such an order temporarily, revive the operation of such an order or provision so suspended, further vary an order previously varied under this section or further suspend or revive the operation of an order or provision previously suspended or revived under this section; and, without prejudice to the generality of the foregoing, an order under this section may require the divesting of any property vested in a person under or by virtue of an order to which this section applies.

(3) Without prejudice to the generality of section 12 or 13, that part of an order to which this section applies which provides for the making of payments for the support of a dependent member of the family shall stand discharged if the member ceases to be a dependent member of the family by reason of his or her attainment of the age of 18 years or 23 years, as may be appropriate, and shall be discharged by the court, on application to it under subsection (2), if it is satisfied that the member has for any reason ceased to be a dependent member of the family.

(4) The power of the court under subsection (2) to make an order varying, discharging or suspending an order referred to in subsection (1)(e) shall be subject to any restriction or exclusion specified in that order and shall (subject to the limitation aforesaid) be a power—
  (a) to vary the settlement to which the order relates in any person's favour or to extinguish or reduce any person's interest under that settlement, and

(b) to make such supplemental provision (including a further property adjustment order or a lump sum order) as the court thinks appropriate in consequence of any variation, extinguishment or reduction made pursuant to paragraph (a),

and section 19 shall apply to a case where the court makes such an order as aforesaid under subsection (2) as it applies to a case where the court makes a property adjustment order with any necessary modifications.

(5) The court shall not make an order under subsection (2) in relation to an order referred to in subsection (1)(e) unless it appears to it that the order will not prejudice the interests of any person who—

(a) has acquired any right or interest in consequence of the order referred to in subsection (1)(e), and

(b) is not a party to the marriage concerned or a dependent member of the family concerned.

(6) This section shall apply, with any necessary modifications, to instruments executed pursuant to orders to which this section applies as it applies to those orders.

(7) Where the court makes an order under subsection (2) in relation to a property adjustment order relating to land, a copy of the order under subsection (2) certified to be a true copy by the registrar or clerk of the court concerned shall, as appropriate, be lodged by him or her in the Land Registry for registration pursuant to section 69(1)(h) of the Registration of Title Act 1964, in a register maintained under that Act or be registered in the Registry of Deeds.

23 Restriction in relation to orders for benefit of dependent members of family

In deciding whether—

(a) to include in an order under section 12 a provision requiring the making of periodical payments for the benefit of a dependent member of the family,

(b) to make an order under paragraph (a)(ii), (b)(ii) or (c)(ii) of section 13(1),

(c) to make an order under section 22 varying, discharging or suspending a provision referred to in paragraph (a) or an order referred to in paragraph (b),

the court shall not have regard to conduct by the spouse or spouses concerned of the kind specified in subsection (2)(i) of section 20.

24 Method of making payments under certain orders

(1) The court may by order provide that a payment under an order to which this section applies shall be made by such method as is specified in the order and be subject to such terms and conditions as it considers appropriate and so specifies.

(2) This section applies to an order under—

(a) section 11(2)(b) of the Act of 1964,

(b) section 5, 5A or 7 of the Act of 1976,

(c) section 7, 8 or 24 of the Act of 1995, and

(d) section 12, 13, 19 or 22.

25 Stay on certain orders the subject of appeal

Where an appeal is brought from an order under—

(a) section 11(2)(b) of the Act of 1964,

(b) section 5, 5A or 7 of the Act of 1976,

(c) section 7, paragraph (a) or (b) of section 8(1) or section 24 of the Act of 1995, or

(d) section 12, paragraph (a) or (b) of section 13(1) or paragraph (a), (b) or (c) of section 22(1),

the operation of the order shall not be stayed unless the court that made the order or to which the appeal is brought directs otherwise.

26 Orders under Acts of 1976, 1989 and 1995

(1) Where, while an order ('the first-mentioned order'), being—

(a) a maintenance order, an order varying a maintenance order, or an interim order under the Act of 1976,

(b) an order under section 14, 15, 16, 18 or 22 of the Act of 1989,

(c) an order under section 8, 9, 10, 11, 12, 13, 14, 15 or 18 of the Act of 1995,

is in force, an application is made to the court by a spouse to whom the first-mentioned order relates for an order granting a decree of divorce or an order under this Part, the court may by order discharge the first-mentioned order as on and from such date as may be specified in the order.

(2) Where, on the grant of a decree of divorce an order specified in subsection (1) is in force, it shall, unless it is discharged by an order under subsection (1), continue in force as if it were an order made under a corresponding provision of this Act and section 22 shall apply to it accordingly.

27 Amendment of section 3 of Act of 1976

Section 3(1) of the Act of 1976 is hereby amended by the insertion in the definition of 'antecedent order' after paragraph (k) (inserted by the Act of 1995) of the following paragraph:

'(l) a maintenance pending suit order under the Family Law (Divorce) Act 1996, or a periodical payments order under that Act;'.

28 Transmission of periodical payments through District Court clerk

Notwithstanding anything in this Act, section 9 of the Act of 1976 shall apply in relation to an order ('the relevant order'), being a maintenance pending suit order, a periodical payments order or a secured periodical payments order or any such order as aforesaid as affected by an order under section 22, with the modifications that—

(a) the reference in subsection (4) of the said section 9 to the maintenance creditor shall be construed as a reference to the person to whom payments under the relevant order concerned are required to be made,

(b) the other references in the said section 9 to the maintenance creditor shall be construed as references to the person on whose application the relevant order was made, and

(c) the reference in subsection (3) of the said section 9 to the maintenance debtor shall be construed as a reference to the person to whom payments under the relevant order are required by that order to be made,

and with any other necessary modifications.

29 Application of maintenance pending suit and periodical payment orders to certain members of Defence Forces

The reference in section 98(1)(h) of the Defence Act 1954, to an order for payment of alimony shall be construed as including a reference to a maintenance pending suit order, a periodical payments order and a secured periodical payments order.

30 Amendment of Enforcement of Court Orders Act 1940

The references in subsections (1) and (7) of section 8 of the Enforcement of Court Orders Act 1940 (as amended by section 29 of the Act of 1976 and section 22 of the Act of 1995), to an order shall be construed as including references to a maintenance pending suit order and a periodical payments order.

PART IV

INCOME TAX, CAPITAL ACQUISITIONS TAX, CAPITAL GAINS TAX, PROBATE TAX AND STAMP DUTY

31 Payments to be made without deduction of income tax

Payments of money pursuant to an order under this Act (other than under section 17) shall be made without deduction of income tax.

32 Income tax treatment of divorced persons

Where a payment to which section 3 of the Finance Act 1983, applies is made in a year of assessment (within the meaning of the Income Tax Acts) by a spouse who was a party to a marriage that has been dissolved for the benefit of the other spouse and—
(a) both spouses are resident in the State for tax purposes for that year of assessment, and
(b) neither spouse has entered into another marriage,
then, the provisions of section 4 of the Finance Act 1983, shall, with any necessary modifications, have effect in relation to the spouses for that year of assessment as if their marriage had not been dissolved.

33 Exemption of certain transfers from stamp duty

(1) Subject to subsection (3), stamp duty shall not be chargeable on an instrument by which property is transferred pursuant to an order to which this subsection applies by either or both of the spouses who were parties to the marriage concerned to either or both of them.

(2) Section 74(2) of the Finance (1909–10) Act 1910, shall not apply to a transfer to which subsection (1) applies.

(3) (a) Subsection (1) applies to an order under Part III.
(b) Subsection (1) does not apply in relation to an instrument referred to in that subsection by which any part of or beneficial interest in the property concerned is transferred to a person other than the spouses concerned.

34   Exemption of certain transfers from capital acquisitions tax

Notwithstanding the provisions of the Capital Acquisitions Tax Act 1976, a gift or inheritance (within the meaning, in each case, of that Act) taken by virtue or in consequence of an order under Part III by a spouse who was a party to the marriage concerned shall be exempt from any capital acquisitions tax under that Act and shall not be taken into account in computing such a tax.

35   Capital gains tax treatment of certain disposals by divorced persons

(1) Notwithstanding the provisions of the Capital Gains Tax Acts, where, by virtue or in consequence of an order made under Part III on or following the granting of a decree of divorce either of the spouses concerned disposes of an asset to the other spouse, both spouses shall be treated for the purpose of those Acts as if the asset was acquired from the spouse making the disposal for a consideration of such amount as would secure that on the disposal neither a gain nor a loss would accrue to the spouse making the disposal:

Provided that this subsection shall not apply if, until the disposal, the asset formed part of the trading stock of a trade carried on by the spouse making the disposal or if the asset is acquired as trading stock for the purposes of a trade carried on by the spouse acquiring the asset.

(2) Where subsection (1) applies in relation to a disposal of an asset by a spouse to the other spouse, then, in relation to a subsequent disposal of the asset (not being a disposal to which subsection (1) applies), the spouse making the disposal shall be treated for the purposes of the Capital Gains Tax Acts as if the other spouse's acquisition or provision of the asset had been his or her acquisition or provision of the asset.

36   Abatement and postponement of probate tax on property the subject of an order under section 18

Subsection (1) of section 115A of the Finance Act 1993 (which was inserted by the Finance Act 1994, and provides for the abatement or postponement of probate tax payable by a surviving spouse)—
   (a)   shall apply to a spouse in whose favour an order has been made under section 18 as it applies to a spouse referred to in the said section 115A, and
   (b)   shall apply to property or an interest in property the subject of such an order as it applies to the share of a spouse referred to in the said section 115A in the estate of a deceased referred to in that section or the interest of such a spouse in property referred to in that section,
with any necessary modifications.

PART V

MISCELLANEOUS

37   Powers of court in relation to transactions intended to prevent or reduce relief

(1) In this section—
'disposition' means any disposition of property howsoever made other than a disposition made by a will or codicil;

'relief' means the financial or other material benefits conferred by an order under section 12, 13 or 14, paragraph (a) or (b) of section 15(1) or section 16, 17, 18 or 22 other than an order affecting an order referred to in subsection (1)(e) thereof) and references to defeating a claim for relief are references to—

(a) preventing relief being granted to the person concerned, whether for the benefit of the person or a dependent member of the family concerned,

(b) limiting the relief granted, or

(c) frustrating or impeding the enforcement of an order granting relief;

'reviewable disposition', in relation to proceedings for the grant of relief brought by a spouse, means a disposition made by the other spouse concerned or any other person but does not include such a disposition made for valuable consideration (other than marriage) to a person who, at the time of the disposition, acted in good faith and without notice of an intention on the part of the respondent to defeat the claim for relief.

(2) (a) The court, on the application of a person ('the applicant') who has instituted proceedings that have not been determined for the grant of relief, may—

(i) if it is satisfied that the other spouse concerned or any other person, with the intention of defeating the claim for relief, proposes to make any disposition of or to transfer out of the jurisdiction or otherwise deal with any property, make such order as it thinks fit for the purpose of restraining that other spouse or other person from so doing or otherwise for protecting the claim,

(ii) if it is satisfied that that other spouse or other person has, with that intention, made a reviewable disposition and that, if the disposition were set aside, relief or different relief would be granted to the applicant, make an order setting aside the disposition.

(b) Where relief has been granted by the court and the court is satisfied that the other spouse concerned or another person has, with the intention aforesaid, made a reviewable disposition, it may make an order setting aside the disposition.

(c) An application under paragraph (a) shall be made in the proceedings for the grant of the relief concerned.

(3) Where the court makes an order under paragraph (a) or (b) of subsection (2), it shall include in the order such provisions (if any) as it considers necessary for its implementation (including provisions requiring the making of any payments or the disposal of any property).

(4) Where an application is made under subsection (2) with respect to a disposition that took place less than 3 years before the date of the application or with respect to a disposition or other dealing with property that the other spouse concerned or any other person proposes to make and the court is satisfied—

(a) in case the application is for an order under subsection (2)(a)(i), that the disposition or other dealing concerned would (apart from this section) have the consequence, or

(b) in case the application is for an order under paragraph (a)(ii) or (b) of subsection (2), that the disposition has had the consequence,

of defeating the applicant's claim for relief, it shall be presumed, unless the contrary is shown, that that other spouse or other person disposed of or otherwise dealt with the property concerned, or, as the case may be, proposes to do so, with the intention of defeating the applicant's claim for relief.

38 Jurisdiction of courts and venue

(1) Subject to the provisions of this section, the Circuit Court shall, concurrently with the High Court, have jurisdiction to hear and determine proceedings under this Act and shall, in relation to that jurisdiction, be known as the Circuit Family Court.

(2) Where the rateable valuation of any land to which proceedings in the Circuit Family Court under this Act relate exceeds £200, that Court shall, if an application is made to it in that behalf by any person having an interest in the proceedings, transfer the proceedings to the High Court, but any order made or act done in the course of such proceedings before the transfer shall be valid unless discharged or varied by the High Court by order.

(3) The jurisdiction conferred on the Circuit Family Court by this Act may be exercised by the judge of the circuit in which any of the parties to the proceedings ordinarily resides or carries on any business, profession or occupation.

(4) The Circuit Family Court may, for the purposes of subsection (2) in relation to land that has not been given a rateable valuation or is the subject with other land of a rateable valuation, determine that its rateable valuation would exceed, or would not exceed, £200.

(5) Section 32 of the Act of 1989 shall apply to proceedings under this Act in the Circuit Family Court and sections 33 to 36 of that Act shall apply to proceedings under this Act in that Court and in the High Court.

(6) In proceedings under section 13, 14, 15(1)(a), 16, 17, 18 or 22—
    (a) each of the spouses concerned shall give to the other spouse and to, or to a person acting on behalf of, any dependent member of the family concerned, and
    (b) any dependent member of the family concerned shall give to, or to a person acting on behalf of, any other such member and to each of the spouses concerned,
such particulars of his or her property and income as may reasonably be required for the purposes of the proceedings.

(7) Where a person fails or refuses to comply with subsection (6), the court on application to it in that behalf by a person having an interest in the matter, may direct the person to comply with that subsection.

39 Exercise of jurisdiction by court in relation to divorce

(1) The court may grant a decree of divorce if, but only if, one of the following requirements is satisfied—
    (a) either of the spouses concerned was domiciled in the State on the date of the institution of the proceedings concerned,
    (b) either of the spouses was ordinarily resident in the State throughout the period of one year ending on that date.

(2) Where proceedings are pending in a court in respect of an application for the grant of a decree of divorce or in respect of an appeal from the determination of such an

application and the court has or had, by virtue of subsection (1), jurisdiction to determine the application, the court shall, notwithstanding section 31(4) of the Act of 1989 or section 39 of the Act of 1995, as the case may be, have jurisdiction to determine an application for the grant of a decree of judicial separation or a decree of nullity in respect of the marriage concerned.

(3) Where proceedings are pending in a court in respect of an application for the grant of a decree of nullity or in respect of an appeal from the determination of such an application and the court has or had, by virtue of section 39 of the Act of 1995, jurisdiction to determine the application, the court shall, notwithstanding subsection (1), have jurisdiction to determine an application for the grant of a decree of divorce in respect of the marriage concerned.

(4) Where proceedings are pending in a court in respect of an application for the grant of a decree of judicial separation or in respect of an appeal from the determination of such an application and the court has or had, by virtue of section 31(4) of the Act of 1989, jurisdiction to determine the application, the court shall, notwithstanding subsection (1), have jurisdiction to determine an application for the grant of a decree of divorce in respect of the marriage concerned.

40 Notice of proceedings under Act

Notice of any proceedings under this Act shall be given by the person bringing the proceedings to—

    (a) the other spouse concerned or, as the case may be, the spouses concerned, and

    (b) any other person specified by the court.

41 Custody of dependent members of family after decree of divorce

Where the court makes an order for the grant of a decree of divorce, it may declare either of the spouses concerned to be unfit to have custody of any dependent member of the family who is a minor and, if it does so and the spouse to whom the declaration relates is a parent of any dependent member of the family who is a minor, that spouse shall not, on the death of the other spouse, be entitled as of right to the custody of that minor.

42 Social reports in family law proceedings

Section 47 of the Act of 1995 shall apply to proceedings under this Act.

43 Cost of mediation and counselling services

The cost of any mediation services or counselling services provided for a spouse who is or becomes a party to proceedings under this Act, the Act of 1964 or the Act of 1989 or for a dependent member of the family of such a spouse shall be in the discretion of the court concerned.

44 Determination of questions between persons formerly engaged to each other in relation to property

Where an agreement to marry is terminated, section 36 of the Act of 1995 shall apply, as if the parties to the agreement were married to each other, to any dispute between them, or claim by one of them, in relation to property in which either or both of them had a beneficial interest while the agreement was in force.

45 Amendment of Act of 1989

The Act of 1989 is hereby amended—
 (a) in section 3(2)(a), by the substitution of the following subparagraph for subparagraph (i):
  '(i) is satisfied that such provision exists or has been made, or',
 (b) in section 7, by the deletion of subsection (7), and
 (c) by the insertion of the following section before section 8:

'7A Non-admissibility as evidence of certain communications relating to reconciliation or separation

An oral or written communication between either of the spouses concerned and a third party for the purpose of seeking assistance to effect a reconciliation or to reach agreement between them on some or all of the terms of a separation (whether or not made in the presence or with the knowledge of the other spouse), and any record of such a communication, made or caused to be made by either of the spouses concerned or such a third party, shall not be admissible as evidence in any court.'.

46 Amendment of Act of 1965

Section 117(6) of the Act of 1965 is hereby amended by the substitution of '6 months' for 'twelve months'.

47 Amendment of Pensions Act 1990

The Pensions Act 1990, is hereby amended as follows:
 (a) in subsection (4)(a) (inserted by the Pensions (Amendment) Act 1996) of section 5, by the substitution of 'paragraph (c) or (cc) of section 10(1)' for 'section 10(1)(c),',
 (b) subsection (4) (inserted by the Pensions (Amendment) Act 1996) of section 5 shall apply and have effect in relation to section 17 as it applies and has effect in relation to section 12 of the Act of 1995 with the modifications that—
  (i) the reference to the said section 12 shall be construed as a reference to section 17,
  (ii) the reference in paragraph (c) to the Family Law Act 1995, shall be construed as a reference to the Family Law (Divorce) Act 1996,
  (iii) the references to subsections (1), (2), (3), (5), (6), (7), (8), (10) and (25) of the said section 12 shall be construed as references to subsections (1), (2), (3), (5), (6), (7), (8), (10) and (25), respectively, of section 17, and
  (iv) the reference to section 2 of the Act of 1995 shall be construed as a reference to section 2, and
 (c) in section 10(1), by the substitution for paragraph (cc) (inserted by the Pensions (Amendment) Act 1996) of the following paragraph:

'(cc) to issue guidelines or guidance notes generally on the operation of this Act and on the provisions of the Family Law Act 1995, and the Family Law (Divorce) Act 1996, relating to pension schemes (within the meaning of section 2 of the Family Law Act 1995 and section 2 of the Family Law (Divorce) Act 1996);'

48 Amendment of Criminal Damage Act 1991

Section 1(3) of the Criminal Damage Act 1991, is hereby amended—
  (a) in paragraph (a), by the insertion after '1976,' of the following:
  'or a dwelling, within the meaning of section 2(2) of the Family Home Protection Act 1976, as amended by section 54(1)(a) of the Family Law Act 1995, in which a person, who is a party to a marriage that has been dissolved under the Family Law (Divorce) Act 1996, or under the law of a country or jurisdiction other than the State, being a divorce that is entitled to be recognised as valid in the State, ordinarily resided with his or her former spouse, before the dissolution', and
  (b) in paragraph (b), by the substitution of the following subparagraph for subparagraph (i):
  '(i) is the spouse of a person who resides, or is entitled to reside, in the home or is a party to a marriage that has been dissolved under the Family Law (Divorce) Act 1996, or under the law of a country or jurisdiction other than the State, being a divorce that is entitled to be recognised as valid in the State, and'.

49 Amendment of Criminal Evidence Act 1992

Section 20 of the Criminal Evidence Act 1992, is hereby amended in section 20—
  (a) by the insertion of the following definition:
  '"decree of divorce" means a decree under section 5 of the Family Law (Divorce) Act 1996 or any decree that was granted under the law of a country or jurisdiction other than the State and is recognised in the State;', and
  (b) by the substitution of the following definition for the definition of former spouse:
  '"former spouse" includes a person who, in respect of his or her marriage to an accused—
  (a) has been granted a decree of judicial separation, or
  (b) has entered into a separation agreement, or
  (c) has been granted a decree of divorce;'.

50 Amendment of Powers of Attorney Act 1996

The Powers of Attorney Act 1996, is hereby amended—
  (a) in section 5(7), by the substitution of the following paragraph for paragraph (a):
  '(a) the marriage is annulled or dissolved either—
    (i) under the law of the State, or
    (ii) under the law of another state and is, by reason of that annulment or divorce, not or no longer a subsisting valid marriage under the law of the State,',
  (b) in Part I of the Second Schedule, by the insertion of the following paragraph:
  '2A The expiry of an enduring power of attorney effected in the circumstances mentioned in section 5(7) shall apply only so far as it relates to an attorney who is the spouse of the donor.'.

51 Amendment of Act of 1996

The references in sections 2 and 3 of the Act of 1996 to a spouse shall be construed as including references to a person who is a party to a marriage that has been dissolved under this Act or under the law of a country or jurisdiction other than the State, being a divorce that is entitled to be recognised as valid in the State.

52 Amendment of Act of 1995

The Act of 1995 is hereby amended—
  (a) in section 8—
      (i) in subsection (1), by the insertion of 'or at any time thereafter' after 'separation',
      (ii) in paragraph (c)(i) of that subsection, by the insertion of 'or' after 'so specified', and
      (iii) in subsection (4), by the substitution of 'the spouse, or any dependent member of the family, in whose favour the order is made or the other spouse concerned' for 'either of the spouses concerned',
  (b) in section 9(1), by the insertion of 'or at any time thereafter' after 'separation',
  (c) in section 10—
      (i) in subsection (1), by the insertion of 'or at any time thereafter' after 'separation', and
      (ii) by the insertion after subsection (2) of the following subsection:
          '(3) Subsection 1(a) shall not apply in relation to a family home in which, following the grant of a decree of judicial separation, either of the spouses concerned, having remarried, ordinarily resides with his or her spouse.',
  (d) in sections 11(2)(a), 12(23)(b) and 25(1), by the substitution of 'proper provision, having regard to the circumstances,' for 'adequate and reasonable financial provision', in each place where it occurs,
  (e) in section 12—
      (i) in subsection (1), in the definition of 'relevant guidelines', by the substitution of 'paragraph (c) or (cc) of section 10(1)' for 'section 10(1)(c)', and
      (ii) in subsection (18), by the substitution of '40' for '41',
  (f) in section 15—
      (i) in subsection (5), by the substitution of '10(1)(a)' for '10(1)(a)(ii)', and
      (ii) by the insertion of the following subsection after subsection (5):
          '(6) This section shall not apply in relation to a family home in which, following the grant of a decree of judicial separation, either of the spouses concerned, having remarried, ordinarily resides with his or her spouse.',
  (g) by the insertion of the following section after section 15:

'15A Orders for provision for spouse out of estate of other spouse

(1) Subject to the provisions of this section, where, following the grant of a decree of judicial separation, a court makes an order under section 14 in relation to the spouses concerned and one of the spouses dies, the court, on application to it in that behalf by the other spouse ("the applicant") not more than 6 months after representation is first granted under the Act of 1965 in respect of the estate of the deceased spouse, may by order make such provision for the applicant out

of the estate of the deceased spouse as it considers appropriate having regard to the rights of any other person having an interest in the matter and specifies in the order if it is satisfied that proper provision in the circumstances was not made for the applicant during the lifetime of the deceased spouse under section 8, 9, 10(1)(a), 11 or 12 for any reason (other than conduct referred to in subsection (2)(i) of section 16 of the applicant).

(2) The court shall not make an order under this section if the applicant concerned has remarried since the granting of the decree of judicial separation concerned.

(3) In considering whether to make an order under this section the court shall have regard to all the circumstances of the case including—
   (a) any order under paragraph (c) of section 8(1) or a property adjustment order in favour of the applicant, and
   (b) any devise or bequest made by the deceased spouse to the applicant.

(4) The provision made for the applicant concerned by an order under this section together with any provision made for the applicant by an order referred to in subsection 3(a) (the value of which for the purposes of this subsection shall be its value on the date of the order) shall not exceed in total the share (if any) of the applicant in the estate of the deceased spouse to which the applicant was entitled or (if the deceased spouse died intestate as to the whole or part of his or her estate) would have been entitled under the Act of 1965 if the court had not made an order under section 14.

(5) Notice of an application under this section shall be given by the applicant to the spouse (if any) of the deceased spouse concerned and to such (if any) other persons as the court may direct and, in deciding whether to make the order concerned and in determining the provisions of the order, the court shall have regard to any representations made by the spouse of the deceased spouse and any other such persons as aforesaid.

(6) The personal representative of a deceased spouse in respect of whom a decree of judicial separation has been granted shall make a reasonable attempt to ensure that notice of his or her death is brought to the attention of the other spouse concerned and, where an application is made under this section, the personal representative of the deceased spouse shall not, without the leave of the court, distribute any of the estate of that spouse until the court makes or refuses to make an order under this section.

(7) Where the personal representative of a deceased spouse in respect of whom a decree of judicial separation has been granted gives notice of his or her death to the other spouse concerned ("the spouse") and—
   (a) the spouse intends to apply to the court for an order under this section,
   (b) the spouse has applied for such an order and the application is pending, or
   (c) an order has been made under this section in favour of the spouse,
the spouse shall, not later one month after the receipt of the notice, notify the personal representative of such intention, application or order, as the case may be, and, if he or she does not do so, the personal representative shall be at liberty

to distribute the assets of the deceased spouse, or any part thereof, amongst the parties entitled thereto.

(8) The personal representative shall not be liable to the spouse for the assets or any part thereof so distributed unless, at the time of such distribution, he or she had notice of the intention, application or order aforesaid.

(9) Nothing in subsection (7) or (8) shall prejudice the right of the spouse to follow any such assets into the hands of any person who may have received them.

(10) On granting a decree of judicial separation or at any time thereafter, the court, on application to it in that behalf by either of the spouses concerned, may, during the lifetime of the other spouse or, as the case may be, the spouse concerned, if it considers it just to do so, make an order that either or both spouses shall not, on the death of either of them, be entitled to apply for an order under this section.',

(h) in section 16(1)—
    (i) by the insertion of '15A,' after '14',
    (ii) by the substitution of 'exists or will be made' for 'is made', and
    (iii) by the substitution of 'proper' for 'adequate and reasonable',
(i) in section 18, in subsection (1)(h), by the insertion of 'insofar as such application is not restricted or excluded by section 12(26)' after 'section 12',
(j) in section 25—
    (i) in subsection (1), by the substitution, as respects applications under that section made after the commencement of the Family Law (Divorce) Act 1996, of '6 months' for '12 months', and
    (ii) by the substitution of the following subsections for subsection (7):
        '(7) The personal representative of a deceased spouse in respect of whom a decree of divorce has been granted in a country or jurisdiction other than the State shall make a reasonable attempt to ensure that notice of his or her death is brought to the attention of the other spouse concerned and, where an application is made under this section, the personal representative of the deceased spouse shall not, without the leave of the court, distribute any of the estate of that spouse until the court makes or refuses to make an order under this section.
        (8) Where the personal representative of a deceased spouse in respect of whom a decree of divorce has been granted in a country or jurisdiction other than the State gives notice of his or her death to the other spouse concerned ("the spouse") and—
            (a) the spouse intends to apply to the court for an order under this section,
            (b) the spouse has applied for such an order and the application is pending, or
            (c) an order has been made under this section in favour of the spouse,
        the spouse shall, not later than one month after the receipt of the notice, notify the personal representative of such intention, application or order, as the case may be, and, if he or she does not do so, the personal representative shall be at liberty to distribute the assets of the deceased spouse, or any part thereof, amongst the parties entitled thereto.
        (9) The personal representative shall not be liable to the spouse for the assets or any part thereof so distributed unless, at the time of such

distribution, he or she had notice of the intention, application or order aforesaid.

(10) Nothing in subsection (8) or (9) shall prejudice the right of the spouse to follow any such assets into the hands of any person who may have received them.',

(k) in section 29, by the insertion of the following subsection after subsection (10):
'(11) In this section a reference to a spouse includes a reference to a person who is a party to a marriage that has been dissolved under the Family Law (Divorce) Act 1996.',

(l) in section 35(1)—
   (i) by the insertion in the definition of 'relief', of '15A,' after '13,', and
   (ii) by the insertion in that definition, after paragraph (a), of the following paragraph:
      '(aa) an order under section 11(2)(b) of the Act of 1964 or section 5, 5A or 7 of the Act of 1976, or',

(m) in section 36—
   (i) in subsection (7)(a)(i), by the insertion of 'or dissolved', after 'annulled', and
   (ii) in subsection (8), after paragraph (c), by the insertion of the following paragraph:
      '(cc) either of the parties to a marriage that has been dissolved under the law of the State,',

(n) in section 38(7), by the insertion of '15A,' after '14,',

(o) in section 43—
   (i) in paragraph (a), by the substitution of the following subparagraph for subparagraph (ii):
      '(ii) in the definition of "dependent child" the substitution of "18" for "sixteen" and "23" for "twenty-one", and ', and
   (ii) by the substitution of the following paragraph for paragraph (e):
      '(e) in section 23, after subsection (2), the insertion of the following subsections:
         "(3) In proceedings under this Act—
            (a) each of the spouses concerned shall give to the other spouse and to, or to a person acting on behalf of, any dependent member of the family concerned, and
            (b) any dependent member of the family concerned shall give to, or to a person acting on behalf of, any other such member and to each of the spouses concerned,
         such particulars of his or her property and income as may reasonably be required for the purpose of the proceedings.
         (4) Where a person fails or refuses to comply with subsection (3), the Court, on application to it in that behalf by a person having an interest in the matter, may direct the person to comply with that subsection.".', and

(p) in section 47—
   (a) in subsection (6), by the substitution of 'This section' for 'Subsection (1)', and
   (b) in subsection (7), by the substitution of '(1)(b)' for '(2)'.

53 Amendment of Maintenance Act 1994

The Maintenance Act 1994 (as amended by the Act of 1995), is hereby amended—
  (a) in section 3, in subsection (1), by the insertion of the following definition:
    '"the Act of 1996" means the Family Law (Divorce) Act 1996;',
  (b) in section 4, by the substitution of the following paragraph for paragraph (a) of subsection (2):
'(a) For the purposes of section 8 of the Enforcement of Court Orders Act 1940, the Act of 1976, the Act of 1988, the Act of 1993 (as amended by this Act), the Act of 1995, the Act of 1996 and this Act, the Central Authority shall have authority to act on behalf of, as the case may be, a maintenance creditor or claimant, within the meaning of section 13(1), and references in those enactments to a maintenance creditor or such a claimant shall be construed as including references to the Central Authority.',
  (c) in section 14—
    (i) in subsection (1)(c), by the substitution of the following subparagraph for subparagraph (i):
      '(i) if the amount of the maintenance sought to be recovered exceeds the maximum amount which the District Court has jurisdiction to award under the Act of 1976 or the request is for a relief order (within the meaning of the Act of 1995) or a maintenance pending suit order, a periodical payments order, a secured periodical payments order or a lump sum order (within the meaning, in each case, of the Act of 1996, make an application to the Circuit Court,', and
    (ii) by the substitution of the following subsection for subsection (3):
      '(3) An application referred to in subsection (1)(c) shall be deemed to be an application for a maintenance order under section 5 or section 5A or 21A (inserted by the Status of Children Act 1987) of the Act of 1976, or the appropriate order referred to in subsection (1)(c)(i), as may be appropriate, and to have been made on the date on which the request of the claimant for the recovery of maintenance was received by the Central Authority of the designated jurisdiction concerned.'.

Appendix 2

CODE OF PRACTICE

ISSUED BY THE FAMILY LAW AND LEGAL AID COMMITTEE OF THE LAW
SOCIETY OF IRELAND

GENERAL

1.1   At an early stage the Solicitor should inform the client of the underlying
approach and ethos which will be adopted by the Solicitor in family law work.

1.2   The Solicitor should advise, negotiate and conduct matters so as to encourage
and assist the parties to achieve a constructive settlement of their differences as
quickly as may be reasonable, whilst recognising that the parties may need time to
come to terms with their new situation.

1.3   The Solicitor should ensure the client appreciates that the interests of the
children should be a primary concern. The client should be appraised of the
advantages to the family of a constructive and non-adversarial approach to the
resolution of the couple's difficulties and advised that the client's attitude and
approach to negotiations can affect not only the family as a whole, but may impact
on their relationship with the children.

1.4   The Solicitor should encourage the attitude that a family dispute is not a contest
in which there is one winner and one loser, but rather a search for fair solutions.
The Solicitor should avoid using words or phrases that imply a dispute when no
serious dispute necessarily exists.

1.5   Because of the involvement of personal emotions in family disputes the Solicitor
should, where possible, avoid heightening such emotions in any way.

1.6   The Solicitor should have regard to the impact of correspondence sent and
received. The Solicitor should always be mindful that correspondence may, at
some stage, be produced to the court. The Solicitor should avoid expressing
personal opinions as to the conduct of the other party.

1.7   The Solicitor should aim to avoid mistrust between parties by encouraging, at an
early stage, full, frank and clear disclosure of information and openness in
dealings.

SOLICITOR AS MEDIATOR

2.1   The Committee is of the view that Solicitors should not not act as Solicitors and
Mediators in the same case.

CONFLICT OF INTEREST GENERAL

3.1 Where a Solicitor has acted for parties in non-contentious matters, and subsequently one or other of the parties return to him or her seeking advice, then the Solicitor has a duty to ensure that the other party has no objection to his or her retainer and that, in the course of the work done for the parties, the Solicitor has acquired no information which could lead to a possible conflict of interest.

3.2 The Committee is of the view that it is unprofessional for a Solicitor or a firm of solicitors to represent both parties in any family dispute.

RELATIONSHIP WITH CLIENT

4.1 The Solicitor should ensure that the relationship with the client is such that objectivity is preserved and personal emotions do not cloud the issues.

4.2 The Solicitor should always ensure that the client is fully aware of how costs will be charged and the impact of costs on any chosen course of action, and should in appropriate cases make the client aware of the existence of the scheme of civil legal aid and advice.

4.3 The Solicitor should ensure that the client is aware of the existence and range of all other services which may be of assistance in bringing about a resolution and helping members of the family through the process of family breakdown. In particular, the Solicitor, having regard to the provisions of Section 5 and 6 of the 1989 Act should discuss with the client:
   (a) the possibility of reconciliation and give the names and addresses of persons qualified to help effect a reconciliation between spouses who have become estranged;
   (b) the possibility of engaging in mediation to help effect a separation on an agreed basis with an estranged spouse and give the names and addresses of persons and organisations qualified to provide a mediation service;
   (c) the possibility of effecting a separation by negotiation and the conclusion of a Deed of Separation or a settlement leading to a Consent Order.

4.4 While recognising the need to advise firmly and guide the client, the Solicitor should ensure that where a decision is made by the client, the consequences of any decision are fully understood by him/her, both as to its effects on the client and on any children.

4.5 The Solicitor should inform the client of all offers made by the other side.

4.6 The Solicitor's correspondence, both with the client and with the other side, should focus on how contentious issues might be resolved rather than emphasising difficulties that have occurred in the past.

DEALINGS WITH OTHER SOLICITORS

5.1 In all dealings with colleagues, the Solicitor should show courtesy and endeavour to create and maintain a good working relationship.

DEALINGS WITH THE OTHER PARTY IN PERSON

6.1   In dealing with another party who is not legally represented the Solicitor should take particular care to be courteous and restrained. Special care should be taken to express letters and other communications clearly, avoiding technical language where it is not readily comprehensible to the person or might be misunderstood.

6.2   In every case the Solicitor should advise the unrepresented party to consult a Solicitor and of the existence of the scheme for civil legal aid and advice and the right to apply for legal services/representation from the Legal Aid Board through a Law Centre.

COURT PROCEEDINGS

7.1   The taking of any action or proceedings which is likely to cause or increase animosity between the parties must be balanced against the likely benefit to the client and the family.

7.2   Where the purpose of taking a particular step in proceedings may be misunderstood or appear hostile, the Solicitor should consider explaining it, at the first practical opportunity, to the other party or their Solicitors.

7.3   A Solicitor should conduct family law proceedings, including preparation, advocacy and implementation, in the most cost-effective manner and in such a way as not to increase hostility unnecessarily and so as to allow reasonable opportunity for settlement.

7.4   The Solicitor should encourage the parties to endeavour to agree as many issues as possible in advance of a court hearing so as to reduce the areas of conflict, and should co-operate with the other side on the production of documents to ensure the smooth running of the case.

FINANCIAL PROVISIONS

8.1   It is inevitable that an income which up to the time of the break-up of the marriage was adequate to maintain a single establishment will not be adequate to maintain two separate establishments and this realisation should be brought to the attention of the parties at the earliest opportunity to avoid unrealistic expectations.

8.2   The Solicitor should ensure that the client is aware of the obligation to make full financial disclosure of all assets, liabilities and income to comply with the Circuit Court Rules No 1 of 1994.

CHILDREN

9.1   The Solicitor should, in advising, negotiating and conducting proceedings, encourage both the client and other family members to regard the welfare of the children as the first and paramount consideration.

9.2   The Solicitor should aim to promote co-operation between parents in decisions concerning the children, and should consider encouraging arrangements to be reached directly between the parties, or through mediation.

9.3   Issues relating to the custody and access of children on the one hand and finance on the other, must be kept separate and independent.

9.4   The Solicitor should avoid direct contact with the client's children except in exceptional circumstances and, if necessary, should encourage the use of appropriate professional services to ascertain the children's interests.

9.5   The Solicitor must keep in mind that the interests of the children do not necessarily coincide with the interests of either parent. In certain cases separate representation may be necessary in order to preserve the independent rights of the child. It is a matter which might be considered by the Solicitor and, if necessary, brought to the attention of the Court.

THE MINOR AS A CLIENT

10.1   There may be occasions when a Solicitor is requested to act on behalf of a minor. In such circumstances, the Solicitor should be aware that in acting for minors, special considerations apply and exceptional care must be taken by the Solicitor in the discharge of his retainer.

CONCLUSION

1   The aim of the Code is to set the tone of professional standards which should be adhered to by Solicitors who practise family law. The underlying approach and attitude embodied in the Code is to encourage a conciliatory approach. Where litigation is necessary it should be approached in a similar manner.

2   Adherence to the Code is not a sign of weakness nor does it expose the client to disadvantage. The approach adopted should be firm and fair. The Solicitor is not prevented from taking immediate and decisive action where this is required. Even where there are on-going discussions, they may often proceed in parallel with Court proceedings, in case negotiations do not produce a settlement.

3   The guide-lines of the Code cannot be absolute rules, but they are recommended to the profession as encompassing a practical set of ground rules and conditions based on which the practitioner can conduct his/her practice. It is to be hoped that this Code of Conduct will act as a ready reference to Solicitors as to what is proper in the many diverse and unique situations in which they find themselves.

Appendix 3

JURISDICTION OF THE COURTS

District court	Circuit court	High Court
1 Custody/access.	1 Decree of divorce and all ancillary relief under the Family Law (Divorce) Act 1996.	1 Decree of divorce and all ancillary relief under the Family Law (Divorce) Act 1996.
2 Maintenance (up to £200) per week for wife) up to £60 per week for child – includes mother seeking maintenance for children born outside marriage.	2 Judicial separation and ancillary relief under the Judicial Separation and Family Law Reform Act 1989 and the Family Law Act 1995.	2 Judicial separation and ancillary relief (under the 1989 and the 1995 Acts).
3 Barring orders (max 3 years).	3 Custody/access.	3 Application under s 36 of the Family Law Act 1995.
4 Safety orders (max 5 years).	4 Maintenance (no limit).	4 Application under the Adoption Acts 1974 and 1987 (High Court only).
5 Protection orders.	5 Barring orders (no limit).	
6 Application under s 9 of the Family Home Protection Act 1976 (re disposal of household goods).	6 Affiliation orders (no limit).	5 Nullity application.
	7 Appeals from the district court.	6 Application under Succession Act 1965.
7 Care orders and fit person orders.	8 Applications under s 36 of the Family Law Act 1995, Partition Acts, Family Home Protection Act 1976, and Family Law Act 1981.	7 Application to have a separation agreement made a rule of court under the Family Law (Maintenance of Spouses and Children) Act 1976.
8 Lump sum orders up to £5,000.	9 Application to have separation agreement made a rule of court under the Family Law (Maintenance and Spouses and Children) Act 1976 and application to have agreement between parents who are not married in relation to child maintenance etc, made a rule of court.	8 Appeals from circuit court.
		9 Applications for declarations as to marital status.
	10 Application under Succession Act 1965.	10 Applications for interim maintenance orders.
	11 Nullity applications (Family Law Act 1995, s 39).	11 Applications for periodical payments pending suit orders.
	12 Applications for declaration as to marital status.	
	13 Interim maintenance orders.	
	14 Periodical payments pending suit orders.	
	(Any property which may be the subject matter of any of the above orders must have a rateable valuation of less than £200).	

Appendix 4
LIST OF AGENCIES

Actuaries: The Society of Actuaries – Ireland
5 Wilton Place, Dublin
Tel: 01 661 2422

Counsellors: Accord (formerly CMAC)
Head Office
39 Harcourt Street, Dublin 2
Tel: 01 478 0866

(Accord have centres nationwide.)

Marriage and Relationship Counselling Services (MRCS)
24 Grafton Street, Dublin 2
Tel: 01 872 0341

Irish Association of Counselling and Therapy
8 Cumberland Street, Dun Laoghaire
Tel: 01 230 0061

Mediators: Family Mediation Service
Block 1, Floor 5
Irish Life Centre
Lower Abbey Street, Dublin 1
Tel: 01 872 8277

Family Mediation Centre
1st Floor
Mill House
Henry Street, Limerick
Tel: 061 312232

Mediators Institute Ireland (MII)
79 Merrion Square, Dublin 2
Tel: 01 661 8488

(A list of all accredited mediators is available from MII. A mediator who is accredited by the Institute may use the designation Registered Family Mediator (MII).)

Legal aid: Legal Aid Board
St Stephens Green House
Carlsfort Terrace, Dublin 2
Tel: 01 661 5811

(A list of full-time and part-time law centres are available from the Board.)

Aim Group Family Law Information, Mediation and Counselling Centre (C)
6 D'Olier Street, Dublin 2
Tel: 01 670 8363

Al Anon Family Groups (C)
Al Anon Information Centre
5/6 Capel Street, Dublin 1
Tel: 01 873 2699 (Monday to Saturday 10.30 am–2.30 pm)

Alcoholics Anonymous
Central Office: 152, Lisburn Road, Belfast BT9 6AJ
Tel: 0801 232 681084
109 South Circular Road, Leonards Corner, Dublin 8
Tel: 01 453 8998, 453 7677

Coolock Community Law Centre
Barryscourt Mall, Northshide Shopping Centre, Coolock, Dublin 17
Tel: 01 847 7804, 847 8602
Fax: 01 847 7563

Financial Information Service Centres (FISC) (C)
87/89 Pembroke Road, Ballsbridge, Dublin 4
Tel: 01 668 2044, 668 0400

Free Legal Advice Centres
49 South William Street, Dublin 2
Tel: 01 679 1554
2 Tuckey Street, Cork

Gamblers Anonymous/GAM-ANON
Carmichael House, North Brunswick Street, Dublin 7
Tel: 01 872 1133

Gingerbread Ireland
29/30 Dame Street, Dublin 2
Tel: 01 671 0291
Fax: 01 671 0352

Irish Society for the Prevention of Cruelty to Children (C)
20 Molesworth Street, Dublin 2
Tel: 01 679 4944
Childline; 1800 666 666

Law Reform Commission
Ardilaum Centre, 111 St Stephen's Green, Dublin 2
Tel: 01 671 5699
Fax: 01 671 5316

The Law Society of Ireland
Blackhall Place, Dublin 7
Tel: 01 671 0711
Fax: 01 671 0704

National Social Service Board
71 Lower Leeson Street, Dublin 2
Tel: 01 661 6422
Fax: 01 676 4908

Rape Crisis Centre
70 Lower Leeson Street, Dublin 2
Tel: 01 661 4911
Freephone: 1800 778888

The Samaritans
112 Marlborough Street, Dublin 1
Tel: 01 872 7700

Womens Aid
FreeFone Helpline, Dublin 1
FreeFone 1800 341 900

INDEX

References are to paragraph numbers.